Dignity and Practical Reason
in Kant's Moral Theory

Dignity and Practical Reason

in Kant's Moral Theory

THOMAS E. HILL, JR.

Cornell University Press

ITHACA AND LONDON

First published 1992 by Cornell University Press.

International Standard Book Number 0-8014-2514-X (cloth)
International Standard Book Number 0-8014-9748-5 (paper)
Library of Congress Catalog Card Number 91-23543
Printed in the United States of America
Librarians: Library of Congress cataloging information appears
on the last page of the book.

⊗The paper in this book meets the minimum requirements of the
American National Standard for Information Sciences—Permanence
of Paper for Printed Library Materials, ANSI Z39.48-1984.

Contents

Sources and Acknowledgments

I gratefully acknowledge the following for permission to reprint my essays.

"The Hypothetical Imperative" was originally published in *The Philosophical Review* 82 (1973): 429–50. It is reprinted by permission of the publisher.

"Humanity as an End in Itself" was originally published in *Ethics* 91 (1980): 84–90, © 1980 by the University of Chicago. Reprinted here by permission of the publisher.

"The Kingdom of Ends" first appeared in *Proceedings of the Third International Kant Congress,* edited by Lewis White Beck (Dordrecht, Holland: D. Reidel, 1972), pp. 307–15. Reprinted by permission of Kluwer Academic Publishers, P.O. Box 17, 3300 AA Dordrecht, Holland.

"Kant's Utopianism." *Akten des 4. Internationalen Kant-Kongresses, Mainz, 1974,* Teil II.2, pp. 918–24. Edited by Gerhard Funke. Berlin and New York: Walter de Gruyter.

"The Kantian Conception of Autonomy." From *The Inner Citadel: Essays on Individual Autonomy,* edited by John Christman. Copyright © 1989 by Oxford University Press, Inc. Reprinted by arrangement.

"Kant's Argument for the Rationality of Moral Conduct" was originally published in *Pacific Philosophical Quarterly* 66, nos. 1 & 2 (January–April 1985): 3–23. Reprinted by permission of the publisher.

During the time when these essays were written, I received financial and other institutional support from the University of California, Los Angeles (1968–84), the National Endowment for the Humanities (1972–73), the National Humanities Center (1982–83), and the University of North Carolina, Chapel Hill (1984–91). This support is gratefully acknowledged.

The notes accompanying each essay acknowledge the help of various individuals, but my philosophical debts extend significantly beyond those specific acknowledgments. Former teachers who stimulated and influenced my thinking about Kant's ethics were Roderick Firth, H. H. Cox, and especially John Rawls. Among the contemporary philosophers from whose writings on Kant I have learned are Henry Allison, Karl Ameriks, Rudiger Bittner, L. W. Beck, Alan Donagan, Stephen Engstrom, David Falk, Dieter Henrich, Barbara Herman, Christine Korsgaard, Jeffrey Murphy, Onora O'Neill, Andrews Reath, John Rawls, Jerome Schneewind, John Silber, and Allen Wood. Colleagues, students, and friends at U.C.L.A., U.N.C., and elsewhere have given me helpful comments and encouragement. Tyler Burge, Jan and Bernard Boxill, David Falk, Gerald Postema, and Geoffrey Sayre McCord have been especially helpful as colleagues and friends. I am grateful to Karánn Durland for her fine work as a research assistant and to the Philosophy Department staff for their help. Special thanks are due to family members for their goodwill and support for many years and most particularly to Robin.

T. E. H.

Abbreviations for Kant's Works

CPrR   *Critique of Practical Reason*, trans. Lewis White Beck (New York: Macmillan/Library of Liberal Arts, 1985).

DV   *The Doctrine of Virtue*, trans. Mary Gregor (New York: Harper & Row, 1964).

G   *Groundwork of the Metaphysic of Morals*, trans. H. J. Paton (New York: Harper & Row, 1964).

LE   *Lectures on Ethics*, trans. Louis Infield (New York: Harper & Row, 1963).

MEJ   *Metaphysical Elements of Justice*, trans. John Ladd (Indianapolis: Bobbs-Merrill, 1965).

MPV   *Metaphysical Principles of Virtue*, trans. James Ellington (Indianapolis: Bobbs-Merrill, 1964).

R   *Religion within the Limits of Reason Alone*, trans. T. M. Greene and H. H. Hudson (New York: Harper & Row, 1960).

Page numbers in brackets refer to the appropriate volumes of *Kant's gesammelte Schriften,* herausgegeben von der Königlichen Preussischen Akademie der Wissenschaften, 23 volumes (Berlin: Walter de Gruyter, 1902). Kant's *Grundlegung zur Metaphysik der Sitten* (abbreviated "G") is in volume IV, pp. 387–463. *Kritik der praktischen Vernunft* (abbreviated "CPrR") is in volume V, pp. 1–164. *Die Metaphysik der Sitten* is in volume VI, pp. 203–494. (MEJ is a translation of the first part of *Die Metaphysik der Sitten* and can be found in volume VI, pp. 203–372; DV and MPV are alternative translations of the second part of this work and can be found in the same volume, pp. 375–491.) *Die Religion innerhalb der Grenzen der blossen Vernunft* (abbreviated "R") is in volume VI, pp. 1–202.

Dignity and Practical Reason
in Kant's Moral Theory

Introduction

Reading Kant's Ethics: Obstacles and Moderate Hopes

Few ethical theories, if any, have been as extravagantly praised, as fervently denounced, or as variously interpreted as Immanuel Kant's. The controversies surrounding Kant's work can be especially intimidating to students and nonspecialists seeking to grasp his basic ideas, and the persistence of deep disagreements should be humbling even to longtime Kant scholars. Readers undaunted by differences of opinion still face the difficulties of Kant's texts themselves. Whatever their merits, these are often highly abstract, heavily laden with special terminology, densely compressed in crucial arguments, and at times seemingly inconsistent. Central doctrines sometimes appear to be hopelessly enmeshed in an outmoded metaphysics while more specific moral opinions seem to be rooted in cultural prejudices of another era. Several works, over many years, address the same or similar issues, and this overlap poses further problems of interpretation. It is not surprising, then, that students and even contemporary moral philosophers are often tempted to abandon any effort to find a reasonably clear and coherent articulation of Kant's main ethical ideas that is worthy of attention and yet faithful to the texts. Though understandable, such pessimism leads one too readily to dismiss or ignore Kant's ethics, to accept familiar oversimplifications or caricatures of it, or simply to attribute to Kant whatever ideas one most favors or opposes.

Despite these obstacles there are good reasons to persist in the effort to understand and appreciate Kant's ethical writings. Library shelves bulge with the products of Kant studies over many years, but each generation undertakes its investigations with its own philosophical commitments, prejudices, and insights. Readers of Kant now can often build upon previous scholarly efforts even when discarding parts and searching for something further. Moreover, the continental tradition of close examination of Kant's texts continues, and recent work on Kant's epistemology, aesthetics, political philosophy, and religion suggests new perspectives on his ethics. A fuller range of Kant's writings is now available in translation, enabling even nonspecialists to read for themselves beyond the familiar *Groundwork of the Metaphysics of Morals.*

Less obviously, there are also reasons for renewed optimism about the study of Kant's ethics in the development of twentieth-century analytic philosophy in the English-speaking world. For all its faults, this many-sided movement has provided resources and standards that have only in recent years begun to be employed in serious efforts to make sense of Kant's ethical theory. Kant, like many early and middle twentieth-century analytic philosophers, attempted to dissect familiar concepts, such as *duty* and *ought,* and to expose the presuppositions of their use. Though often falling short of the ideal, Kant also shared with other analytical thinkers a sense that adequate treatment of some problems requires the careful introduction and rigorous use of a specialized terminology. While dissimilarities of projects and methods should not be overlooked, contemporary moral philosophers have made distinctions, noted fallacies and confusions, and articulated conceptual possibilities that can help in the rereading of Kant's texts, providing new perspectives on what is promising and what is not.

In addition to narrowly focused studies, more systematic and constructive ethical theories have developed within what is, broadly speaking, the same analytical tradition. Several such theories, including prominently John Rawls's theory of justice, develop certain aspects of Kant's thinking in ways that suggest interpretative hypotheses as well as possible modifications. Rawls's work and the increasing dissatisfaction with utilitarianism have generated a renewed interest in Kant's ethics.

Also, by heightening awareness of the advantages of careful attention to language, analytic philosophy has generally raised standards for the understanding and articulation of ideas in ethics. New expectations of this sort should not deter us from studying the works of another era, but they do pose a challenge and an opportunity for those of us who want to rearticulate Kant's main ideas and to find, if possible, positions we can take seriously. In recent years the excellent work of Henry Allison, Barbara Herman, Christine Korsgaard, Onora O'Neill, Jerome Schneewind, and others has taken up this challenge in original and promising ways.

For all these reasons we should not despair of making good sense of Kant's ethics, and in fact we should return to the old texts with renewed interest and hope. To be realistic, however, we must be moderate in our expectations. Only dreamers could imagine that Kant's writings on ethics are like the pieces of a perfectly designed and flawless jigsaw puzzle, merely waiting for devoted and meticulous scholars to put them together. The most insightful reconstructions of central themes may not always square with all passages, and even the most literal or historically faithful readings will no doubt leave some passages in conflict with others. Kant not only pressed questions of moral philosophy to a deeper level but also attempted in his mature years to construct a new and more rationally tenable set of answers. Given his historical context and the wide scope of his vision, it is not surprising that he left us with inadequately explained concepts, incomplete arguments, and unannounced shifts of position. Though understandable, this is still a problem. Perhaps in the end we will conclude that Kant's theory is not merely flawed but unacceptable even under the most sympathetic reading, but we are not yet in a position to make any final judgments. At present the wisest course for both the reader and the commentator is simply to work toward improved understanding without either pessimism or unrealistic hopes.

The pages that follow stem from my efforts, off and on over twenty-some years, to travel this middle course. My ideal has been, where possible, to make good sense of Kant's ethics while remaining faithful in his texts. At times this project requires some reconstructing, filling in gaps, and suggesting modifications. In doing so I have tried to be guided by a sense of Kant's central projects and dominant themes gleaned from many works. This process unavoidably imposes some risk of oversimplifying or distorting Kant's views. I have tried to make clear to the reader when my suggestions extend substantially beyond Kant's texts, at least when I am aware of this; but I fear that in these often condensed topical discussions I may at times present reconstructions, interpretative conjectures, and desired modifications as if they were straightforward readings of unambiguous texts.

My aim has been to find and articulate ideas worthy of contemporary attention rather than to belabor old objections, and I have concentrated on ideas that, in my opinion, have been comparatively neglected, undeveloped, or commonly misunderstood. The essays range over topics and problems representative of most major parts of Kant's systematic treatment of ethics. They were written in the conviction that, whatever one's final assessment, Kant's views on these matters are worth reexamining from new perspectives, are important for contemporary moral philosophy, and can be made more accessible to nonspecialists.

Despite its broad scope, my project is limited in various ways. First, to make it somewhat more manageable, I have focused primarily on Kant's systematic treatment of ethics in the *Groundwork of the Metaphysics of Morals* and the later two-part work *The Metaphysics of Morals,* though Kant's other works helped to guide my interpretations and are frequently cited. The essays collected here are organized by topics, following more or less the order of Kant's treatment in the two works just cited. This arrangement differs somewhat from the order in which the essays were written; the order of writing also reflects my increasing boldness in thinking that I might yet make good sense of some notoriously intimidating aspects of Kant's ethics and so gain a better grasp of the whole.

Second, though I discuss a wide range of topics, there remain some important, and many minor, featues of the *Groundwork* and especially *The Metaphysics of Morals* that I do not address directly. Among these are some topics familiar to every student of ethics, most notably the unqualified goodness of a good will and the universal law formulations of the Categorical Imperative. In my essays on autonomy and practical reason, I make suggestions about interpreting the sensible/intelligible world perspectives insofar as these are relevant to deliberation and choice; but I offer no general account. The selection of subjects is to some extent due to various accidental circumstances, such as invitations to conferences that provided occasions to try out ideas I was developing as parts of a larger project. But the decision to concentrate on the topics raised here, rather than some others, is also based on my conviction that certain other topics have been so often the primary focus of Kant's commentators and critics that they have come to appear more fundamental than they are.

Third, since the papers collected here were written over several years and for different audiences, my treatment of various topics varies somewhat in style, length, and scope. Some essays aim to present an overview of a very large topic without extensive textual references, while others are more sharply focused and detailed in citations. Later essays sometimes expand and slightly modify the interpretation presented in an earlier one, and some take up problems previously left aside. The last essay, contrasting aspects of Kant's ethics with a contemporary analogue, was originally addressed to readers of John Rawls's recent work. I hope that the resulting stylistic differences, minor changes, and occasional overlaps will not be seriously distracting.

To give a more stylistically uniform, comprehensive, and explicitly supported reconstruction of Kant's ethics is a more ambitious project than attempted in these essays. Though I have not abandoned hopes of completing such a project, the essays here may in fact speak more directly to the audiences I would most like to reach, namely, those who will treat them as potentially helpful interpretative hypotheses and constructive suggestions as they read Kant and do moral philosophy for themselves.

The Tasks of Ethics and the Order of Topics

To understand Kant's ethics it is important to identify the various tasks he thought ethical theory could accomplish and some of the special problems he faced in dealing with them. The order in which Kant addresses topics in the *Groundwork* and elsewhere is often determined by the needs of exposition and argument, and so is not a reliable guide to his conception of the distinctness, conceptual priority, or even importance of these tasks. The length and thoroughness of his treatment of various questions is also an unreliable guide, for these can also reflect his sense of how radical his answer is, how important it is to emphasize, and what kinds of proof, explanation, and illustration it admits of. I begin, then, with a sketch of how I conceive some main tasks that Kant undertakes in his ethical writings, so that my essays in this volume can be oriented with respect to these tasks as well as Kant's order of exposition.

(1) Kant recognized a need to provide an explanation, or analysis, of certain concepts expressed by "ought" and "duty" as he believed these are used in common judgments as well as in his theory. His method, of course, is not to survey many samples of ordinary discourse, but nonetheless he attempts to articulate the sense and presuppositions of common concepts. One can speculate that Kant's strong opposition to theories that try to draw basic *moral* conclusions from examples misled him into supposing that linguistic studies would have been irrelevant to his *conceptual* task. In any case he attempted to explain the concepts expressed in common *ought*-judgments, both moral and nonmoral, by a more abstract and indirect procedure.

In the first chapter of the *Groundwork* Kant begins with bold generalizations about the value of a good will and a motive of duty, and then makes an all too brief attempt to show that these are underlying presuppositions of common moral thinking. The motive of duty is then explained in more specialized terms as "reverence (or respect) for moral law" and is sharply contrasted with familiar desires and aversions. These preliminary points in the initial chapter serve at least two immediate purposes. First, they express the core of Kant's ideas about what would make a person worthy of rational and moral esteem and how this esteem-worthy trait would be expressed in the person's motives in acting. Second, Kant uses these ideas to build an argument to show that a certain principle, later to be identified as the Categorical Imperative, underlies common moral judgments and serves, among other things, as an implicit criterion of what our moral duties are. Though being morally worthy and conforming to duty are not the same, Kant makes a transition by supposing that we can at least learn how to conform to duty by studying the principle that would be ever ready and overriding for ideally esteem-worthy persons.

Kant's initial discussion of the motive of duty also sets the stage for his more direct attempt in chapter 2 of the *Groundwork* to explain the common concepts of *ought* and *duty,* employing the specialized terminology deemed necessary in a more rigorous philosophical treatment. Kant then uses the results of this conceptual investigation to suggest another, independent argument to confirm that the principle identified in chapter 1 as the criterion of duty is a fundamental presupposition of moral thinking.

The essays in which I discuss Kant's account of the ideas of *ought* and *duty* most explicitly are "The Hypothetical Imperative" and "Kant's Theory of Practical Reason" (Chapters 1 and 7). The technical terms in which Kant expresses these ideas do not merely mark grammatical distinctions. To call a normative judgment an *imperative* is to claim that it is a rational requirement. The distinction between *hypothetical* and *categorical* imperatives, then, is based on the different sorts of reasons that support the judgment. In brief, particular hypothetical imperatives are rational to follow only because (and so long as) doing so is necessary to achieve ends that one desires and *wills* to pursue but could abandon (or limit). Particular categorical imperatives are based on the general Categorical Imperative, and they prescribe constraints and ends required by reason whether or not one happens to desire them or desire anything to which they serve as a means. Independently of both his account of what our moral duties are and his argument that moral duties are really commands of reason, Kant uses his special terminology to put forward a bold analytical thesis: whenever we conceive an imperative as moral, we regard it as categorical; otherwise we see it as hypothetical.

Examination of the pattern of reasoning behind hypothetical imperatives reveals some initially surprising results. The basic principle behind particular hypothetical imperatives is "analytic," implied in the general concept of a rational agent quite apart from assumptions about particular human desires. As imperatives, these nonmoral *ought*-judgments can be, and often are, violated even though, as conditional, they always leave us with an option. Duty and desire often diverge but, strictly speaking, hypothetical and categorical imperatives cannot conflict; both are rational requirements that one can fully satisfy. Kant's account of these concepts suggests what would be needed to derive an *ought* from an *is,* and why this is so difficult, if not impossible, in the case of moral judgments. *Ought*-judgments purport to express what is *rational*, and conceptual analysis can only partly reveal the latter.

(2) Another task that Kant attributed to ethical theory was to find and explain "the supreme moral principle." He believed that presupposed in the variety of particular moral judgments that virtually everyone makes are some basic principles of duty that philosophers can articulate in general (though somewhat technical) terms. These fundamental ideas, he thought, can even be compressed into one abstract formula, but they are more fully revealed when this initial principle is reformulated in various ways. Whether these alternative formulations introduce new ideas or merely reexpress the initial principle (as Kant suggests) remains a disputed question, but in any case they contribute to a fuller and richer conception of morality than can be found by focusing exclusively on the famous first formulation.

Kant did not suppose that to live a morally decent life everyone needed consciously to articulate and apply his philosophical formulations of the supreme moral principle, but he did suggest that these can help to guide our judgments regarding specific moral problems and make us less susceptible to the corrupting influence of bad moral philosophy. Kant referred repeatedly to his supreme moral principle, in its several versions, as "*the* Categorical Imperative" because he believed that what it expresses is not only presupposed in common moral opinion but is also unconditionally required by reason. However, at least in the *Groundwork,* he sharply distinguishes these two claims. By an "analytic method" he thought he could identify the basic and comprehensive principle behind our *beliefs* about moral right and wrong, but this would still leave open the further task of "establishing" that the principle is, as we presuppose, a requirement of reason.

The supreme moral principle, expressed in the *Groundwork* as versions of the Categorical Imperative, is supposed to be identified in the two arguments mentioned earlier, the first (in chapter 1) starting from ideas about a good will and the motive of duty and the second (in chapter 2) building from a conceptual analysis of duty. The transitional arguments between the several formulas of the categorical imperative can be seen not merely as (dubious) attempts to demonstrate that these formulas are fundamentally the same but also as progressive efforts to articulate more fully a complex set of interrelated ideas implicit, or assumed, in the initial "universal law" formulation.

In "seeking out" the supreme moral principle Kant is aware of the dangers of trying to base moral conclusions on examples, and this awareness seems again to prevent him from testing his general claims about common moral judgments by the methods dominant in moral philosophy today, that is, in this case by working out the implications of general princples for many particular cases, including apparent "counter-examples." In the *Groundwork* he gives four remarkably brief illustrations of how two of his principles might be used as guides to moral decisions, but otherwise he postpones fuller discussion of this matter for his later work *The Metaphysics of Morals*.

Unfortunately, when Kant finally returned to questions about how to apply the Categorical Imperative in this later work, he did so with the assumption that previous theoretical conclusions had already been firmly established and that all that remained to do was to work out the details of a system of more specific moral principles for a less philosophically sophisticated critical audience. Believing that his supreme moral principle was an unconditional requirement of reason, Kant understandably wanted to postpone specific questions of application until he had adequately articulated it, established its claim to rationality, and explored the conception of agency and freedom presupposed by it. But Kant also claimed that his supreme moral principle is the underlying principle behind *common* moral belief and thought, and to defend this claim a fuller treatment of examples at an earlier stage would seem in order. Perhaps such reflection could have led Kant to refinements in his formulas, and in his brief examples, that could make them less open to now familiar "intuitive" objections.

In my second and third essays I present reconstructions of two of Kant's formulations of the supreme moral principle. In "Humanity as an End in Itself" the formula examined is "Act in such a way that you always treat humanity, whether in your own person or in the person of any other, never simply as a means but always at the same time as an end" (G 96 [429]). My suggestions about this formula are developed, and somewhat modified, in my last two essays (Chapters 10 and 11). In "The Kingdom of Ends"

(Chapter 3) I take up the formula that is supposed to combine the preceding ones, namely, "Every rational being must so act as if he were through his maxims always a law-making member in the universal kingdom of ends" (G 106 [438]). I discuss a problem for this formula in "Kant's Utopianism," a practical application in "Making Exceptions without Abandoning the Principle," and a comparison with John Rawls's theory of justice in "Kantian Constructivism in Ethics."

My reconstructions of Kant's views on these topics are unusual in several respects. For example, though "Treat *persons* as ends" and "Treat *humanity in persons* as an end" can be considered equivalent, I argue that the former is an abbreviation for the latter, not the reverse. "Humanity" in a person, as contrasted with a person's "animality," is one's "rational nature." "Never treat it merely as a means" is empty except by contrast with the more inclusive precept "Treat it as an end in itself," and the key to understanding the latter is the concept of dignity. Kant's later writings confirm that he understood this to be an "incalculable" value, and not only by comparison with the value of material objects and "mere" pleasure and pain. Even trade-offs between the dignity of one person and the dignity of many are forbidden, though, despite this restriction, capital punishment and risking innocent lives are not absolutely forbidden.

Kant's "kingdom of ends" principle has been warmly greeted but rarely developed by commentators. This principle draws crucial elements from the famous "universal law" formulas (as well as the dignity principle), but in many respects I think it is more promising. The kingdom (or "realm") of ends, I suggest, may be understood as a model legislative perspective from which to develop and review more specific moral principles for certain presupposed conditions. Construed in this way, the kingdom of ends principle is not open to all of the problems, notoriously raised against the "universal law" formulas, that stem from the fact that "maxims," like actions, can be described in many different ways. Though Kant did not use the principle explicitly in *The Metaphysics of Morals,* it suggests a way of thinking that helps to make sense of Kant's theory of punishment. (See Chapters 9 and 10.) It also may have advantages over Rawls's "original position" as a perspective on some ethical issues beyond the justice of basic political and economic institutions (see Chapter 11).

(3) A third major task that Kant addresses in his ethical writings is to defend belief in the rationality of moral conduct against certain sources of doubt. Kant argued that our moral concepts themselves presuppose that moral constraints are rational requirements: to believe that one has a duty to do something is to believe that it would be contrary to reason to do otherwise. But in the *Groundwork* Kant acknowledges that this conceptual point alone does not prove that our belief that we are subject to rational moral constaints is *true;* for he admits that the "analytical" argument for the point is compatible with the possibility that we *really* have no moral duties. The third chapter of the *Groundwork* argues that this apparent possibility is not in fact one that any rational agent can take seriously. The perspective of rational deliberation and choice itself, he maintains, necessarily commits one to a conception of oneself as rationally bound in a way that leaves no room for moral skepticism, or at least for doubts about the rationality of the supreme moral principle.

Here Kant's focus of attention is not on several forms of skepticism now quite prevalent: (a) the amoralist who grants that he has moral duties but professes not to care, (b) the relativist who draws from cultural disagreements grounds to doubt the universal validity of our particular moral beliefs, or (c) the noncognitivist who doubts that moral judgments can be "true" or "known" in the senses pertinent in science. Also Kant has, in effect, already responded to philosphers who would *reduce* moral judgments to reports, or expressions, of sentiments when he argued (in chapter 2 of the *Groundwork*) that "moral duty" *implies* "rational constraint." The skeptical doubts to which chapter 3 of the *Groundwork* is more relevant, then, come primarily from two sources: philosophers who think that causal determinism in empirical science has moral consequences and those who maintain that practical reason merely prescribes efficient and informed pursuit of self-interest or of whatever ends one most desires.

Kant's attempt to undermine these sources of doubt is reviewed most directly in Chapter 6, "Kant's Argument for the Rationality of Moral Conduct." Here I take seriously aspects of Kant's ethics that have been until recently relatively neglected in contemporary discussions despite the widespread current interest in the topic of practical reason. Kant's argument in the third chapter of the *Groundwork* is usually dismissed as a confusion and error that Kant finally abandoned when he wrote *The Critique of Practical Reason*, but I attempt to reconstruct that argument as a serious and necessary completion of Kant's project in the *Groundwork*, with aspects worth taking seriously.

(4) A further task of moral philosophy, which Kant took as necessary for adequate treatment of the rest, is to give some account of the ideas of desire, reason, freedom, and "will" as they are used in his argument and presupposed in any practical reasoning. Unfortunately, Kant's treatment of these matters is heavily laden with a specialized conceptual apparatus that requires (and almost defies) interpretation in contemporary terminology. Nonetheless in two essays I try to describe some main features of these concepts and their practical import. "The Kantian Conception of Autonomy" distinguishes contemporary views of autonomy from the fundamental Kantian idea, the neglect of which Kant believed to be the source of error in all previous moral philosophies. Again stepping back from textual details, in "Kant's Theory of Practical Reason" I summarize some main features of Kant's theory, as I understand it, for purposes of comparison with recent "Kantian" and other theories of practical reason.

The papers concerning autonomy, Kant's argument that our commitment to morality is rational, and practical reason (Chapters 5, 6, and 7) concern the most fundamental and difficult features of Kant's ethics. At first I had been primarily interested in Kant's moral principles as a systematic alternative to utilitarianism, but increasingly I have become convinced not only (as I always feared) that the moral principles must be understood in the context of the whole theory but also (as I never anticipated) that Kant's discussions of freedom and practical reason may be the most profound and richly suggestive aspects of his work. To those of us steeped in a tradition that respects only rigor and precision in formal systems and plain speaking in the rest of philosophy, these aspects of Kant's theory are at first daunting, and always frustrating. But beneath the surface obscurity and before one falls into a metaphysical nightmare there is, I believe, a layer of practical wisdom worth taking seriously.

A central idea throughout these essays (5, 6, and 7) is that Kant's main project in the *Groundwork* was not to resolve metaphysical issues but to answer concerns of rational human beings reflecting on the traditional ethical questions, *What ought I to do? What ends are rationally worth pursuing, and in what order?* and *Why?* In taking seriously such questions, one sees the world (and oneself) from the standpoint of an agent, facing options for choice and concerned to find good reasons for choosing. From this point of view even one's own desires, hopes, and previous decisions become part of the background against which, as a reflective agent, one must now affirm a goal and a plan. Hidden causal mechanisms and "unconscious desires" may, or may not, be needed for the explanatory and predictive purposes of empirical science, and becoming more aware of the particular tendencies and limits that these impose can be practically useful. From the deliberative point of view, however, one's questions are normative ones, one's options are defined within the range of one's awareness, and one's presumption must be that one faces a choice among options that are still "open" in an appropriate sense.

How to understand that sense, of course, is a long disputed question. About this issue Kant makes two strong claims. First, empirical science, even construed deterministically, does not contradict or undermine the necessary presuppositions of practical deliberation. Second, compatibilists such as Hume are deeply misguided in their attempts to understand the ideas of reason, freedom, and "will," as these are presupposed in rational deliberation, solely within the conceptual framework appropriate for explaining and predicting causally related sequences of events (empirically observed or inferred). Although Kant's treatment of these matters at times seems to cross the boundaries of both good sense and his own critical philosophy, at least some aspects of what is often read as crossing that line into forbidden metaphysical territory can also be construed as significant points about practical reasoning from a deliberative agent's standpoint.

One major theme embedded in Kant's discussion of freedom, apart from any supposed threats to morality from deterministic science, is his opposition to the idea that what practical reason demands is merely informed pursuit of self-interest or selection of the best available means to one's preferred ends, whatever those may be. That Kant rejects these views is obvious once one understands what he means in asserting that there are categorical imperatives. But the question remains: how can we understand a rational requirement to act contrary to our self-interest and even our desires? In what sense is this even possible?

To understand Kant's position, I suggest, we must see it as a part of his attempt to express what we presuppose about the relation between our desires and our normative reasons to act when we deliberate about what we ought to do. As often in the first *Critique,* Kant combined a stronger and more dubious thesis with a weaker and more persuasive thesis. The more modest claim is that recognition of rational constraints on the pursuit of desire and self-interest is *possible* for us and is even inherent in *our* conception of ourselves as rational/moral agents in deliberation. The more extreme thesis, which even Kant in the end realized he could not prove, is that acknowledgment of these rational constraints is *necessary* because inherent in practical deliberation by *any* possible rational agent with desires.

(5) Once the foundations of ethics have been identified and established, Kant thought, a remaining task for moral philosophers is to work out a complete system of rational moral principles. Ideally this would be a consistent and coherent set of moral principles, rationally grounded in the Categorical Imperative, neatly divided into types indicating where, to whom, and with what stringency each principle applies. The principles are supposed to be morally and rationally binding for all human beings, but they could be presented (Kant thought) in a somewhat informal style, with examples, for a popular audience.

The Metaphysics of Morals was Kant's main effort to sketch a rational system of moral principles. Though far from the ideal for such a system, what Kant says there is important. It reveals more specifically than the *Groundwork* the sort of morality Kant thought to be rationally defensible, and it provides clues for understanding Kant's general moral theory as well as suggestions for working on particular moral issues in a Kantian spirit.

The system of principles, except for the supreme moral principle itself, is meant to be the result of applying considerations valid for any rational being to recurring human problems. Thus, despite Kant's occasional remarks to the contrary, we should not expect arguments for these principles to be completely free from empirical assumptions. The arguments should, in fact, take into account general facts about the human condition. If, as Kant thought, certain teleological claims about "nature's purposes" are defensible, then one could also use these claims, as Kant did, in arguing for specific moral principles. The principles themselves are not supposed to be dependent on local facts, that is, on conditions that vary from one place or time to another. To apply any principle to a particular case, however, requires *judgment,* and good judgment requires understanding the context of the problem. Even the principles of perfect duty cannot be put into practice in ignorance of the facts of one's situation, and informed judgment is needed in deciding when, how much, and to whom to carry out the widest "duties of virtue" (such as beneficence).

My last four essays concern Kant's plan and efforts to develop a rational system of moral principles grounded in the Categorical Imperative. The first of these, "Kant on Imperfect Duty and Supererogation," attempts to explain how Kant distinguishes types of duty and how he thought moral worth varies not only according to the agent's motive but also according to the type of duty in question. Kant's set of categories for evaluating actions turns out to be richer and more complex in *The Metaphysics of Morals* than it appears to be in the *Groundwork.* The scheme even seems to leave a place, under another name, for what some contemporary philosophers call *supererogatory* acts.

The essay titled "Kant's Anti-Moralistic Strain" calls attention to several ways in which, contrary to its popular image, Kant's ethical theory makes our duties to others largely independent of what we judge their moral merits and demerits to be. Even in justifying punishment and its appropriate measure ("an eye for an eye"), Kant's theory, I argue, does not rest on the retributivist idea that people should prosper or suffer according to their inner deserts.

The next essay, "Making Exceptions without Abandoning the Principle," raises the question how, if at all, Kant's idea of human dignity could allow the killing of terrorists and the endangering of innocent hostages even when extraordinary circumstances seem to demand this. This question raises a more general issue, crucial for Kantian ethics, namely, how a reasonable moral agent could maintain any action-guiding principle as exceptionless in the face of all the horrible choices we may be forced to make. My tentative proposal draws from Kant's rationale for capital punishment and makes use of the interpretations of "humanity as an end" and "the kingdom of ends" presented in Chapters 2 and 3.

The final essay, "Kantian Constructivism in Ethics," contrasts Kant's legislative perspective for determining moral principles with John Rawls's "original position" for choosing the principles of justice. This essay was initially written largely as a warning against the tendency in "applied ethics" to extend Rawls's theory of justice uncritically to other moral issues. It seems too often assumed, though not by Rawls, that an ideal choice perspective carefully constructed to resolve questions of institutional justice would automatically be an appropriate perspective for addressing all moral issues. The essay is included here (with slight modifications) because it contrasts Kant's theory, as presented in my previous essays, with the most important and influential development of Kant's work in recent times.

1

The Hypothetical Imperative

Commentators on Kant's theory of practical reason have devoted much attention to his concept of the Categorical Imperative and its several formulations. Comparatively little has been said about the principle which I shall call "the Hypothetical Imperative." An understanding of this principle, however, is essential for an undistorted view of Kant's theory. Neglect of the Hypothetical Imperative results in failure to see both the striking parallels and the important differences between Kant's account of moral reasoning and his account of prudential reasoning. My objects in this paper are, first, to sketch an interpretation of the principle I refer to as "the Hypothetical Imperative"; second, to explain a sense in which it is a hypothetical imperative, though a very special one; and, finally, to explain why, despite the similarities between the Categorical Imperative and the Hypothetical Imperative, Kant assigned a special sublimity to actions based on the Categorical Imperative.

I

The Hypothetical Imperative may be expressed provisionally as follows: *If a person wills an end and certain means are necessary*

This paper owes much to the lectures of John Rawls at Harvard in 1962. In addition I have received helpful comments from several sources, including John G. Bennett, Sharon Bishop Hill, and the editors of the *Philosophical Review*.

to achieve that end and are within his power, then he ought to will those means. Kant never explicitly states the imperative in this ("ought") form, but he does mention "the imperative which commands the willing of the means to him who wills the end" as a principle presupposed in both imperatives of skill and imperatives of prudence (G 86 [419]). Moreover, that there is such an imperative for men is implied by his repeated contention that whoever wills an end, if he is fully rational, wills also the necessary means to that end which are in his power. For to say that a principle is an imperative for men is simply to say that it is a rational principle for men to follow expressed in one of those special forms (for example, "One ought . . . ") in which rational principles are appropriately addressed to imperfectly rational wills—that is, to those who can follow them but who might fail to do so. The Hypothetical Imperative merely expresses what Kant regards as a fundamental rational principle in the "ought" form appropriate for us as imperfectly rational beings.

The Hypothetical Imperative, as I understand it, is a principle of conduct and not simply an explication of what it is to *will* an end. It states how men ought to act, even though sometimes, irrationally, they fail to comply. Often, however, Kant is understood in a quite different way. The slogan "Who wills an end, wills the means" is construed not as a principle of rational conduct but as an analytic truth concerning the concept of willing an end. On this reading Kant's point is that anyone who wills an end necessarily *does* will the means. No one is to be condemned for irrationally failing to will the means to his ends; for such failure is conceptually impossible. This common (though, I think, mistaken) interpretation is not a stupid one; some passages do suggest it. Nevertheless, I believe for several reasons that it cannot represent Kant's dominant line of thought. First, Kant usually states the allegedly analytic proposition in a qualified way that shows that what is intended is *"If a person is fully rational and wills an end, then he wills the necessary means."* Consider, for example:

> Whoever wills the end, *so far as reason has decisive influence on his action,* wills also the indispensably necessary means to it that lie in his power. (G 84–85 [417]; my italics)

Whoever wills the end wills also (*necessarily according to reason*) the only means to it which are in his power [my italics].[1]

If I *fully* will the effect, I must also will the action necessary to produce it. (G 85 [417]; my italics)

Since "will" is sometimes identified with "practical reason," "fully will" may mean "choose as a completely rational and informed person"; but, in any case, "fully will" contrasts with simply "will" and thus the last quotation does not deny that one can will an end without willing the necessary means in his power. Second, Kant explicitly refers to "the imperative which commands him who wills the end to will the means," and there could be no such *command* or *imperative*, by Kant's doctrines, if failure to conform were impossible (G 86 [419]). Third, if it is a necessary truth that anyone who wills an end also wills the necessary means, then there is no imperative "Whoever wills an end, *ought* to will the necessary means"; and, if this is so, then there is no valid way of justifying particular hypothetical imperatives. For typically a particular hypothetical imperative is of the form "If one wills A (a certain end), then one *ought* to will B (a certain means)," and such "ought" propositions cannot be supported by empirical facts (for example, B is a necessary means to A) alone. A general "ought" premise, the Hypothetical Imperative, is also required.

Now assuming that I am right in thinking of the Hypothetical Imperative as a principle of conduct, what is its practical import? A partial answer has already been suggested: the Hypothetical Imperative serves as a general, though rarely articulated, premise in arguments for various nonmoral "ought" judgments. The pattern of such arguments would be as follows:

(1) Whoever wills an end also wills the sole means which are in his power if he is fully rational.
(2) Whoever wills an end ought to will the sole means which are within his power. Or, in other words, if a person wills an end and

---

[1] *Foundations of the Metaphysics of Morals*, trans. L. W. Beck (Indianapolis: Bobbs-Merrill, 1959), p. 35. Kant's words are: *"wer Zweck will, will auch (der Vernunft gemäss notwendig) die einzigen Mittel, die dazu in seiner Gewalt sind."* Paton's translation, I think, is misleading at this point. See G 85 [418].

certain means are necessary to achieve that end and are within his power, then he ought to will those means.
(3) A is the sole means to B and is generally available (within everyone's power).
Therefore,
(4) If one wills B, one ought to will A.
(5) Q (a person) wills B.
Therefore,
(6) Q ought to will A.

(1) is a proposition which Kant held to be analytic; (2) is the Hypothetical Imperative, an expression of (1) in imperative form; (3) and (5) must express empirical facts; and (4) is the typical form of Kant's particular hypothetical imperatives. Used in an argument of this sort, the Hypothetical Imperative is an essential step in the support of particular hypothetical imperatives. Together with certain empirical facts it backs up particular judgments, such as "I ought (to will) to get new tires for my car" and "I ought (to will) to lose a few pounds." One way of failing to obey the Hypothetical Imperative, then, is to fail to do what can be inferred that one ought to do, given the Hypothetical Imperative and the facts about one's ends and the necessary means to them.

The Hypothetical Imperative can also be viewed in another way, apart from its role in arguments for particular hypothetical imperatives. That is, the Hypothetical Imperative can function as a general proscription of a kind of duplicity that we associate with neurotic behavior. What it condemns is the irrational failure to follow through on our own morally permissible projects. What it prescribes is that we decide to take the requisite steps to achieve goals that we have already decided to pursue. The paradigm of a person who offends against the imperative is the man who continues to declare himself for a goal, takes many steps toward it, and half hopes to achieve it even though he systematically refuses to take some means obviously necessary to reach the goal. For example, a man solemnly resolves to lose ten pounds of excess weight, buys smaller clothes, weighs himself each day hopefully, but rarely chooses the lighter meals that are required to do the job.

To clarify this second function of the Hypothetical Imperative, it may be useful to consider some natural objections to it. Consider, for example, the following: "A person typically has many desires and aims at the same time, and an act that is necessary as a means to the satisfaction of one of these may lead to the frustration of many others. It is often foolish, therefore, to take the means to an end one has even if it is the only means within one's power. The cost may simply be too high." To meet this objection we need to make clearer what the Hypothetical Imperative prescribes. It does not say that one should take the necessary means to every end that one has, still less that one must take the requisite steps to satisfy every desire. The imperative prescribes only the means necessary to ends *that one wills*. To will an end, I take it, is not simply to have an indeterminate goal which one hopes somehow to reach; it involves deciding, resolving, or setting oneself to go for the goal. A fully rational being, presumably, would will an end only after duly reflecting on what is required to achieve it, weighing the cost, and so forth. Thus the principle that a fully rational being would accept, stated more completely, is (roughly) to do whatever is a necessary means within his power to an end that, after due deliberation, he actually sets himself to pursue.[2] The person who offends against the principle, then, is not in general the person who lets his opportunity pass to achieve some ideal goal or to satisfy some desire; it is the man who deliberates carefully and resolves, in the light of all relevant circumstances, to pursue a certain goal but who balks when the anticipated means present themselves.

Another natural objection to the Hypothetical Imperative is this. "The Hypothetical Imperative seems to say that if one has already decided to pursue an end, then one must carry through with the necessary means. The dieter's neurotic balking at the means to his goal does seem irrational; but is it always unreasonable to change one's mind after one has decided to pursue a goal? Suppose a man decides to become a doctor and attends a year of

[2]Strictly speaking, the principle is to *will* the necessary means, not to *take* them or to *do* what is required. We can assume for all practical purposes, however, that anyone who *wills* some means *within his power* also takes those means. Thus I shall not always state the principle in the strict way.

medical school. The second and third years of training are necessary means to his end, but he has doubts about his goal and
suspects that he would rather be a philosopher. The Hypothetical
Imperative seems to demand that he finish his training regardless
of his doubts simply because he earlier decided to become a phy-
sician. But, surely, there need be no irrationality in his anticipated
change of profession." This objection, I suspect, is a result of a too
simple identification of "willing" with "deciding." If we understand "willing an end" as simply "deciding to pursue an end,"
then this suggests that willing an end takes place at a rather specific time and then is done. Thus the precept "If one wills an end,
one ought to will the means" becomes "If the act of willing the
end has taken place, then one must decide to take the necessary
steps to implement it." Reconsideration and changes of goal are
prohibited once the required event, willing the end, has taken
place. Now, although willing is in some respects like deciding, the
suggestion that it is an act or even that it takes place at a specific
time may be misleading. Willing is in some respects like wanting
and believing; whether one wills an end is determined by a complex pattern of thoughts, actions, and dispositions over a period of
time. Because of this, the precept "If one wills an end, one ought
to will the means" might be better rendered as "If one has decided
to pursue a certain end and remains constant in his commitment to
it, then one ought to will the necessary means within his power."
This expresses the idea of "willing an end" in a clumsy and imperfect way but it avoids the suggestion that it refers to a momentary occurrence.

Now, with the last point in mind, we can answer our second
objection to the Hypothetical Imperative. The objection stems
from the idea that the Hypothetical Imperative demands that
one carry through on every project on which one at some time or
other decided. But this is not what the Hypothetical Imperative
requires. If "willing an end" is understood as I have suggested,
then the Hypothetical Imperative demands only that a person
follow through in practice the commitments he has made and
does not withdraw. It does not prohibit reconsideration but only
the irrational refusal to implement decisions that one continues
to reaffirm. To the man who doubts his earlier decision, it says,
in effect: "Face the fact that you cannot reach your goal with-

out these means—either give up your resolve to reach the goal or decide to take the means." What the Hypothetical Imperative condemns is not the changing of one's aims; it is the irrationality of continuing to profess, work toward, and hope for certain ends even though one is unwilling to take some essential means to realize them.

A third objection might be put as follows: "The use of certain means is immoral; or, even if there are some ends that would justify the means (not Kant's view), at least some of our lesser ends do not warrant the means necessary to them. Sometimes the moral thing to do is to let the only chance to achieve our ends pass because the ends are of too little value to justify our taking the shocking means required to reach them. On some occasions to will the necessary means to one's end is immoral." Now it is abundantly clear that Kant would not condone, and still less encourage, a person to achieve his ends by taking means contrary to the Categorical Imperative, even if the ends could be achieved in no other way. What is perhaps not so clear is how this attitude squares with what he says about the rationality of taking the necessary means to one's ends. It is tempting to say that the Hypothetical Imperative was intended to express only a prima facie requirement of rationality and that the Categorical Imperative was meant to take precedence in case of conflict. This way of putting the matter, however, is unsatisfactory. For imperatives are supposed to tell us that certain acts are *necessary*, not merely that there is a prima facie case for them; and, as principles of reason, imperatives should never fall into an irreconcilable conflict. That is, one imperative should never demand unequivocally that we do something prohibited unequivocally by another imperative. A rational man should not have to choose between obeying one objective principle or another.

The resort to prima facie requirements, moreover, is unnecessary. The proper reply to the third objection is to point out that it wrongly assumes that, unless qualified, the Hypothetical Imperative sometimes prescribes unequivocally that a person take immoral means. The Hypothetical Imperative does in fact imply that there is some irrationality in the man who remains committed to a certain end but nevertheless refuses to take the necessary but immoral means to it. This does not mean, however, that the Hypothetical Imperative demands that he use the immoral means; for there is another alternative. He can abandon the end. Insofar as this remains a possibility, what the Hypothetical Imperative prescribes, in effect, is "Take the necessary means or else give up the end." If we assume with Kant that moral rules are backed by a Categorical Imperative which expresses an unqualified requirement of reason, then the rational person will have to give up his ends when they can be achieved only by immoral means. The Hypothetical Imperative poses an alternative, and in some cases the Categorical Imperative eliminates one of these options.

To illustrate, consider the Nazi officer who must kill thousands of prisoners in order to advance himself in the party, an end to which he is fanatically committed. He balks, failing to release the gas, even though he remains firmly set in his ambition and he knows that the killing is necessary as a means. According to the Hypothetical Imperative, the man is irrational; for he fails to take the necessary means to his ends. He could avoid *that* irrationality by going ahead with the killing, but then he would run afoul of the Categorical Imperative, another principle of rationality. The only rational course, then, is to abandon the end of advancement in the party. In this way he can completely satisfy the requirements of both rational principles.

This reply depends, of course, upon Kant's belief that the use of immoral means is contrary to a categorical imperative. A categorical imperative, by definition, is an unconditional principle of rationality; and nothing would count as such a principle if it resulted in irreconcilably conflicting commands. Thus, while it is notoriously difficult to show that there is a categorical imperative behind our moral beliefs, it is not difficult to show that, if there is one, it will never both demand the pursuit of an end and yet prohibit the only means to it. If, as Kant supposed, morality is rational, it does not lead to irresolvable moral dilemmas. Thus when the Hypothetical Imperative confronts us with a choice of taking certain means or abandoning an end, we know that the Categorical Imperative (if there is one) will condemn only one option, not both. The first principle of a rational morality would not prohibit us from satisfying other principles of rationality.

Kant apparently believed that a person can always abandon his ends when they require immoral means, but this belief is not presupposed in our reply to the third objection.[3] We must take for granted that a fully *rational* person can give up his ends when rational principles so direct, but we need not assume that everyone is always capable of complete rationality. If a compulsive person were unable to abandon an end when he saw that it required immoral means, he would simply be unable to act rationally. He might still refuse to take the means but without making the adjustments in his life plans which the Hypothetical Imperative demands. In such a case he would demonstrate a capacity for satisfying one principle of rationality, the Categorical Imperative, but not both. Kant and modern psychologists would no doubt disagree about the extent to which we are capable of rational action, but that is not the issue. The answer to the third objection is that the prescriptions of the Hypothetical Imperative are always compatible with those of a rational morality, not that we always have the psychological capacity to satisfy both.

[3]The idea that a person can always abandon his ends when they require immoral means, I take it, is a consequence of Kant's radical notion of free will. To will something is not the same as to desire it. For our desires are given, so to speak, but Kant says that the distinctive feature of humanity is the power to set oneself an end, *any end whatsoever* (DV 51 [390]). Again, Kant says that "adoption of any end whatsoever is an act of freedom on the agent's part, not an operation of nature" (DV 43–44 [384–85]). Thus no matter how much a person may desire an end, he still has the ability not to pursue it if doing so is immoral.

An apparent counter-example arises from Kant's claim that all men have happiness as their end by "natural necessity" (G 83 [416]). Happiness, on Kant's view, is not a particular end (like winning a race) but an indeterminate idea of the realization of all one's ends. Since one's ends do not form a clearly understood or even coherent set, there is rarely, if ever, an occasion to say that a particular act is a necessary means to happiness. Prudential imperatives give only "counsel," rather than definite requirements, and often we can come as close to that amorphous ideal of happiness by replacing our specific ends as by pursuing them. Still, if we understand "happiness" in an ordinary way, there may be times when unless we do something immoral we shall lose all hope of happiness. Then if we cannot abandon the end of happiness, we cannot satisfy both the Categorical and the Hypothetical Imperative. Faced with this problem, we might salvage Kant's main points by making a distinction between *having* an end and *willing* an end. All men, one might say, have happiness as their end—that is, desire it—by natural necessity; but it is contrary to the doctrine of free will to say that men on all occasions necessarily *will* happiness as their end—that is, set themselves to pursue it.

II

When Kant introduced the distinction between categorical and hypothetical imperatives, he was apparently thinking of the contrast between the Categorical Imperative and particular hypothetical imperatives, such as "If you aim to get well, you ought to take this medicine." Nevertheless, it is clear that he would classify what I call "the Hypothetical Imperative" as an imperative and as hypothetical. I shall try to explain briefly why this is so.

The idea of an *imperative* presupposes Kant's distinction between objective and subjective principles. (G 81 [413]). A subjective principle is a principle on which one person (or "subject") acts. Thus both "Seek peace" and "Annihilate your enemies" are subjective principles. An objective principle is one which every rational person would follow if he were acting in a completely rational way. It is not, of course, a principle that all rational persons happen, by some coincidence, to follow; it is a principle they adopt because they are rational. Whether anyone actually acts on a principle is irrelevant to whether it is an objective principle. The supreme moral principle, for example, is held to be an objective principle even though Kant says that it is uncertain whether anyone ever acted entirely on that principle (G 75 [407]). The same principle can be both objective and subjective. In fact, whenever a person acts on a rational principle, his subjective principle is also objective.

Objective principles can be stated either in a general way applicable to all rational beings (including the "divine will") or in a way appropriate only for "imperfect wills" (such as we have). When objective principles are stated generally, they can be expressed with the words "to do . . . ," "to avoid . . . ," and the like, as in "The over-riding principle is to preserve the peace."[4] The principle of autonomy is stated in this way: "Never to choose except in such a way that in the same volition the maxims of your choice are also present as universal law" (G 108 [440]). When expressed in the general way applicable to the divine will, objective principles will not include the terms "ought," "obligation," and "duty." Imperatives, however, express objective principles (or ap-

---

[4]This point I take from Rawls.

plications of these) less generally, in a way appropriately addressed only to imperfectly rational wills (G 81 [414]). These are the wills of persons who can follow the principles but might not. Kant's idea is that if a person necessarily conforms to a principle it is inappropriate to say that he *ought* to do so, that it is his *duty*, and so forth. Human beings, however, always have imperfect wills. Because they are rational and have free will, they can follow objective principles; because they also have sensuous desires, they might not. This is true of the best men along with the worst. The human condition, as it were, guarantees that imperative forms of expressing objective principles are never inappropriate for us.

Kant's imperatives should not be identified with the class of linguistic expressions that serve to convey the idea that something ought to be done or avoided. Imperatives, in Kant's terminology, are not simply "ought" sentences or statements, nor are they (like ordinary commands) merely complex speech acts. They are, rather, formulae that express objective principles (or principles derivable from these). In order to state an imperative it is necessary, but not sufficient, to use "ought" or some equivalent. One must also formulate a principle, or an application of a principle, to which any fully rational person would conform. That is, imperatives are formulae which present principles that actually are objective; they are not merely expressions through which someone purports to state an objective principle.[5] The category of imperatives, then, is no more a linguistic (or grammatical) category than is that of *true* indicative sentences.

To say that a given principle is an imperative, then, is to make a claim about its rationality as well as its form and linguistic propriety. That is, a principle is an imperative for human beings if, but only if, it is appropriate to express the principle to human

[5]This point makes clear some of Kant's remarks which otherwise would be inexplicable. E.g., if an imperative were simply an utterance which purports to express an objective principle, then the question "How are imperatives possible?" would be pointless. See G 84 [417]. Again, at several points Kant implies that it is a formidable task to establish that a certain principle, the principle of autonomy, "is an imperative for human beings" (G 86–87 [419–20], 92 [425], 108 [440]). If principles could be made into imperatives simply by expressing them in an "ought" formula, there would be no problem. In fact, Kant paraphrases the statement "this rule (the principle of autonomy) is an imperative" with the words "that is, . . . the will of every rational being is necessarily bound to the rule as a condition" (G 108 [440]).

beings in "ought" form *and* the principle is one (or the application of one) that any fully rational person would follow. Now the principle which the Hypothetical Imperative expresses, stated generally, is "to will the necessary means to one's ends if they are within one's power." There is no impropriety in addressing this principle to ourselves in "ought" form insofar as we can follow the principle but might not. Any fully rational person would follow the principle, according to Kant, for the concept of a fully rational person is, at least in part, the concept of a person who does not hesitate to take the requisite steps toward the ends which he affirms (G 84–85 [417–18]). If so, it follows that the principle is an objective principle and its expression in "ought" form, which I have called "the Hypothetical Imperative," is an imperative.

To explain why the Hypothetical Imperative is a *hypothetical* imperative is more difficult. So far it seems to share the most striking features of Kant's conception of the Categorical Imperative: it is a principle that any fully rational person would follow, it expresses a stringent rather than a prima facie requirement of reason, and to establish its rationality we do not need any contingent premises about what human beings desire. Moreover, the Hypothetical Imperative does not, like particular hypothetical imperatives, "declare a possible action to be practically necessary as a means to the attainment of something else that one wills (or that one may will)" (G 82 [414]). The Hypothetical Imperative is a general principle that does not mention particular ends or means; it tells us only that we ought to will the means to our ends, whatever these may be. If the Hypothetical Imperative is hypothetical, then, there must be some more general account of what makes imperatives hypothetical.

A tempting but inadequate proposal is that hypothetical imperatives can be distinguished from categorical ones by form. Thus the distinctive form of a fully stated hypothetical imperative would be "If one wants (seeks, and so forth) A, then one ought to do X." The typical form of a categorical imperative, in contrast, would be simply "One ought to do X." A major problem with this way of distinguishing the types of imperatives is that the distinction does not coincide, as Kant intended, with the distinction between moral and nonmoral imperatives.[6] Moral imperatives are supposed to be categorical and nonmoral ones hypothetical. But consider the following. The principle "If you want to kill someone for money, you ought to restrain yourself" has some credibility as a moral one; but it is hypothetical in form. Similarly, the supposedly moral imperative in Kant's example concerning a man tempted to suicide might be expressed: "If one wants to end one's life merely to minimize one's pains, one ought to resist the temptation." Again, a nonmoral imperative might be expressed in categorical form: for example, "One ought to treat a headache with aspirin." One might argue that after proper analysis this would be stated in hypothetical form, but it would not be easy to say what constitutes a "proper analysis" without begging the question at issue. The examples just considered have been particular imperatives, but the same point can be made with Kant's most general ones. What Kant calls "the Categorical Imperative," for instance, can be stated in the form "If you want to do something X but cannot will acting on that want to become a universal law, then you ought not to do X." Again, the Hypothetical Imperative can be expressed in categorical form: "You ought always to take the necessary, available means to your ends." The natural linguistic form of an imperative may provide a good clue concerning whether it is hypothetical or categorical, but it does not adequately reflect the distinction Kant wanted to make.

Again, one might think that hypothetical imperatives are distinguished from categorical imperatives by the fact that in the absence of empirical data they give no substantive prescriptions about what one ought to do. Particular hypothetical imperatives tell us the means to our ends, or at least they are based on such information; and, though the Hypothetical Imperative neither gives nor is based upon empirical data, it yields no advice until information about particular means and ends is supplied. The Categorical Imperative, by contrast, is supposed to be an a priori principle which is the foundation of a purely rational system of ethical principles. It may seem, then, that the Categorical Imperative is distinct from the Hypothetical Imperative in that it can

[6]See L. W. Beck's "Apodictic Imperatives," *Kant-Studien*, Band 49, Heft 1 (1957–58).

give us substantive commands which are not based on empirical facts and so hold regardless of empirical conditions. Kant does sometimes suggest this contrast; but it is not one to which he consistently held, and on closer view it appears highly implausible. Kant's own examples of the application of the Categorical Imperative usually, if not always, rely upon empirical information.[7] Moreover, even if the general principles in *The Metaphysics of Morals* could be derived a priori, they could hardly be applied in any real case without empirical information about the case at hand. One cannot follow the principle to promote the ends of others, for example, without knowing what these are.

What is needed is a general account of hypothetical imperatives which will appropriately classify principles of different forms and levels of generality as hypothetical. Each of the following, for example, should turn out to be hypothetical: (a) the Hypothetical Imperative, (b) "If one aims to be a concert violinist, one ought to practice," and (c) "Jack Glatzer ought to practice his violin." What these have in common is simply that they are parts of a certain pattern of argument for particular prescriptions, such as (c). (See pp. 19–20.) If we think of particular prescriptions as imperatives prescribing unequivocally what a particular person ought to do at a certain time, then we can characterize hypothetical imperatives in general as follows. Imperatives are hypothetical if *either* they support particular prescriptions for a person only in conjunction with premises describing that person's ends *or* they cannot themselves be supported without premises describing the ends of the person to whom they are directed. No information about an agent's ends is required to support (a) and (b) above, but these will not tell a particular person specifically what he ought to do until such information is supplied. The Hypothetical Imperative, then, is like more specific imperatives of the typical "If one wills . . . , one ought . . . " type in this respect: they are hypothetical because no specific unequivocal directives can be derived from them until we know what ends the agent in question wills. Particular prescriptions such as (c) above are hypothetical for a different reason:

[7]See Jonathan Harrison, "Kant's Examples of the First Formulation of the Categorical Imperative," *Philosophical Quarterly* 7 (Jan. 1957); 50–62. Also consider Kant's arguments for the principles of duty in DV.

although they express unequivocal prescriptions to an agent, those prescriptions cannot be rationally defended without information about the agent's ends.

In either case, there is no route from first principles of reason to particular prescriptions for an individual until the individual has committed himself to certain goals, and the character of the resulting prescriptions is contingent upon the nature of those goals.

Categorical imperatives, by contrast, can be defined as imperatives which are not hypothetical.[8] If there are categorical imperatives, we can expect at least one to be a general principle of rationality and others to be specific "ought" judgments derived from this: for example, on Kant's view, the Categorical Imperative and the more specific prohibition against lying. To any categorical imperative we should be able to add "regardless of what you will," or something similar. The most general categorical imperative, like the Hypothetical Imperative, should be rational independent of contingent facts about which means are necessary for various ends; but particular categorical imperatives must be independent only of facts about what the agent's ends are. Both the Hypothetical Imperative and the Categorical Imperative might support a particular imperative, such as "I ought to tell the truth now," but then the imperative will be categorical because information about the agent's own ends is not *necessary* to establish the rationality of the prescription. The issue whether moral principles really *are* categorical imperatives is simply the issue whether there is a general principle of rationality, distinct from the Hypothetical Imperative, which can support those moral principles and their specific applications without relying at any stage upon a certain type of empirical information—namely, what the agent in question wills to pursue as an end. It is this independence of the

[8]An apparent counter-example is the following case. Suppose I promise a friend that if I choose (will) to run for political office I shall tell him immediately. Then I decide to run. The imperative "I ought to tell my friend now" cannot be supported without the information that I willed a certain end, and so it must be classified as hypothetical even though it seems obviously a moral imperative. Though bizarre, this consequence need not be too troublesome. For the imperative "I ought to tell my friend now" is based on moral principles, and one could still regard these as categorical imperatives. The relevant categorical imperatives would be "One ought to keep promises (unless . . .)" and "I ought to tell my friend now or change my plan to run for office."

commitments of the agent, and not independence of all empirical facts whatever, that makes moral prescriptions categorical (if they are).

III

So far the Hypothetical Imperative has been presented as the expression of a principle which any fully rational person would adopt and which men ought always to follow. Moreover, I have suggested that it is misleading to say that the Categorical Imperative takes precedence over the Hypothetical Imperative, for, properly understood, the two principles cannot conflict. The main difference between the principles which has appeared so far is that the Hypothetical Imperative can be applied only when information about the agent's ends is supplied. This difference, however, hardly seems sufficient to account for the sublimity which Kant accords to the Categorical Imperative. There must be some further distinction which explains the extraordinary importance Kant placed on the Categorical Imperative and his comparative neglect of the Hypothetical Imperative.

One difference, of course, is that Kant held the Hypothetical Imperative to be easier to follow and to justify than the Categorical Imperative. The Categorical Imperative often demands the sacrifice of self-interest whereas the Hypothetical Imperative, typically, is in the service of long-term self-interest. The Hypothetical Imperative rarely calls for the sort of internal struggle that the Categorical Imperative demands. Moreover, on Kant's view, the Hypothetical Imperative can be inferred rather simply from a proposition analytic of the ordinary concept of rationality whereas the Categorical Imperative can be justified, if at all, only by a long, tortured argument employing both "analytic" and "synthetic" methods. These differences no doubt help to account for the fact that Kant devoted so much more space to the Categorical Imperative, but they do not explain the boundless esteem Kant felt for the man who acts out of respect for the Categorical Imperative. Why should he not have equal esteem for the man who, following the Hypothetical Imperative, overcomes immediate impulse for the sake of some long-range goal?

The Categorical Imperative, unlike the Hypothetical Imperative, is supposed to be a synthetic principle. Although this does not, by itself, explain the special importance of the Categorical Imperative, it does provide a clue. For, when we consider why the Categorical Imperative is synthetic, we discover that the reason has to do with a distinctive connection between the Categorical Imperative and positive freedom (autonomy); and this connection, I suggest, is what makes the Categorical Imperative uniquely important to Kant.

Why is the Categorical Imperative synthetic? To say that the Categorical Imperative is synthetic, strictly speaking, is to say that it is not an analytic proposition that any fully rational person would follow the principle expressed in the Categorical Imperative. This proposition is synthetic because the idea of the subject—that is, a fully rational person—does not "contain" the idea of the predicate—that is, following the principle expressed in the Categorical Imperative. In other words, the proposition that a person is completely rational does not, by itself, entail that the person will follow the principle. Nevertheless, the idea of a fully rational person is supposed to be *necessarily* connected with the idea of following the principles expressed in the Categorical Imperative. That is, that any fully rational person would follow the principle is a necessary, synthetic truth. The argument seems to be this.[9]

(1) Any fully rational and *positively free* person would follow the principle expressed by the Categorical Imperative.
(2) Any person ("will") that is negatively free is also positively free.
(3) Any rational person is negatively free.
Therefore,
(4) Any fully rational person would follow the principle expressed by the Categorical Imperative.

The first and second premises are supposed to be established by conceptual analysis in the *Groundwork of the Metaphysics of Morals*, chapter 2 and the first three paragraphs of chapter 3. The third premise, (3), cannot be obtained by conceptual analysis even

---

[9]Here I reconstruct what I take to be the main lines of Kant's argument in the *Groundwork*, primarily in chap. 3.

though Kant argues (in chapter 3) on a priori grounds that it is, for practical purposes, a reasonable assumption. One cannot infer that a person is negatively free simply from the premise that he is rational. One needs intermediate steps, employing a "third term," the idea of an intelligible world. The argument for (3), it seems, runs as follows.

(P$_1$) Any rational person is a member of an intelligible world.
(P$_2$) Any member of an intelligible world is negatively free.
Therefore,
(3) Any rational person is negatively free.

At least one of the intermediate steps, (P$_1$) and (P$_2$), is not obtained by conceptual analysis, and therefore (3) is synthetic. Because (4) cannot be established without (3), (4) is also synthetic.

The noteworthy feature of this argument for the Categorical Imperative is the essential role played by the idea of positive freedom (or autonomy). This idea need not enter into the justification of the Hypothetical Imperative, for the Hypothetical Imperative is simply the expression in imperative form of the allegedly analytic proposition that if any fully rational person wills an end then he wills the necessary means within his power. The Categorical Imperative, then, is connected with autonomy in a way that the Hypothetical Imperative is not. The nature of the connection can be summarized as follows. Any rational person with desires is bound by the Categorical Imperative if and only if he has an autonomous will. In fact, the Categorical Imperative is, on Kant's view, simply one way of expressing the constraints that all rational and autonomous persons would impose on themselves. One must make one's conduct conform to the Categorical Imperative, then, in order to avoid acting contrary to principles that one freely adopted. And when respect for the Categorical Imperative is the motive for one's conduct, one's actions express one's nature as an autonomous person. Thus, in a sense, the man who acts from respect for the Categorical Imperative is the most completely free.

These remarks require explanation. They may lead one to infer that a person is free only when he acts morally, but this inference would be mistaken. Kant distinguishes two different kinds of freedom. The first is what he calls "negative freedom." This is "the property (of a will) of being able to work independently of determination by alien causes" (G 114 [446]). All men, good and bad, have this freedom, which consists of being able to choose to do things without one's choices being entirely the result of prior causes. In saying that men have autonomous (or positively free) wills, Kant attributes to them a second kind of freedom. This is "the property of being a law to oneself" (G 114 [446–47], 108 [440]). A person is a law to himself, I take it, if he adopts principles for himself and regards himself bound by them and if he was not caused or even motivated to adopt them by any contingent circumstances (such as his desires). A person who is autonomous in this sense gives himself principles without accepting them on authority, out of fear, or even from an interest in his own or others' welfare. He regards himself as bound by these principles and is disposed to follow them, but does not always do so. All men, Kant held, are autonomous in this sense. And, in fact, the only principles they adopt as autonomous persons are those expressed in the various formulations of the Categorical Imperative.

Now consider three possible life patterns open to those who are both negatively and positively free. First, imagine a man who, with his negatively free will, elects on some occasions to act contrary to the Categorical Imperative. He is thereby acting contrary to principles which he himself adopted independently of his particular fears, wants, authorities, and so forth.[10] Though he remains free in Kant's two senses, there is a further sense in which he is not completely free. He, like the incontinent man, is not perfectly "self-governing"; for he fails to follow principles that he freely adopted. Admittedly, he may be following other principles—for example, maxims of self-interest—which he also willed; but he can hardly be completely self-governing if he has adopted principles which conflict with one another. Because he freely adopted his principles, he is autonomous in a way that he would not be if he had blindly taken all his principles on

[10]One is naturally inclined to object that one never actually took the step of adopting moral principles; but Kant's argument that men "give themselves" the moral law is not based on observation of the "phenomenal" experience of deciding to accept them.

authority. Nevertheless, insofar as he does not completely live by his principles, he fails to express or manifest his autonomy in the most complete way.

Now contrast this person with those who always conform to the Categorical Imperative. Their personal maxims never direct them to act contrary to the principle they have adopted as autonomous persons. They at least lack the incontinence of the person who fails to live by his own principles; and they are not divided against themselves in the manner of those who adopt personal maxims that conflict with the Categorical Imperative. Nevertheless, if their conformity to the Categorical Imperative was a result of fortunate desires rather than respect for the Categorical Imperative, then they are still not expressing their nature as autonomous persons. They give themselves principles as autonomous persons, but these principles are inoperative in their lives. Their lives are just what they would be if they had lacked autonomous wills.

The person who most completely lives as an autonomous person, then, is the one for whom the disposition to follow the Categorical Imperative is most effective. That is, the person not only conforms to freely adopted principles but does so *because* these are principles that he or she freely and rationally adopted. This is the person most completely "self-governing."

Why, then, did Kant hold conscientious adherence to the Categorical Imperative in such high regard? It was, I suggest, to a large extent because he felt that the noblest feature of humanity is the capacity to be self-governing, to adopt principles without being influenced by sensuous motives and then to live by them whatever the contingencies. On Kant's theory, the person who best realizes this capacity is the person who acts from respect for the Categorical Imperative.

I conclude with two brief comments. First, if my explanation of the importance of moral conduct is correct, then Kant should not be viewed as a man obsessed with duty for duty's sake. He believed, of course, that one ought always to do one's duty and also that only acts motivated by respect for moral law have moral worth. What is uniquely important to Kant about moral conduct, however, is not its difficulty, orderliness, or purposelessness; it is rather the fact that moral conduct is the practical exercise of the noble capacity to be rational and self-governing, a capacity which sets us apart from the lower animals and gives us dignity. Kant's ethics is as much an ethics of self-esteem as it is an ethics of duty. [11]

Finally, without overlooking the important differences between the Categorical Imperative and the Hypothetical Imperative, we may note a further similarity. Both principles, as it turns out, enjoin a person to follow through on what he himself wills. The Hypothetical Imperative tells him not to balk at the necessary means to the ends he wills, and the commands of the Categorical Imperative are simply the constraints he himself adopts as a rational and autonomous person. To put the point paradoxically, we could summarize the demands of practical reason by saying, "Do what you will."

[11] This idea I take from Rawls's lectures.

2

Humanity as an End in Itself

Few formulas in philosophy have been so widely accepted and variously interpreted as Kant's injunction to treat humanity as an end in itself. For some it is a specific antidote to utilitarianism, prohibiting all kinds of manipulation and exploitation of individuals for selfish or even altruistic ends. For others it is a general reminder that "people count," that no one's interests should be disregarded. Sometimes the formula is viewed as a principle of benevolence. The fact that the formula seems so adaptable for the expression of different ideas may, in fact, explain some of its appeal. Without denying that there are elements in Kant's writing which suggest alternative interpretations, I shall reconstruct what seems to me the main line of his thought about humanity as an end in itself. The interpretation I propose enables Kant to meet many of the objections that critics have raised against his formula, but it also reflects an extreme moral stand that few of us, I suspect, could accept without modification.

I

Kant's principle, the second formulation of the Categorical Imperative, is introduced as follows: "Act in such a way that you always treat humanity, whether in your own person or in the person of any other, never simply as a means but always at the same time as an end" (G 96 [429]). The first problem of interpretation is to see what is meant by the phrase "humanity *in* a person." On the usual reading this is treated as a quaint way of saying "a human person." That is, treating humanity in persons as an end is just to treat human beings as ends. "Humanity," on this view, refers to the class of human beings, and what is meant is simply that each member of the class is to be treated as an end. This reading is a natural one, for Kant does speak of persons and "rational beings" as ends in themselves (G 97 [430]; 104 [436]; 105 [437]), and human beings are the only persons and rational beings we know. Translators sometimes encourage this interpretation by rendering *"Menschheit"* as "man" instead of "humanity." There is no temptation to think of "man" as referring to something in a person, or a characteristic of a person, though "humanity" can be so understood, for example, when we contrast a person's animality with his humanity or when a theologian contrasts the divinity of Jesus with his humanity.

A review of Kant's repeated use of "humanity in a person" in *The Metaphysics of Morals* and elsewhere strongly suggests that, contrary to the usual reading, Kant thought of humanity as a characteristic, or set of characteristics, of persons. Kant says, for example, that we can even contemplate a rogue with pleasure when we distinguish between his humanity and the man himself (LE 196–97; DV 107 [441]; MPV 104 [441]). Again, humanity is contrasted with our animality; and it is said to be something entrusted to us for preservation (DV 51 [392]; 85 [423]; MPV 50, 84). Its distinguishing feature is said to be "the power to set ends," and we are supposed to respect it even in those who make themselves unworthy of it (DV 51 [392]; 133 [463]; MPV 50, 128). Thus, though Kant probably intended "persons are ends" and "humanity in persons is an end" to be equivalent for all practical purposes, I suggest that the former is best construed as an abbreviation for the latter rather than the reverse (as the usual reading has it).

Unfortunately the texts are not unequivocal about exactly what characteristics make up our humanity. In the *Groundwork* the "rational nature" of human beings is clearly intended to be included under, if not identified with, their humanity. Kant writes, for example, of the paradox that "the mere dignity of humanity, that is, of rational nature in man . . . should function as an inflexible precept for the will . . . " (G 106 [439]). In the original German, however, it is not so definite that rationality is the only feature of humanity. The phrase "*die Würde der Menschheit als vernünftiger Natur*" could as well be "the dignity of humanity as (i.e., insofar as it includes) rational nature." Another passage suggests that various human talents are part of our humanity. "Now there are in humanity [*Menschheit*] capacities for greater perfection which form part of nature's purpose for humanity in our person. To neglect these can admittedly be compatible with the maintenance of humanity as an end in itself, but not with the promotion of this end" (G 97–98 [430]). These "capacities for greater perfection" are the same as what is referred to earlier as "fortunate natural aptitudes," "natural gifts," and "powers . . . given . . . for all sorts of possible ends" (G 90 [423]). In *The Metaphysics of Morals,* however, Kant seems to distinguish these powers from humanity in persons. He says that the characteristic of humanity, as distinct from animality, is "the power to set an end . . . any end whatsoever" (DV 51 [392]; MPV 50). The development of talents is not said to *be* an instance of promoting humanity but rather what must be done to make us *worthy* of humanity (DV 51 [392]; MPV 50). Another passage implies at least that physical abilities are not part of humanity in us, for humanity is identified with our noumenal personality as distinct from the phenomenal, or observable, person (DV 85 [423]; MPV 84). Given Kant's repeated insistence on formulating the supreme moral principle independently of contingent assumptions, I think it is most reasonable to construe "humanity" as including only those powers necessarily associated with rationality and "the power to set ends."

More specifically, these characteristics in Kant's view entail the following. First, humanity includes the capacity and disposition to act on principles or maxims, at least in the broad sense which encompasses all acting for reasons (G 80 [412]). Second, humanity includes the capacity and disposition to follow rational principles of prudence and efficiency, that is, hypothetical imperatives, at least so far as these do not conflict with more stringent rational principles (G 82–83 [414–15]). Third, as a "power to set any end whatsoever," humanity is thought to include a kind of freedom which lower animals lack—ability to foresee future consequences, adopt long-range goals, resist immediate temptation, and even to commit oneself to ends for which one has no sensuous desire (G 114–16 [446–49]). Fourth, humanity as rational nature necessarily (though not analytically) includes acceptance ("legislating to oneself") of certain unconditional principles of conduct, that is, categorical imperatives, independently of fear of punishment and promise of reward (G 83–84 [416], 108 [440]). This implies that anyone who has humanity has a capacity and disposition to follow such principles; but since his rationality may be imperfect or counteracted by other features, he may not always follow these principles (G 81 [413–14]). Fifth, as rational nature encompasses theoretical as well as practical reason, humanity must also include some ability to understand the world and to reason abstractly.

Humanity, so conceived, is attributed by Kant to even the most foolish and depraved persons (LE 197; DV 133 [463]; MPV 128). Although he sometimes writes as if certain acts amount to "throwing away" one's humanity, he repeatedly implies that a person's humanity remains, and so must be respected, even though he defiles, abases, violates, dishonors, or rejects it.[1] With a confidence difficult to maintain in the present age, Kant held that the spark of goodness, and therefore of rationality, is inextinguishable in us (R 41 [45]; LE 197; DV 134 [463]; MPV 129).

II

Kant's formula, in effect, has two parts, namely: (1) Act in such a way that you never treat humanity simply as a means; and (2) act in such a way that you always treat humanity as an end. The first seems to have an instant intuitive appeal, but it cannot, I think, be understood independently of the second. To treat something *simply* as a means is to fail to treat it in some other appropriate way while one is treating it as a means. But (1), by itself, does not indicate what the appropriate treatment in question is. Obviously for Kant the answer is supplied by (2). One treats

[1]DV 85 [422], 87 [424], 88 [425], 92 [428], 113 [463], 143 [471], 122 [454]; MPV 83, 85, 86, 89, 128, 137, 118.

humanity simply as a means if and only if one treats it as a means but not as an end. The meaning of (1), then, depends upon the meaning of (2), and (1) will always be satisfied if (2) is satisfied.

Furthermore, (2) goes beyond (1). That is, the requirement to treat humanity as an end demands more than the requirement to avoid treating humanity merely as a means. This is suggested by the fact that Kant's discussion of the examples of the imperfect duties of developing one's talents and giving aid to the needy does not refer to the idea of using someone as a means (G 97–98 [430]). The point is confirmed in *The Metaphysics of Morals* when Kant says explicitly that being indifferent to someone satisfies the command not to use humanity merely as a means but fails to meet the requirement to treat humanity as an end (DV 55–56 [395]; MPV 54).

There are good reasons, then, to focus attention on (2) rather than (1). The crucial question is, What is it to treat humanity as an end? The question is especially puzzling because "humanity," as a set of rational capacities and dispositions, is not the sort of thing which is an end, or goal, in the ordinary sense. Kant acknowledges this when he says that it is not an end to be pursued but a "self-existent" end. Everyone has humanity, and the moral imperative is not to produce more of it but something else. But what?

The natural temptation at this point is to ignore the text and supply intuitive answers. Kant uses "as an end" as a technical term for the appropriate additional ways to treat humanity when using it as a means. So we naturally fill in the gap as we feel it should be filled. The point, some say, is to take everyone's interests into account. Thus, for example, a person fails when he employs a servant at the lowest possible wage without regard for the servant's welfare. But taking the individual's interests *into account* may seem insufficient, for it often seems inappropriate to use a person, or his humanity, as a means to some larger social ends which might be thought to override the individual interest. The injunction not to use humanity merely as a means seems to condemn not just selfish disregard of others' interests but also utilitarian manipulation of individuals for the general welfare. "I will not be used" is not always a defense against selfishness; it can also oppose abuse of the individual for altruistic purposes. In fact the charge "He is using me as a mere means, an object, a thing" often complains of neglect of one's unique qualities as an individual, as if the agent viewed one as expendable, replaceable by anyone who could serve similar functions.[2]

Whatever the merits of these intuitive reflections in general, they are no substitute, if the aim is to understand Kant, for examination of the puzzling details of Kant's texts. Let us review, then, what Kant says about *ends* in the sense in which humanity is regarded as an end.

(1) Humanity is not a "relative end" but an "objective end" or an "end in itself" (G 95 [427–28]). Relative ends are ends which individuals have because they like, want, and hope for various things as sensuous beings. Objective ends, or ends in themselves, are ends "valid for all rational beings." Their value is contrasted with that of relative ends, which "provide no universal principles, no principles valid and necessary for all rational beings and also for every volition" (G 95 [427]). This does not tell us exactly in what sense humanity is an end, but it does imply that humanity is not an end because it is something desired and that its being an end implies principles which should be recognized by all rational beings.

(2) An end, in general, is defined as "what serves the will as the (subjective) ground of its self-determination" (G 95 [427]). In the typical case this would be some future state of affairs for the sake of which one sets oneself to do something, for example, being financially secure as a goal for which a person might work and save. But humanity is not an end of this sort. In calling it an end, or "ground of self-determination," Kant evidently had in mind something more general, beyond the ordinary use of "end," namely, a reason for acting. This is, to acknowledge that something, such as humanity, is an end is to grant that one has a "ground" for choosing, or "determining oneself," to do or refrain from doing various things. But what, specifically, one has reason to do is not yet clear.

(3) Humanity is a "self-existent" end, not an end to be produced (G 105 [438]). The point, apparently, is that whenever humanity

[2]Note that Kant's view, as should be clear in what follows, is quite different from this; he urges us not to value a person's individuality but rather something which he has in common with others, his "humanity."

exists it is an end by virtue of what it is and that to say that humanity is an end is not to say that something which does not yet exist should be produced or that the quantity of something desirable should be increased.

(4) Humanity, as an objective end, is one "such that in its place one can put no other end to which (it) should serve simply as a means . . . " (G 96 [428]). Construing "ends" in the broad sense of "reasons for choosing," we may understand this as saying that when a person's humanity gives one a reason for doing or refraining from something, whatever this may be, that reason takes precedence over other reasons; for example, even if neglecting, impairing, or dishonoring a person's humanity were to cause many people pleasure, this would not be a rational exchange.

(5) Objective ends are "a supreme condition limiting the use of every means," "a condition limiting all merely relative and arbitrary ends," and "a limit on all arbitrary treatment" of rational beings (G 105 [438], 104 [436], 96 [428]). Thus the fact that humanity is an end in itself is supposed to set a rational and moral limit to the ways we may treat people in the pursuit of our relative ends, but just what this limit is remains to be seen.

(6) Objective ends are to be "conceived only negatively—that is, as an end against which we should never act . . . " (G 105 [437]). This remark is puzzling. There is no problem if it is merely a reiteration of point (3) above, that to say that humanity, or a rational being, is an end in itself is not to name some goal to be achieved. However, if it means, as it seems to, that treating humanity as an end in itself requires only restraint, a "hands-off" attitude, rather than positive effort to help others, then it flatly contradicts what Kant says elsewhere, for example, that one must "agree positively" with humanity as an end in itself. "For the ends of a subject who is an end in himself must, if this conception is to have its full effect in me, be also, so far as possible, my ends" (G 98 [430]). At least at this point Kant is definite that, though humanity is not itself a goal to be achieved, the contention that it is an end in itself is meant to have the consequence that we ought to promote the ends of others.

(7) In his second example Kant implies that one at least partially satisfies the requirement to treat humanity as an end if one treats persons as "beings who must themselves be able to share in the

end of the very same action." A lying promise is wrong, for example, because "the man whom I seek to use for my own purposes by such a promise cannot possibly agree with my way of behaving to him, and so cannot himself share the end of the action" (G 97 [429]). This seems at first to imply that one should never do anything to a person that he does not want done, but Kant makes clear in a footnote that he does not intend such an absurdly extreme principle. Even the similar principle "Don't do unto others what you don't want done to yourself," if unqualified, is said to be unacceptable because it gives the criminal a basis for disputing with the judge who (justly) punishes him (G 97 [430]).

It would be obviously absurd to say that one cannot use a person's services unless that person, quite literally, shared all of one's ends in doing so—for example, to say that carpenters employed to build an opera house must have among their goals the increased enjoyment of opera. The point is that, insofar as they are used as means, they must *be able* to adopt the agent's end, under some appropriate description, without irrational conflict of will. If the carpenters are in need of work and are decently paid, they can without irrationality adopt the immediate end of building an opera house, whether they care for opera or not. Similarly, at least in Kant's opinion, the criminal can rationally—though he may not—adopt the ends of deterrence and even retribution for which he may be punished. What is relevant is not whether the person who is treated as a means happens to like the ends in question or could psychologically bring himself to value them all for their own sakes; it is rather that the maxim on which the agent acts ("Do this for the sake of that") is such that there is no irrationality in anyone's willing it as a universal law. The first formula of the Categorical Imperative asks us to test maxims from the agent's point of view; the second, insofar as the remarks about shared ends indicate, asks us to consider maxims from the point of view of those who are treated in accord with the maxims. But the main question is the same: Is the maxim one which any human being can, without irrational conflict of will, accept when applied to oneself and to everyone else?

Several considerations favor this interpretation. First, Kant was thinking of the "beings who must be able to share in the end" as rational beings, for he says: "For then it is manifest that a violator of the rights of man intends to use the person of others merely as a means without taking into consideration that, *as rational beings*, they ought always at the same time to be rated as ends—that is, only as beings who must themselves be able to share in the end of the very same action" (G 97 [430]).

Second, in the *Critique of Practical Reason* Kant states as the condition of treating a person as an end that his autonomy as a rational being be subjected to no purpose unless it is in accord with a law that might arise from the will of the person affected (CPrR 90 [87]). Here the restriction on the purposes or ends to which a person may be subordinated is more explicitly the compatibility of such purposes with laws which the affected person, as a rational being, could accept. Third, the present reading helps to make understandable (though not entirely correct) Kant's belief that the first and second formulas of the Categorical Imperative are equivalent, at least for practical purposes (G 103 [436]). Fourth, the more literal alternative readings yield obviously absurd conclusions.

Although Kant's remarks about the ability to share ends do give a sense to his second formula, it would be a mistake, I think, to suppose that it represents his whole understanding of the matter—or even his most dominant line of thought. The remarks occur in a discussion of only one example, and they have little to do with his use of the idea of humanity as an end in *The Metaphysics of Morals*. Moreover, the requirement that the recipient of an act must be able to share its end is subject to all the familiar, even notorious, problems that can be raised to the first formula of the Categorical Imperative. Until a maxim, including the appropriate description of the end of an act, is specified, the test cannot be used; and, while there are no adequate rules for characterizing the maxim, how one does so makes all the difference in the results of the test. Moreover, it is difficult, if not impossible, to explain the sort of irrational conflict of will in question such that the test condemns just those maxims which morally should be condemned, and not others. For these reasons, I think, it is well to look further for clues regarding what it means to treat humanity as an end.

III

In describing a "kingdom of ends" Kant distinguishes (relative) personal ends from ends in themselves by saying that the latter have *dignity* whereas the former have only price (G 102 [434]). This idea, repeated in various ways elsewhere,[3] may be a key to understanding the sense in which humanity is supposed to be an end in itself.

Dignity is attributed by Kant to things which are related but of different types: (1) humanity (rational nature, human nature[4]); (2) morality (moral law—references at G 93 [425], 102 [435]; CPrR 152 [147]; (3) persons (rational beings—references at G 105 [436]; MPV 96–97 [433–34]); (4) persons who conform to duty (G 107 [439–40], 102 [434]); and (5) moral disposition (to do duty for duty's sake—reference at G 103 [435]). The attribution of dignity to dutiful persons (4) and moral disposition (5) might suggest that one acquires dignity only by conforming to moral law and so that only morally good people have dignity. But other passages make clear that humanity in each person has dignity, no matter how immoral the person may be (DV 99 [435]; MPV 97; LE 196–97; DV 45 [387]). Autonomy is said to be the ground of dignity, and this is a property of the will of every rational being, namely, the property of legislating to oneself universal (moral) laws without the sensuous motives of fear, hope for reward, and the like (G 103 [436], 108 [440]). Dignity is repeatedly ascribed to "every rational being" and "rational nature" (G 103 [436], 105 [438], 106 [439]). As far as human beings are concerned, this amounts to saying that humanity in persons has dignity; and, as we have seen, Kant does not think that one loses one's humanity when one acts immorally.

Dignity is characterized as "an unconditional and incomparable worth" (G 103 [436]). The first point, that dignity is an unconditioned worth, is that it is a value not dependent upon contingent facts. Thus, for example, whatever has dignity has value indepen-

---

[3]For example, MPV 97 [434], 127 [462]. In the first passage Kant explicitly identifies being an end in itself and having dignity.

[4]G 102 [435], 103 [436], 106 [436]; MPV 80 [420], 90 [429], 97 [435], 98 [436], 124 [459], 127 [462].

dently of any effects, profit, or advantage which it might produce. In Kant's terms, it has value regardless of any *market price* which it may have, that is, regardless of what one could get from others in exchange for it on account of its ability to satisfy universal needs and inclinations. Its value is also independent of *fancy price*, that is, independent of what one could get in exchange for it on account of someone's happening to want it quite apart from its utility in satisfying universal human needs and inclinations (G 102 [434–35]). What has dignity has value whether in fact valued by anyone or not. Thus when Kant speaks of dignity as an "intrinsic value" he does not imply that, as a matter of fact, people value what has dignity for its own sake. The point is rather that a perfectly rational person would so value it.

The second point, not entailed by the first, is that dignity is an "incomparable" worth, "exalted above all price," and "admits of no equivalent" (G 102 [434–35]). This means at least that whenever one must choose between something with dignity and something with mere price one should always choose the former. No amount of price, or value dependent on contingent needs and tastes, can justify or compensate for sacrifice of dignity. We may express this by saying that what has dignity is *priceless*.

While it is clear that Kant thought that dignity should always take precedence over price, it is not so obvious whether he took a more extreme position. That is, did he hold that what has dignity is *irreplaceable* in the sense that there are no legitimate trade-offs among things which have dignity? Is his view, for example, that there are two scales of value, price and dignity, such that things can be ranked comparatively on each scale even though nothing on the scale of dignity can be overweighed by any amount of value on the scale of price? This would allow that some things may have more dignity than others, and that the sacrifice of dignity in one sphere might be justified by its enhancement in another. This is compatible with the claim that dignity is above all price. Or, alternatively, is Kant's view that dignity is something that cannot be quantified, so that it does not make sense to say that dignity of humanity in one person can fairly and reasonably be exchanged for the sake of a greater amount of dignity elsewhere? On this view to say that something has dignity is to say that it can never be sacrificed for anything with mere price, but it tells us nothing about what to do if one must choose between dignity in one sphere and dignity in another.

The first interpretation may well be more congenial to most readers because it obviously allows the sacrifice of humanity in one person for the sake of humanity in many persons in extreme circumstances. One can imagine a spy story, for example, in which suicide, the use of brain-damaging drugs, and contemptuous mockery of another human being, all of which Kant regards as contrary to the dignity of humanity, are necessary means to the prevention of a holocaust. In such a case, admittedly rare, many people would readily grant that it is justified to sacrifice the humanity of one person for the preservation of life, prevention of misery, and even furtherance of rationality in many persons. The second interpretation, however, seems to be implied by what Kant says. The definition of *price* is that "something else can be put in its place as an equivalent," and *dignity*, by contrast, "admits of no equivalent." Strictly construed, this must mean that what has dignity cannot morally or reasonably be exchanged for anything of greater value, whether the value is dignity or price. One cannot then, trade off the dignity of humanity in one person in order to honor a greater dignity in two, ten, or a thousand persons. This may seem to imply that there can never be a justification for impairing the rationality or sacrificing the life of any human being, but this is not necessarily so. What is implied, strictly, is only that one may not sacrifice something with dignity *in* exchange for something of greater value. Thus, if the sacrifice of something with dignity is ever justified, the ground for this cannot be "this is worth more than that" or "a greater quantity of value is produced by doing so." Kant in fact takes a quite rigoristic stand regarding acts contrary to the dignity of humanity in a single person; for example, suicide, drunkenness, and mockery are said to be violations of "perfect," that is, exceptionless, duties. To say that one should never, for any reason, damage the rational capacities of any person would probably not come hard for one who held that it is wrong to tell a lie to save a friend from murder. However, the thesis that humanity has an incomparable worth which "admits of no equivalent" does not, strictly speaking, commit Kant to such a view. One cannot trade off a person's rational capacities for anything alleged to be more valuable, but comparisons of quantities of value may not be the only justifications. When we turn to Kant's more specific moral opinions, especially regarding the preservation of human life, we find that Kant sometimes even demands the destruction of a person with humanity of incomparable worth.

IV

What are the practical implications of the thesis that humanity in persons has an unconditional and incomparable worth? Since humanity is our rationality and capacity to set ends, it seems natural to suppose that one would acknowledge its special value in the following ways. First, and most obviously, one would refuse to do anything which damages or impairs a person's rational capacities, whether the person is oneself or another. For example, drugs or frontal lobotomies that render a criminal nonviolent at the cost of making him permanently cowlike would be forbidden. Even temporary impairment of reason through drugs, at least in one who had a viable alternative to use reason, would be suspect. Second, one who sufficiently valued persons' rational capacities would presumably not want to destroy the persons themselves. Thus killing human beings seems to be ruled out. Third, if rational capacities have an incomparable value, then surely one should try to develop them and improve them in oneself and others. Fourth, it seems equally obvious that one should strive to exercise these capacities as far as possible. Thus if, as Kant thought, acting from respect for the moral law is a use of reason, then one should try to do so. And, more surprisingly, even prudence is required so far as it is compatible with unconditional rational principles of morality. Fifth, since the exercise of rationality is something to be cherished, in trying to influence others one should appeal to their reason rather than try to manipulate them by nonrational techniques. Sixth, valuing highly the setting and rational pursuit of ends even in other persons, one should leave them freedom to set and pursue their ends in a rational (moral and prudential) way, subject only to, whatever further constraints reason imposes. Finally, certain attitudes and symbolic gestures, and avoidance of others, may be required. If humanity is of incomparable value, it should be honored and respected or at least not mocked, dishonored, or degraded. This is especially suggested by the term dignity (*Würde*), which is Kant's label for this special value.

Kant's own use of the idea of humanity as an end is for the most part in line with these natural applications, and at least some of the discrepancies can be explained as a result of certain special beliefs he held. Let us consider Kant's view on each point in turn.

(1) Kant does not discuss lobotomy and other means of causing permanent brain damage, but he does condemn drunkenness and the use of opium as making one temporarily animal-like, with a weakened "capacity to use his powers purposively" (MPV 88 [427]). Even gluttony is prohibited because it leaves one "temporarily incapacitated for activities which require adroitness and deliberation in the use of one's powers" (MPV 88 [427]). The principle behind these conclusions, as well as the requirements to develop one's natural talents, is: "It is one's duty to raise himself out of the crudity of his nature, out of his animality . . . more and more to humanity, by which alone he is capable of setting himself ends" (MPV 44–45 [387]).

(2) In both the *Groundwork* and *The Metaphysics of Morals* Kant argues that suicide is wrong because it reflects an undervaluation of humanity in one's own person. He does not, however, draw the general conclusion that killing human beings is always wrong. Execution for murder is said to be a requirement of justice, and killing in a just war is regarded as permissible at least in certain stages of history (MEJ 102 [333], 122–23 [349]). Thus if Kant was consistent, he understood the incomparable value of humanity in persons in a sense that does not imply that the life of every person with humanity must always be preserved. In fact the argument against suicide does not imply that *life* is irreplaceable. What is at issue is suicide for the purpose of ending a painful existence or "as a mere means to some end of one's own liking," and this is said to be wrong not because it destroys something priceless and irreplaceable but because it "degrades" humanity in one's own person. That is, suicide for such reasons reflects an attitude that devalues humanity (G 97 [429], 89 [421–22]; MPV 84 [423]) and counts lesser things as more important. Although suicide contravenes a "perfect duty," still Kant leaves open "casuistic questions," for example, whether it is wrong to kill oneself in anticipation of an

unjust death sentence, or in order to save one's country, or to escape an impending madness resulting from the bite of rabid dog (MPV 84–85 [423–24]).

Kant's view, I think, may be best reconstructed as follows. First, to take the life of someone with humanity for the sake of something of mere price is always wrong, an undervaluation of humanity. Pleasure and pain, and the particular goals one has because of what one desires to achieve, are thought to have only conditioned value, or price, and so suicide or the killing of others for the sake of increasing pleasure, diminishing pain, or achieving any contingently desired goal is wrong. Second, the proper attitude about humanity is not that each bit of it has a value which one can weigh against the value of other bits to calculate reasonable trade-offs. One should not try to determine what to do by calculating whether destroying or degrading humanity in one case is warranted by its consequences of preserving or developing it in another. But nevertheless, third, the fact that such calculation is inappropriate does not imply that there is no reason, ever, for ending the life of a being with humanity. Analogously, perhaps, a parent of three children faced with the awful choice of saving two or one might on some ground choose to save the two without having to grant that two are *worth* more than one, that the reason is that the quantity of something valuable in the world has been maximized. What the ground could be would need to be explained by other formulas of the Categorical Imperative, despite Kant's (mistaken) belief that the formulas are equivalent; but I expect that the intuition here is not uncommon.

(3) As we would expect, Kant argues for a duty to develop one's rational capacities, "powers of the spirit" (e.g., in mathematics, logic, and metaphysics of nature) and "powers of the mind" (e.g., memory, imagination, and the like), and again the general ground seems to be "the worth of humanity in his own person, which he should not degrade" (MPV 109–10 [445–46]). The duty is regarded as an "imperfect" one, but the point is not that one may choose to neglect these powers but only that the principle in question does not specify "the kind and degree" of action needed to satisfy it. Kant does not, however, conclude that it is a duty to develop the rational powers of others. The reason is not that the development of their perfection is unimportant or less important but

rather that, in Kant's opinion, such development can only be achieved by the person himself (MPV 44 [386]). As the old quip has it, "you can lead a youth to college, but you can't make him think." The idea that one should at least help to provide opportunity for others' rational development is not discussed, though in his own life Kant was obviously committed to it.

(4) To strive to exercise reason in moral contexts, Kant implies, is a duty, but to use it to promote one's own happiness, barring special circumstances, is not a duty. Kant says that it is a duty to strive for moral perfection, which consists of a disposition to do one's duty from a sense of duty, which in turn is supposed to be a disposition to act from pure reason as opposed to sensuous inclination (MPV 110 [446]). Despite the incomparable value of rationality, however, Kant does not conclude that the exercise of prudential reason in normal contexts is a duty (even when compatible with other moral principles). The explanation is not that such use of reason is unimportant or that the idea of humanity as an incomparable value fails to commend it; it is rather that human beings are so disposed by nature to pursue their own happiness that it is inappropriate to speak of a "duty" to do so. "Duty" implies constraint, possible disinclination and failure to comply (MPV 43 [385–86]). Thus, though rational prudence is not demeaned, the only *duty* to promote one's own happiness is indirect and concerns special circumstances; that is, the duty, strictly speaking, is to avoid unnecessary pain, adversity, and poverty insofar as these are temptations to vice rather than a general duty to maximize one's (morally permissible) satisfactions (MPV 46 [388]).

(5) The idea that one should try to reason with others rather than to manipulate them by nonrational techniques is manifest in Kant's discussion of the duty to respect others. No matter how stupid a person may appear, it is wrong to censure him "under the name of absurdity, inept judgment, and the like," and no matter how immoral he may seem, one must not treat him as worthless or incapable of improvement (MPV 128 [463–64]). Moral education—as illustrated in Kant's sample moral catechism—is to be by a rational process of question and answer, never by citing examples to emulate (MPV 145–53 [477–84]).

(6) One of the most significant consequences of placing a special value on a human being's capacity to set and rationally pursue ends

is that there is a strong prima facie case for allowing individuals freedom to form and pursue their own life plans subject only to the constraint that others be allowed a similar freedom. This is essentially Kant's "universal principle of justice," the foundation of his treatment of rights and juridical duties (MEJ 35 [230–31]). Even in the private sphere the duty of respect for persons is one which requires us to reject arrogance and make room for others; in contrast with beneficence, it is a negative duty and requires that even friends "halt at a suitable distance from one another" (MPV 113–14 [449–50], 130 [464–65], 136 [470]). Thus not only must we allow others "external" freedom but we should also leave even the best of friends a certain private space. We should value not only their happiness but that they set their own ends and pursue them in a rational way.

Valuing someone's rational pursuit of his own ends is not the same as wanting him to have what he desires, or what he will most enjoy, by any (morally permissible) means. The latter is general beneficence, and it is noteworthy that in *The Metaphysics of Morals* Kant's argument for general beneficence has nothing to do with the dignity of humanity (MPV 116–18 [450–54]). Indeed it is hard to see how such a duty would follow from the principle to treat humanity as an end, despite Kant's remark in the *Groundwork* that to accept fully humanity in others as an end one must regard their ends as one's own. If one could paternalistically give another pleasure and diminish his pain by ignoring his own life plan and thwarting his own rational pursuit of his ends, then this would be placing something with mere price (e.g., his comfort) over something with dignity (his capacity to set and rationally pursue ends). If our interpretation is right, what the dignity of humanity should require is that one should help others to set their own ends and rationally pursue them rather than try to make their lives pleasant independently of their own goals. This might well involve removing obstacles, providing opportunities, and all manner of "positive" activity distinct from a passive "hands-off" attitude. In fact Kant's example of beneficence in the *Groundwork* really has to do with helping someone in need rather than with general beneficence, and one is urged to be concerned with his ends, not with what one believes will make him best off (G 90 [423], 98 [430]; MPV 46 [388]). In respecting the dignity of humanity in a person, one is to value another's achievement of a (morally permissible) end because it is an end *he* adopted rather than because one expects it will bring him pleasure or something regarded as intrinsically valuable apart from his choice.

(7) Kant's arguments in *The Metaphysics of Morals* also accord with the final natural application of the idea of the dignity of humanity in persons, namely, that human rationality is to be honored in word and gesture as well as in deed. Kant is unusual, at least compared to moral philosophers today, in stressing the moral importance of attitude and gesture aside from their consequences. Mockery is opposed, whether or not it is effective for the purpose of reform or deterrent, because it reflects a disrespectful attitude toward the humanity of others (MPV 132 [467]). Servility, as often revealed in groveling, flattery, simpering, and self-disparagement, is condemned because it symbolizes an attitude which does not place the dignity of one's own humanity above all price (MPV 96–98 [434–36]).

V

My purpose has not been to defend Kant but to understand him. Nevertheless, it is worth noting that, if my account is more or less correct, certain objections to Kant's formula regarding humanity as an end turn out to be off the mark. For example, it is sometimes said that this formula is "empty," having no implications independently of other formulations of the Categorical Imperative.[5] Although fine questions about the relations among the formulations must await proper interpretation of each, my reconstruction of Kant's second formulation certainly appears to be independent of others and, in fact, to go beyond the famous first formula, as the usual interpretations would have it, in declaring a rather substantive value judgment with significant practical implications. Another objection that has been raised to the second formula is that it prohibits what is impossible, namely, treating

[5]See, for example, M. G. Singer, *Generalization in Ethics* (New York: Knopf, 1961), p. 235.

oneself merely as a means.[6] On the present account, however, a person can, and too often does, treat humanity in his person merely as a means; for this means, among other things, being willing to trade or sacrifice his rational capacities for something of value merely because he happens to want it. Again, it has been objected that Kant's formula prohibits noble self-sacrifice for the improvement of the human condition as, for example, when a medical researcher undergoes dangerous experiments in hopes of finding a cure for a disease that kills hundreds of thousands.[7] As I understand Kant, however, such self-sacrifice is not necessarily wrong. The second formula condemns sacrifice of life for what has mere price (for example, money, fame, and even cessation of pain) and more controversially, it forbids quantitative calculation of value among things with dignity, but it does not unequivocally prohibit the sacrifice of one's life. Another objection has been that Kant's principle leads to irreconcilable moral dilemmas, as when a typhoid carrier who has done no wrong must be quarantined for the safety of many other people.[8] Treating the individual as an end, it has been alleged, is incompatible with treating other people as ends. Possible conflicts of duties may remain a problem, but the situation in question is not a definitive example. Liberty is a high priority according to the second formula, but it is limited by a concern for the liberty and rational development of all. It should not be curtailed for the sake of anything of minor value or even the highest value by the measure of price, but that does not entail that there is never a reason to limit it.

A more serious worry about Kant's formula is that it places a comparatively higher value on rational capacity, development, control, and honor than most morally conscientious and reasonable people are prepared to grant. Kant has arguments for his view, which I have not considered; and common opinion is hardly decisive. Nevertheless, the striking implications of Kant's view, as I understand it, should not be ignored and his rationale deserves critical scrutiny. Hedonistic utilitarians surely must recoil; for Kant's view implies that pleasure and the alleviation of pain, even

[6]Ibid., p. 236.
[7]C. D. Broad, *Five Types of Ethical Theory* (New York: Harcourt, Brace, 1930), p. 132.
[8]Ibid.

gross misery, have mere price, never to be placed above the value of rationality in persons. Kant apparently had faith that unequivocal commitment to this ranking of values would lead, in some indescribable world, to the deserved happiness of every conscientious person; but those of us who do not believe this must question his ranking, however strong its intuitive appeal in particular cases.

3

The Kingdom of Ends

Philosophers of the British and American analytic school have, quite understandably, taken much interest in the formulations of the Categorical Imperative concerned with universal law and laws of nature. Recital of standard objections to these formulas is now part of almost every elementary course in the history of ethics. Polite notice is often given to Kant's injunction to treat humanity as an end in itself, but little attention, unfortunately, has been paid to the imperative to regard oneself as a legislating member of a possible kingdom of ends. I propose to sketch an interpretation, or reconstruction, of this form of the Categorical Imperative, treating it, as at least in part it was meant to be treated, as a guide for moral living. More specifically, I want to suggest that the formula of the kingdom of ends combines the main ideas of the other formulations, just as Kant implies that it should, and that his formula is in important respects an improvement over the much discussed first formulation. At the end I shall consider two natural objections to the kingdom of ends principle. These objections, unlike the familiar objections to the first formulation of the Categorical Imperative, raise questions about the most central features of Kant's ethical theory.

The idea of a kingdom of ends is the idea of a state or, as Kant says, "a systematic union of different rational beings through common laws." For us a kingdom of ends is merely possible; it would become actual if all men acted and willed as they should.

Kant mentions three elements of a kingdom of ends: the members, the sovereign, and the private ends which the members have. The *members* are fully rational, autonomous persons, who give themselves universal laws and abide by them. They are ends in themselves: that is, of unconditioned and incomparable worth. They are thought of abstractly: that is, in thinking of persons as members of the kingdom, we abstract from (or ignore) their "personal differences." The *sovereign* is distinguished from the members by virtue of the fact that he is not subject to the laws of the kingdom. This does not mean, however, that he is entitled to break the laws, but only that his nature is such that he cannot break them. The sovereign, who is presumably God or the holy will, serves as the exemplar of an ideal legislator but not as an external lawgiver. For purposes of this paper, he can be ignored. The *private ends* of the members come into the picture in two ways. First, we are to think of each member of the kingdom as having a set of personal ends. Since we must "abstract from personal differences," however, we can know nothing of the particular nature of these ends. Members of the kingdom, for example, are not thought of as power-seekers, peace-lovers, money-grubbers, or bird-fanciers. As members, they are neither egoists nor altruists. Second, in speaking of a harmonious system of personal ends analogous to a system of natural ends, Kant seems to be referring to the set (or sets) of possible ends which would be satisfied if all men did their duty and if God and Nature were cooperative. It is the first idea of personal ends, not the second, that is important for his model of moral legislation.

How, then, does this idea of a kingdom of ends serve as a moral standard? Briefly, the formula of the kingdom of ends enjoins us to follow those rules that we would make as legislating members of such a kingdom. It requires us to work out a set of rules that we would legislate if we were doing so from a certain ideal point of view. Before we can apply the formula, we must reconstruct those ideal legislative conditions from Kant's description of the kingdom. Expanding upon the letter but not the spirit of the text, I suggest that Kant's main conditions are the following:

First, the members are to legislate only laws that are universal in form. That is, the rules which they make must be devoid of proper names: they will be of the form "Anyone in conditions C

must do x," where C and x do not mention particular persons, places, or times.

Second, in trying to decide which rules to make, the members will "abstract from personal differences." That is, they will disregard the various factors which distinguish individuals: for example, differences in appearance, height, weight, sex, race, family, heritage, special talents, social roles, and so on. It follows that their rules will be universal in intent as well as in form. They will not, for example, adopt rules like the restriction upon guest lectures imposed by the regents of the University of California, a rule which was universal in form but actually designed to apply to one individual, Eldridge Cleaver, and which was repealed before it could be applied to a significant number of other cases. Moreover, a member cannot simply choose rules that are universal in form but which actually serve to benefit himself as a white, an American, a general, or whatever. When one legislates as a member of the kingdom, it is as if he were ignorant of his own special traits and circumstances. More generally, the second condition entails that the laws of the kingdom will include no parochial rules. Ignoring the factors which distinguish one man from another, the legislators will have no reason to make regulations concerning the special rights and duties of men and women, the old and the young, or the weak and the strong. Such rules, if morally valid, could only be applications of the more general laws of the kingdom to particular human conditions—applications which we must make as men, with judgment and in the light of our empirical knowledge.

A third condition is that the members of the kingdom must make laws as fully *rational* legislators. From this we can infer that they think logically, that they make no rules without a reason, that they are legislating for persons whose private ends are more or less ranked, and that the set of rules they seek is consistent, never gives conflicting orders for the same situation, and is not self-frustrating or self-defeating. Also, they will follow the rules that they adopt. This is important: for it means that they need not be bothered with questions about whether a proposed law is enforceable or whether it is likely to be abused by an unscrupulous leader. Many of the practical worries that shape our legal systems will have no place in the kingdom of ends.

A fourth condition for legislating in the kingdom is that the lawmakers must be autonomous. This is Rousseau's ideal that they make laws such that each man in obeying them is obeying only himself. For Kant, this implies that the legislators are not causally determined, or even sensuously motivated, to adopt the rules which they do. In legislating, they will be unmoved by appeals to authority and tradition. Unlike our Congressmen, they cannot even appeal to their antecedent moral convictions to guide them in deciding which laws to make. They are the moral lawmakers: there are no moral truths to be discovered independently of their wills.

So far the conditions mentioned have been largely negative. They indicate factors which will *not* determine the legislative decisions of members of the kingdom; but they do not tell us what positive reasons a legislator could have for preferring one rule to another. Some reasons are suggested, however, in Kant's remark that the members of the kingdom are ends in themselves. From this and the rationality of the members we can infer a fifth condition, namely, that in legislating each member regards himself and every other member as an end in himself. This, I suggest, has three implications for Kant. First, that each member grants to every other whatever rights and respect he is entitled to. This is a formal requirement and is of little help here. Second, the legislators regard the rationality of each member as unconditionally and incomparably worth preserving, developing, and honoring. The set of traits Kant calls "rational nature" or "humanity" is not something which distinguishes one man from another but is something which men have in common and which marks them off from animals. In the *Groundwork* Kant argues that rationality is the one value (or end) which all rational beings necessarily have. Insofar as the legislating members share this value, they have a reason for making general rules concerning the preservation, development, and respect for the rational personality of each member. A third (and perhaps derivative) implication of the idea that members regard each other as ends in themselves is that they have a prima facie concern to see each person's ends realized, or at least to ensure each person freedom to pursue his ends. Persons necessarily have ends, and one way of showing our special respect for persons is to favor rules which enhance their opportunity to satisfy their ends. Thus members of the kingdom have some reason to adopt very general rules concerning freedom, the development of resources, mutual aid, and so on.

It should be evident that the kingdom of ends principle combines the main ideas of the other formulations of the Categorical Imperative. It asks us to consider what we can (rationally) will as universal law and requires us to act accordingly. It incorporates the injunction to regard humanity as an end in itself into the conditions for moral legislation; and the idea of autonomy is included in the same way.

The fact that the kingdom of ends principle encompasses the main ideas of the other formulations only partly explains its advantages. Some of these advantages are the result of the way the various ideas are combined in a legislative model. To see this, let us review some familiar objections to the "universal law" formulations.

These tell us to act only on maxims which we can will to become universal laws (or universal laws of nature). To apply the test, we must first specify a principle as *the* principle of an actual or proposed action. How are we to do this? If a principle had to be consciously formulated in order to be a maxim, Kant's test would be inapplicable to most of our conduct. Thus, apparently, the maxim of an act is simply some statement of its nature and purpose: but which statement? Notoriously, the same act can be correctly described in a variety of ways. For example, the same act might be characterized simply as "a lie," or as "answering a depressed patient in the only way that can prevent his suicide," or as both of these together with a host of more specific facts about the case. The results of Kant's test depend upon which description we decide to call "*the* maxim." If the maxims selected are too general, the test becomes rigoristic; if they are too specific, it becomes permissive. That is, the more we focus upon the very general features of acts, such as "being a lie," the more likely we are to get simple, unqualified rules, such as "Never lie," which a morally sensitive person could not accept. If instead we concentrate upon the details of each case and allow maxims to be quite specific, then it seems we can will as universal law the maxim of virtually any act that we are willing to do. Obviously the requirement that one must be willing to accept anyone's acting on one's maxim would not be a serious constraint if one could characterize one's maxim as specifically as one might tell one's story after doing something: for example, "lying to a short, white-haired magazine salesman who looks like my youngest maternal uncle and who on Tuesday, while I am in an elevator with six other people, asks me whether I have ever read any of his eleven cooking publications."

Some of these details, of course, are likely to be irrelevant to a person's reason for acting, and the description of a maxim is more plausibly restricted to features that the agent considers salient in determining what to do. But this alone does not remove the problem, for it seems that some would be all too willing for everyone to accept their actual (but morally objectionable) policies, such as "to lie to rich, pushy tourists who ask for directions." There are various ways to qualify, supplement, or amend the universal law formula, but attempts to make the formula more workable as a guide always face the persistent problem of determining exactly what is, and what is not, to count as a maxim.

Furthermore, as commonly interpreted, the universal law formulations lead to a moral relativism that Kant would have found abhorrent. For, on this account, to say that one cannot will a maxim to become universal law is simply to say that one is unwilling for the sort of conduct indicated in the maxim to become a general practice; but what one is willing to accept as a general practice depends upon one's particular values, beliefs, and personality structure. Since these vary from person to person, it follows that moral right (and wrong) will vary accordingly. Also, what is right even for one person turns out to depend upon contingent, empirical facts in a way Kant wanted to avoid.

Another objection is that the universal law formulations invite us to consider each maxim, in universal form, by itself, whereas a rule that is acceptable in one matrix of rules may be highly unacceptable in another. Strict divorce laws may be desirable where marriages are hard to get but undesirable where marriages are easy. Some universal practices we could accept under more ideal conditions but not in the world as it is. We cannot say *in general* whether we would choose a maxim to become universal law: it may depend upon the background of rules and practices against which we consider it.

Finally, how are the universal law formulations supposed to give us imperfect duties, such as the duty of beneficence described in the *Doctrine of Virtue*? For each maxim, either I can or I cannot

will it to become universal law. If I can, it is permissible to act on
the maxim; if I cannot, it is wrong. If I cannot will as universal law
the maxim not to do a certain thing, *x*, then it must be my duty to
do *x*. This accounts for the obligatory, the forbidden, and the
merely permissible; but how could the procedure generate a principle of beneficence that, as Kant says, leaves a "play-room for free
choice" and does not specify how, when, or to what extent one
must help others, a principle which makes beneficent acts meritorious but does not (except in one case) hold us guilty for our
omissions of beneficent acts?

Most of these objections turn upon quasi-technical flaws in the
universal law formulations when these are construed as stating a
moral decision procedure. The objections do not seem to strike at
the heart of Kant's ethical theory. It is a merit of the kingdom of
ends principle, I suggest, that it expresses many of Kant's main
ethical ideas without raising those problems. In the first place,
while the kingdom of ends principle can be applied to maxims, it
need not be. It asks us to work out a system of moral principles
analogous to the laws of a state. Some of these principles might
enjoin us to adopt certain maxims and to avoid others; but other
principles could prohibit or require actions directly. There is no
need to decide upon one act-description as *the* maxim of an action.
Assuming that we can derive a system of moral principles, we can
(in theory at least) check the moral status of each act by comparing
it, under every true description, against the system of principles.

Moreover, the kingdom of ends principle cannot lead to moral
relativism. Insofar as he is a legislating member of the kingdom of
ends, each person is exactly like every other. If one has sufficient
reason to select (or reject) a rule, then all will have the same reason. Though it may be difficult to show that the members would
adopt any substantive laws, there is no question of their disagree-
ing. Their votes must be unanimous simply because, as members,
they necessarily lack all the features which make men disagree.

Again, the kingdom of ends principle avoids the problems of
treating each maxim in isolation from other rules. It asks us to
work out an ideal system of rules: the matrix for considering each
proposed universal law is the set of all the other rules that every
member in the kingdom, as defined, would necessarily accept.

Finally, there is no *special* problem about generating imperfect duties from the kingdom of ends principle. The members make a system of principles, and there is no reason why some of these should not be principles of the sort "Sometimes, somehow, to some extent promote the ends of others." There may, in fact, be reasons why members of a moral legislature would want principles that make some beneficent acts good but not obligatory. To make them obligatory might be an unwarranted restriction of each person's freedom; whereas to make them merely permissible would not sufficiently encourage the realization of the various ends of the members.

My discussion of the objections to the universal law formulations has taken for granted what seems to be the most common interpretation. There is, however, an extended interpretation, according to which the principle is "Act only on maxims which you can, *as a rational being,* will to become universal law." On this account, a maxim is condemned only if there is some irrationality in willing it as a universal law. The question is not whether a person happens to like or dislike a certain general practice; it is whether the general practice is irrational. This interpretation, which has some merit, brings the universal law formulations closer to the kingdom of ends principle. Both place a restriction on what is to count as ability to will a universal law; but, even on the extended interpretation, the universal law formulations only hint at one of Kant's legislative conditions and they are still subject to all of the objections we have considered except the charge of moral relativism.

The kingdom of ends principle, of course, raises some problems of its own. Let me briefly mention two. First, like all theories which appeal to the idea of an ideal observer, judge or legislator, Kant's principle arouses the suspicion that it cannot support particular moral judgments. Lacking the familiar empirical motives for deciding upon principles, the abstractly defined members of the kingdom may adopt no rules whatsoever. This is a serious problem, cutting to the heart of Kant's ethical theory. To resolve it adequately one would need to construct arguments to show which substantive, though very general, principles members of a kingdom of ends would necessarily adopt. This is a formidable task, of course; but let me mention some considerations which lead me not to despair too readily. First, as indicated earlier, members of a kingdom of ends are not altogether without reasons for making rules. They necessarily value the preservation, development, and honor of the rational side of human nature, and they have a prima facie concern for the freedom and satisfaction of each member. Moreover, we should not be discouraged at the obvious fact that members of the kingdom would have no reason to adopt *particular* moral rules, such as "Treat animals kindly" and "Don't call anyone 'Nigger.' " These rules may be derivative from more general rules which can be justified by the kingdom of ends principle—derivative, of course, in the light of empirical facts, which at some stage (as Kant fully knew) must be consulted. Again, the fact that members of the kingdom would have no opinion about certain matters on which we would like guidance should not, in itself, be regarded as an objection to the principle; for in this case the proper inference, assuming that derivative principles do not apply, is that the matters are morally indifferent—neither obligatory nor forbidden, neither good nor bad. Surely some things, perhaps far more than tradition allows, are morally indifferent from the point of view of rational ethics. Finally, one may draw some encouragement from the similarity between Kant's kingdom of ends principle and the contractual model of justice developed by John Rawls. If significant principles of justice are generated from Rawls's ideal contract situation, there is likely to be moral juice in its Kantian prototype.

A second natural objection to the kingdom of ends principle cannot, I suspect, be met without important revisions. This is the charge that Kant's principle supports utopian, or "clean hands," arguments of an untenable sort. Briefly, it demands that we determine our principles of conduct by considering what rational legislators would will for a community of perfectly rational citizens, ignoring in the process the fact that we must live in a world of imperfectly rational men. The problem is that acting in this world by rules designed for another can prove disastrous. In a world of perfectly rational rule-followers perhaps the imperative "Never lie" would make sense; but not in our world. Once I know that an act is my duty, I should do it regardless of how irrationally others behave; but it does not follow that I should disregard their irrationality when I am trying to determine what my duty is. To adopt our principles *as* ideal legislators seems a good idea; but to make them *for* ideal law-followers does not.

4

Kant's Utopianism

Kant's critics have for centuries bemoaned the abstract, empty, otherworldly character of his ethical theory while at the same time berating him for being unduly rigoristic. His disciples, on the other hand, praise him for the formalistic, general, and a priori nature of his theory while they also admire him for not yielding to demands for a wavering, changeable set of moral principles. The enthusiasm of both sides tends to obscure some important distinctions and to divert attention from the task of evaluating which of the alleged features of Kant's ethics are defects and which advantages. This paper is an attempt to sort out some of these diverse claims about Kant's ethics. Some are simply misplaced, others are quite accurate characterizations of his theory but are not, or are not obviously, defects; and yet nevertheless there remains, I think, at least one serious problem which cannot be lightly dismissed. This is what I call the problem of utopianism. Roughly it is the problem of whether Kant draws illegitimate inferences concerning what we should do in this imperfect world from premises about what perfectly rational beings would do in an ideal world. The problem is not of minor importance for Kant's theory: for obviously it is a fundamental methodological assumption for Kant that the imperatives for human beings are the principles that purely rational beings would necessarily follow. This problem, moreover, is connected with two others, one practical and one theoretical. The theoretical problem is whether Kant was mistaken in insisting on an a priori method of discovering and establishing the supreme principle of morality. The practical problem is to determine when, if ever, morality requires a "clean hands" attitude: that is, an unwillingness to soil one's hands by cooperating with, or adjusting to, irrational and immoral people, even for the sake of good ends. I shall argue that Kant did not adequately face the problem of utopianism, and that this failure stems in part from his conflation of a legitimate insistence on an a priori method in ethics with an unnecessary and untenable corollary. Finally, I shall suggest that insofar as Kant is committed to rigorism and to "clean hands" principles this is a result of the unnecessary corollary rather than the most central doctrines of his ethical theory.

I

In order to isolate the more important issues, let us distinguish among Kant's views several which tend to be conflated under the general charge that Kant was a purist.

First, Kant had some uncompromising ideas about how moral education should proceed. It should elicit recognition of general moral principles by a more or less rational process.[1] Examples are of use only to focus issues and sharpen judgment; they are not to provide the standards. One is not to teach morality by citing examples of good men to emulate. Moreover, moral education should not proceed by concentration on extraordinary acts of heroism and supererogation. Simple duties regularly done should be the focus, not the unusual, the super-noble. All the more, moral principles should not be taught in a watered-down form, less stringent than they are, in order to win acceptance for them. They must be presented in all their purity and strictness, whatever this may be, even if that is not the form in which people are ready to hear them. So far there is nothing to imply that moral principles are especially rigorous, nor is anything implied about how they are derived. The point is just that, whatever these prin-

---

[1]See, for example, "Ethical Didactic" in DV [477–84].

ciples are and wherever they come from, they should be taught in a certain way.

Second, Kant was convinced that only a certain kind of pure motive could confer moral worth on any act. The only morally worthy acts, if indeed any have occurred, are acts motivated by respect for moral law; and respect, it turns out, is a unique motive, the only one which manifests our nature as members of a non-empirical, intelligible realm. Only a good will makes a person morally good, and a good will is utterly different in kind from the familiar feelings of sympathy, pity, love, and desire to share with others. Here again there is nothing about what moral principles are and how they are justified. The point is that, whatever moral principles there are, moral worth is attained only by following them from a pure motive of respect, a motive which is not fully explainable in the terms of empirical psychology.

Third, many of the particular moral principles in Kant's system are rigoristic and deontological. They are rigoristic in the sense that they are simple, unqualified principles, demanding or forbidding fairly specific acts without leaving room for exceptions. It is, for example, notorious that Kant viewed the perfect duty not to tell a lie in this way, though he took a more flexible view of imperfect duties such as beneficence.[2] His principles are typically deontological as well: that is, they require or forbid acts, such as obeying the state and lying, without describing these acts as the furthering of some good end; and moreover they imply that an act must be done or avoided regardless of its actual consequences. There can be no doubt that Kant believed that there were substantive moral principles of this sort, but it is more controversial whether this view was required by his formulations of the Categorical Imperative or by his general analysis of the difference between morality and prudence.

Fourth, and more significantly, Kant held that the appropriate method for moral philosophy, at least in its primary tasks, is an a priori one. More specifically, the supreme principle of morality cannot be discovered or justified by the observation of how people

---

[2]Kant's rigorism is most evident in the discussion of perfect duties in *The Metaphysics of Morals*. The more flexible attitude towards beneficence is evident in Part II, *The Doctrine of Virtue*. Interpretative comment is given in my paper "Kant on Imperfect Duty and Supererogation," reprinted in this volume.

behave, or by any other empirical studies; it must be shown to be a principle that any fully rational person would accept, whatever his circumstances. As a result, Kant thought that the supreme moral principle must be "formal" at least in the sense that it makes no reference to peculiarly human laws, prescriptive or descriptive, nor to peculiarly human ends, such as pleasure. And, insofar as it makes use of the model of a kingdom of ends, it must "abstract from personal differences" which distinguish one person from another. The central idea might be put this way: Moral judgments presuppose that there are rules one ought to follow, whether one wants to or not; and to say one *ought* to follow them implies that any fully rational and free person would follow them. Moral judgments, therefore, presuppose that there is some principle, however general and formal, which backs these judgments and which any fully free and rational person would follow. Are there any such principles? The most obvious candidate is a familiar one: a fully rational person would follow the principle to will the necessary means to the ends which, after due reflection, he wills to pursue. This principle, however, will obviously not support moral judgments, for these demand and forbid acts regardless of what ends one wills to pursue. Thus, if moral judgments are not based on a false presupposition, there must be some other principle of rationality: a principle which, together with empirical facts, will support ordinary moral judgments, which demands more than taking the necessary means to one's ends, but which is a principle that any fully rational (and free) person would follow. How could one discover such a principle and establish its credentials? Clearly not by observing how human beings behave, or even by finding the general principles of human psychology. What is required is an investigation of the necessary features of rationality; and this is not a task for empirical science.

This view of the a priori nature of the first tasks of ethics does not, of course, imply that empirical facts are altogether irrelevant to moral issues; nor did Kant think that they were. The acceptance of an a priori method is simply a consequence of the belief in the rationality of morals together with an analysis of morality which makes it impossible to rationalize it as the most effective device for achieving one's own ends. If moral judgments are justified, there must be some true principle, besides the means–ends principle, which says, "Any fully rational (and free) human being, faced with the conditions of human life, would do such-and-such." But then the question arises: what is there about human beings and their circumstances that makes acting in that way rational? The answer ultimately must have this form: "To be fully rational is necessarily to follow the principle . . . ; human nature and circumstances are—————; and hence any fully rational human being, faced with human circumstances, would do such-and-such." This first part of this answer is a necessary truth about rationality, that is, about what any fully rational (and free) person would necessarily do. If one believes in the rationality of morals it is hard to see how one could avoid the task of finding such a principle; and it is even harder to see how this task could be accomplished by empirical methods.

II

Each of the ideas which I have just sketched is controversial, and my object is not to defend Kant on these matters. Indeed there are many points with which I am in disagreement. Some of these, such as Kant's rigorism, seem inessential to the main tenets of his ethical theory; other points, such as the insistence on non-empirical motives as a condition of moral worth, evoke a sympathetic response but not conviction. The point which I wish to stress, however, is that one should not confuse one's doubts about these ideas with another, quite different ground for thinking that Kant may be too much of a purist. This is the suspicion that his ethical theory is utopian.

A theory is utopian if it describes an ideal state of affairs and then draws illegitimate inferences from this to propositions about what we, in a world far from ideal, ought to do. Some inferences from ideal worlds to actual duties are quite legitimate; some are not. It is one of the most important tasks of moral philosophy to explain which of these inferences are legitimate, and why; and, as far as I know, the task has not been successfully accomplished. Still, some paradigms of overstepping the bounds of legitimacy seem clear; and I believe that Kant, through a failure to make an important distinction, sometimes takes the fateful step.

The problem is that, in his formulations of the Categorical Imperative and elsewhere, Kant suggests that one can decide what is morally right in isolation from facts about the frailty and corruption of other human beings. To be sure, Kant was well aware of human weakness and immorality. The fact that human beings have "imperfect wills" is what, on Kant's view, explains why unconditional rational principles are *imperatives* for us. Nevertheless, at crucial points Kant implies that the right-minded man can ignore the fact that others are immoral and weak when he seeks to determine what he must do. There is, of course, some truth in this; but not as much as Kant suggests.

Kant's utopianism emerges at several points. First, consider the universal law formula of the Categorical Imperative. This tells us to try to conceive a world in which everyone adopts and acts on the maxim which we propose to follow. If we could not rationally will such a world, if we had the choice, then the formula implies that it would be wrong for us to act on that maxim; otherwise, it is permissible. Suppose, for example, I propose to act on the maxim to give only my "fair share" to charity; that is, I propose to give just what would be required to alleviate poverty if everyone were equally, or proportionately, charitable. Since I could rationally will a world in which everyone acted on that maxim, I conclude, by Kant's formula, that it is permissible for me to do so. My conclusion that it is permissible is quite independent of my assessment of how much others will in fact give; I need not, for example, take account of the fact that vast numbers of affluent people are too selfish to take seriously their obligations to the poor, or too weak to act on them. But can one really decide how much one ought to give independently of such facts? Given that others will not do their part, my adherence to the "fair shares" maxim may mean that people will starve even though I could help them at comparatively little cost to myself. Surely a conscientious person will consider not only what *would* be the case *if* everyone acted likewise but also what *will* be the case if one acts this way or that. Perhaps a suitable rewriting of the "relevant" maxim would dispel the problem; but, in the absence of convincing criteria for doing so, such a move looks suspiciously like an ad hoc attempt to save Kant's formula rather than a genuine application of it.

The principle that humanity ought to be treated as an end in itself does not so readily invite the charge of utopianism. Nevertheless, had Kant faced the problem squarely, certain problems of interpretation might have been avoided. The principle affirms that one is never to treat humanity in any person merely as a means, and, as Kant applies it, this implies the unequivocal condemnation of suicide, adultery, mockery, servility, false promises, and much besides.[3] But, given a corrupt world, one wonders, might not special situations arise in which these are necessary in order to further humanity as an end in itself? In a world of thoroughly moral persons, one might never have to make a false promise to one person in order to preserve the lives or dignity of others; but it can happen in the real world. A principle which tells us without qualification to treat each person as an end in himself leaves us in doubt when, due to human weakness and corruption, our only apparent choice is to sacrifice one end in himself to preserve others. At one point Kant suggests that the test of whether we are treating someone as an end in himself is whether that person does, or can, "share the end" of our action.[4] While he denies in a footnote that this is to be construed so as to give a criminal grounds for disputing with the judge who sentences him, it is never clear how the implication is to be avoided. In a world of perfectly moral men, we could more closely approximate the ideal of never treating someone as a means to ends which he does not, or cannot, share; for there our ends would presumably be in greater harmony than in fact they are. But meanwhile, in the real world, what are we to do?

Kant's "kingdom of ends" principle raises the utopian problem most dramatically. It tells us to live in this corrupt world, come what may, by the laws that would be legislated by a community of perfectly rational, autonomous persons, who acknowledge each other as ends in themselves and make their laws in abstraction from personal differences.[5] Legislators under those ideal condi-

[3]The principle is articulated in G [429] and elsewhere. Many of the applications, however, are in *The Metaphysics of Morals.*

[4]See the second example to the ends-in-themselves formula, G [429–30].

[5]My interpretation of the kingdom of ends formulation of the Categorical Imperative, together with a hint of the utopian problem is contained in my paper "The Kingdom of Ends," reprinted in this volume.

tions would have no reason to consider the effects of promulgating those laws in a world of weak and corrupt men. Unlike us, they could take for granted universal compliance. But some laws which would be ideal if everyone followed them may be undesirable if followed by only a conscientious and strong-willed fraction of the community. The benefits of some laws may be chain-linked; that is, if every link is strong and does its part, then the benefits are substantial; but if some links are weak, there are no benefits at all, perhaps even harm. The requirement to live by the rules rational in a perfect law-abiding community amounts to a demand to ignore, as irrelevant to moral decision, the fact that we often have to deal with people who murder, lie, cheat, and exploit others in thousands of complex ways. But a principle which implies that these facts are morally irrelevant is dangerously utopian.

III

Is utopianism essential to the central tenets of Kant's ethical theory? I have suggested that various formulations of the Categorical Imperative, without modification, raise the utopian problem; and other passages, I think, also suggest Kant's liability to this sort of objection. Nevertheless, the problem is not at the core of Kant's theory; and in particular, is quite independent of Kant's primary thesis that, unless morality is an illusion, there is behind ordinary moral judgments a Categorical Imperative, that is, a principle, other than the means-ends principle, which any free and rational person would accept, whatever his circumstances, particular desires, etc. It might be thought that the search, by a priori methods, for such a principle would inevitably result in utopianism; for, after all, the fact that human beings are often weak and corrupt is a contingent, empirical fact, not the sort that can be a premise in the derivation of a Categorical Imperative. The commitment to an a priori search for a Categorical Imperative, however, does not actually require utopianism. One need not assume weakness and corruption as an inevitable precondition of all rational choice in order to acknowledge that at some stage rational moral decision must take these factors into account. Kant could have avoided the utopianism problem, I suggest, if he had more sharply distinguished his central thesis that a rational ethics presupposes a Categorical Imperative, not based upon any special facts about the human condition, from the supposed corollary that such a Categorical Imperative can be applied to real human problems without taking the special facts of human weakness and corruption into account. The former has much to recommend it; but the latter is untenable. At first, the latter might seem to follow from the former; but it does not. Acknowledgment of this fact might require some changes in the formulations of the Categorical Imperative; but the changes, I suspect, need not be radical ones.

Finally, does the theoretical problem raised here have any practical import? An increasingly important part of the unarticulated life-style of many students is an acceptance of the principle "Never compromise with evil." Administrators, they believe, are corrupt; and so "don't play along with the system." To participate in a system which contains injustices is to be co-opted; to work within it for reform is to commit the crimes against humanity that the Nazi judges were convicted of at Nürnberg. In many cases, I agree, co-operation with evil can be quite wrong; and no doubt many who say that they stay with a corrupt scheme in order to reform it are deceiving themselves. But, taken in a sweeping way, the "No compromise" rule suffers from the same defect as Kant's most rigoristic principles. It generates "clean hands" arguments: "Never mind what will happen, don't stain your hands by dealing with those people" or "Don't touch dirty money." The troublesome practical consequence of utopianism, as sometimes suggested by Kant, is that it lends support to this unthinking "clean hands" attitude. A theory which affirmed the purity of morals without utopianism would encourage more intelligent moral judgment about when it is wrong to cooperate with imperfect leaders and when it is not.

5

The Kantian Conception
of Autonomy

Autonomy is a central concept in contemporary moral debates as well as in discussions of Kant; but the only thing that seems completely clear about autonomy in these contests is that it means different things to different writers. Though no one denies the importance of autonomy in Kant's moral theory, there is surprisingly little agreement even about how Kant conceived autonomy. This is not entirely the fault of the commentators, of course, for what Kant says about autonomy is not only deep and richly suggestive but also incomplete, ambiguous, and (at times) opaque. Even those who seem confident that they have grasped what Kant was getting at are deeply divided about the value of Kant's idea of autonomy. To some it is the most central and profound concept in moral philosophy, but to others it is an inapplicable relic of an unduly optimistic age, a desperate metaphysical flight from the implications of science and critical philosophy. Our topic, then, lies in an area where one understandably hesitates to "rush in," even though the ground is not completely untrod by angels.

Nevertheless, I propose to sketch here what I think the main Kantian conception of autonomy is, and what it is not. My main

Earlier versions of this paper were presented at conferences at the University of South Carolina, the University of Virginia, and Virginia Polytechnic and State University. Thanks are due to the participants in those conferences and to colleagues at the University of North Carolina for their helpful comments.

focus is on Kant's *Groundwork of the Metaphysics of Morals,* but the view of autonomy there, I believe, is generally consistent with Kant's later ethical writings. I do not offer detailed analyses of particular texts but rather summarize some main implications of Kantian autonomy, as I understand it, and then discuss briefly some objections to it. My main thesis is not that all Kant's claims about autonomy are correct but just that they have important implications concerning rational deliberation that are, to a large extent, independent of his most troublesome metaphysical ideas and his special understanding of the moral law.

More specifically, my plan is this: First, I will survey some familiar conceptions of autonomy in order to distinguish them from the Kantian conception. Second, I describe some main features of Kantian autonomy, distinguishing these from the claims Kant makes about the connection between autonomy and morality. Third, I highlight some implications of the Kantian conception, especially its relevance to contemporary views about rational choice. Finally, I take up briefly the objections that Kantian autonomy is incompatible with physical determinism and with the explanation of human action by reference to the agent's beliefs and desires.

I. What Kantian Autonomy Is Not

The term "autonomy" appears frequently in philosophical theories of quite different sorts, and recently it has become a favorite term in practical disputes about politics, education, developmental psychology, and feminism. To avoid confusion, then, it may be well to begin by separating our special subject matter, Kantian autonomy, from some familiar but distinct ideas of autonomy.[1] Kant's conception of autonomy may well have inspired some of these contemporary notions, but in important ways they have been cut loose from their Kantian roots.

First, autonomy is sometimes conceived as a sort of psychological maturity, which some people have and others do not and which we attribute to people in various degrees on the basis of

---

[1]Some of these distinctions are discussed in my paper "Autonomy and Benevolent Lies," *Journal of Value Inquiry* 18 (1984): 251–67.

empirical evidence. An autonomous person, in this sense, has a kind of independence of judgment which young children and unthinking conformists lack. One shows a deficiency of autonomy when one blindly follows parental wishes, peer pressures, traditional norms, church authorities, or local fads, fashions, or folk heroes. Impulsive rebellion against custom and authority, however, does not mark one as autonomous, for autonomy is typically associated with a high degree of rational self-control. Compulsive gamblers and drug addicts, for example, are common paradigms of the nonautonomous. Some apparently think of autonomous persons as being, in addition, emotionally independent of others, self-reliant, and secure in their self-esteem. Other common criteria of autonomy include a propensity to think abstractly, to listen to alternative viewpoints, and to weigh reasons for acting.

A particular version of this idea of autonomy as a variable psychological trait serves for some as both a descriptive category and a normative ideal for moral agents. For example, this seems to be the role of autonomy in Kohlberg's account of moral development, which Carol Gilligan has criticized as reflecting a masculine bias.[2] The ideal includes not only reflectiveness, self-control, and independence of judgment, but also commitment to general principles, apart from hope of reward or fear of punishment; and it requires making moral decisions from this loyalty to abstract principle rather than from compassion for particular persons. Autonomous agents, on this view, make moral decisions from an impartial perspective, detached from the special feelings that stem from their particular personal relationships.

Now, though we can easily recognize here several ideas Kant would have applauded, there are some crucial differences between these psychological conceptions of autonomy and Kantian autonomy. For one thing, autonomy in the psychological accounts is an empirically discernible trait, attributed in various degrees to people on the basis of what they are observed to say and do in various circumstances. Kant, on the other hand, treats autonomy as an "Idea" of reason, attributed on a priori grounds to all rational

[2]See Carol Gilligan, *In a Different Voice* (Cambridge: Harvard University Press, 1982), and Lawrence Kohlberg, "Stage and Sequence: The Cognitive Development Approach to Socialization," in *The Handbook of Social Theory and Research,* ed. D. A. Goslin (Chicago: Rand McNally, 1969), pp. 347–480.

wills. Despite some appearances to the contrary, Kant typically treats autonomy as an all-or-nothing trait that grounds a basic respect due to all human beings, as opposed to a variable respect earned only by the most conscientious. Because they have autonomy of the will, Kant argues, all (minimally) rational human beings have basic moral obligations. Though special obligations vary with circumstances, being under moral obligation at all presupposes autonomy, not as the special achievement of the few but as a universal condition of moral agency.

Further, many of the particular features of the psychologically autonomous person are not essential for Kantian autonomy: for example, emotional independence from others, special propensity for abstract thinking, and exceptionally critical attitudes toward current social norms. Even acting from internalized moral principles, contrary to social norms and without concern for reward and punishment, would not guarantee the possession of Kantian autonomy for that autonomy requires acknowledging the principles not only as "self-imposed," in some sense, but also as unconditional requirements of *reason*. With an optimism less common today, Kant believed that virtually all adult human beings acknowledge basic moral laws in this way. Thus, on the Kantian view, even those who are knowingly immoral and those whose most effective loyalties are to individuals rather than to impartial principles still have wills with the property of autonomy, though of course they fail to express their autonomy by living up to the commitments it entails.

Another current conception of autonomy treats autonomy as a right rather than an empirical trait. To be an autonomous person, on this view, is to have a moral right to make certain decisions for oneself, to control certain aspects of one's life without interference. The working analogy here, apparently, is with autonomous states, which are such not because they are governed in a particularly effective or high-minded way but because they have a right that other nations not interfere in their internal affairs. This right-sense, I take it, is what is presupposed when people complain that blue laws, coercive threats, and even well-intended manipulative lies violate their autonomy as persons.

The nature of the right may be spelled out in different ways, but however this is done, the conception of autonomy as a right will be significantly different from Kant's conception. Kant believed, of course, in rights to a high degree of self-determination in practical matters, and he thought all rights are grounded in some way in the fact that human beings have autonomy. But autonomy itself is not a right but a property of all rational wills, a property implying the possessor's recognition of rational principles other than desire-satisfaction but not by itself implying the wrongness of the specific forms of coercion, manipulation, and control that modern appeals to autonomy typically condemn. The confessed murderer on the gallows, I take it, has forfeited most of his rights to determine his future, but he has not thereby lost his Kantian autonomy.

Philosophers sometimes attribute to us a kind of autonomy that, unlike rights, makes no moral claim on others and yet, unlike psychological maturity, is attributed to everyone independently of empirical evidence. I have in mind what I call, without scholarly pretensions, Sartrean autonomy. This consists in part of a denial that human choices are subject to causal determination: we choose free from determination by the sort of causal factors that work in the nonhuman realm. Further, it implies a denial that there are objective moral and rational constraints on our choices: that is, we choose free from any "authoritative" principles not of our own making. To deny this sort of autonomy to persons is not to deny their rights or underestimate their maturity but to pretend that they "have to" make certain choices either because of the laws of nature or because of laws of reason or morality.

Most obviously this Sartrean conception is not Kant's. Choosing for oneself, on the Sartrean view, is not listening to the voice of one's reason amidst the din of "alien" desires; it is turning a deaf ear to any claim that one's choices are objectively constrained by reason, moral obligation, desire, or physical forces. The Sartrean applauds Kant's critique of mindless acceptance of norms as given, by tradition, by divine command, or by human nature; and, like Kant, he does so in the name of "freedom." This freedom is attributed to all as something that can be denied and belied but not escaped; and whatever the grounds of believing in Sartrean freedom, they are not of the ordinary empirical kind. But despite these Kantian overtones, the essential element of Kantian autonomy is missing: the agent's commitment to rational principles of a special sort.

Another similar but distinct notion of autonomy should perhaps be mentioned: this is Rousseau's idea of "moral liberty."[3] This is what citizens would have in a state so ideal that all its laws were backed by the "general will" of the people, and to obtain it, Rousseau argues, it is necessary and rational to abandon "natural liberty" by joining others in a social contract. When there is a general will behind all the laws, then the laws are approved by at least the "public will" of each citizen, that is, by each public-spirited citizen setting aside factionalism and aiming for the common good. If a citizen's "private," or self-interested, will is reluctant to obey these laws, he may be justly coerced to obey; but then, Rousseau tells us, he is only "forced to be free." The relevant sense of freedom here is "moral liberty," which is the condition of being constrained only by laws which you give to yourself.

This had an obvious Kantian ring, and Kant's debt to Rousseau has often been noted. But, importantly for our purposes, there is for Rousseau a political interpretation of "being constrained only by laws which you give to yourself": the constraining is by law backed by police, and one can give laws to oneself by participating in a political process in an informed and public-spirited way. The resultant laws, according to Rousseau, are necessarily just, but they are not necessarily acknowledged as rational independently of the citizens' (other-regarding) feelings and desires. Kantian autonomy may have been inspired by Rousseau, but Kant transforms Rousseau's "moral liberty" for more general use in the controversies about reason and morals.

Finally, I need to distinguish Kantian autonomy as I understand this from a conception of autonomy often attributed to Kant by students and at times by professional commentators.[4] The background of the latter is an interpretation of the *Groundwork* according to which there are just two mutually exclusive ways in which human beings can act. First, one can act from inclination; and, in this case, the act is nothing but a product of natural forces, unfree, causally "determined" by desire, and "heteronomous." Though we may speak of a "heteronomous will," strictly such acts are not

[3]Jean-Jacques Rousseau, *The Social Contract* (Baltimore: Penguin, 1968), bk. I, chaps. 7 and 8.
[4]In many respects this seems to be the view of Robert Paul Wolff in *The Autonomy of Reason* (New York: Harper & Row, 1973).

willed at all because "will" is identical with "practical reason," which chooses only the rational and the good. Second, one can act from moral principle; and, in this case, the act is a product of causally undetermined choice, free, and perfectly rational. The will, on this picture, cannot freely choose between acting from inclination and acting from moral principle because the will, as practical reason, is directed exclusively toward what is rational and moral. Nature sometimes, inexplicably, takes over a person, who then "acts" unfreely; but sometimes, inexplicably, the will is in control and then the person is free in the sense "uncaused and yet following reason." Autonomy, on this view, is just the freedom we have in our better moments, when willing rationally, guided by moral principles. Some have autonomy, some do not; or, more likely, sometimes one has it, sometimes not. When it is operative, we act autonomously; when not, we act heteronomously; but, strictly speaking, we do not *will* to do the one rather than the other because the will, by definition, is always on the side of the angels.

This conception of autonomy has several striking consequences that should give pause to anyone tempted to attribute it to Kant. Most obviously, all "immoral" acts prove to be unfree and not even willed by the agent. The adulterer is almost literally "carried away" by his lust as is the thief by his greed; and even minor, relatively passionless crimes must be construed on the same model. Further, since autonomy is the ground of human dignity, dignity and so the respect owed to human beings must vary with one's level of moral achievement. Again, since Kant argues both that negative freedom is inseparable from autonomy and that it is a necessary condition of moral obligation, we would have to conclude that whenever one lacks autonomy one is not under moral obligation. Thus the apparently immoral thief, acting from greed, is not merely excused from responsibility; he was not even acting contrary to a moral obligation.

The interpretation in question must also treat Kant's later distinction between *Wille* and *Willkur* as a radical departure from the *Groundwork*. Within the *Groundwork* many passages will become baffling, for example, passages implying that reason sometimes fails to "determine the will." Admittedly, there are other passages in the *Groundwork* that suggest the dualistic picture that I am opposing here, but on balance the evidence weighs heavily against it.

II. Main Features of Kantian Autonomy

In the *Critique of Pure Reason* Kant attempts to prove that all empirically discernable events are governed by causal laws, and yet he says that we can "think" of another sort of causation in which causes are themselves uncaused. Causes of this alternative kind, he tells us, are possible but cannot be known or even "comprehended." Kant defends the compatibility of belief in such causes with the (allegedly) proven fact that all empirical events have causes by denying that uncaused causes are spatiotemporal events.

According to Kant's strictest statements about the merely negative role of the idea of *noumena,* these expansive remarks about non-empirical causes are not to be understood as metaphysical speculations but merely as reminders that all that we can understand and know about the world is dependent upon our conceptual and perceptual frameworks.[5] Kant allows himself to write dramatically of our world as a world of "appearance" as opposed to "things in themselves"; but, strictly speaking, by his own doctrine "reality" is a "category" for empirical understanding, and so any working distinction between what is "real" and what merely "appears" must be empirically based.[6] The urge to read Kant as proposing a metaphysical picture of two worlds is hard to resist, but despite his own lapses, Kant repeatedly insists that we can have neither an "intuition" nor a "concept" of anything beyond experience.

Notoriously, Kant *seems* to ignore these warnings in his works on ethics, for he often writes of "the intelligible world," God, and "freedom" as a non-empirical property of human "wills." At the same time Kant insists that such usage is only for "practical," not "theoretical," purposes, and that none of his earlier warnings about metaphysics has been abandoned or violated.

Some readers take Kant's disclaimer that he speaks only from a "practical" perspective to be simply an admission that he has nothing but weak, pragmatic arguments for his metaphysical speculations about "the will," and so forth. Far from removing our

---

[5]Immanuel Kant, *The Critique of Pure Reason,* trans. Norman Kemp Smith (London: Macmillan, 1956), especially pp. 257ff.

[6]Kant, *The Critique of Pure Reason,* pp. 111–19.

worries about the intelligibility of the two-worlds view, this interpretation would compound the problem by casting doubt on the *grounds* for believing what is admitted to be impossible to *understand*. A more sympathetic and profitable interpretative strategy, I suggest, is to try to construe Kant's disclaimer not so much as a remark about the *grounds* for belief as a clue about *how* we are to read his claims about freedom, the will, and so on. That is that, so far as possible, the content of such claims should be understood as "practical," or normative, rather than as metaphysical. Perhaps the metaphysics cannot be entirely eliminated; the effort to construe the problematic concepts normatively has textual support and yields more interesting results.

These preliminary remarks lead to my first suggestion about the Kantian idea of autonomy, namely, that we take it less as a metaphysical account of what we are like than as a normative idea about the task, attitudes, and commitments of *rational* agents when deliberating about what to do. It has more to do with what we should count as reasons for acting, and with what we should hold ourselves responsible for, than with how human action fits into a metaphysical picture of what there is in the world.

Second, autonomy is said to be a property of human *wills;* to have a will Kant says, is to have "the power to act in accordance with [one's] idea of laws . . . [or] principles" or "a kind of causality belonging to living things so far as they are rational" (G 80, 114). The basic idea, I take it, is that in saying we have *wills* we are saying that we can "make things happen" for reasons, or according to policies or principles. We cannot isolate a particular physical or introspectible "event" as the "act of will," but we make sense of practical talk of doing things for reasons as opposed, say, to twitching, sneezing, and sleepwalking. Autonomy, then must have something to do with the reasons, or principles, for which we act.

Next, and more controversially, I contend that Kant viewed autonomy as a property of (the wills of) virtually all adult, sane human beings, not as a special feature of the most perfectly rational or morally conscientious persons. This follows, I would argue, from his contention that autonomy is inseparable from "negative freedom," which in turn is a necessary condition for being under moral obligation (G 114). The error of all previous moral philosophers, Kant implies, is their failure to recognize that moral obligation is grounded on the fact that the human will has autonomy. They misidentified the supreme moral principle because they tried to derive moral obligations from the idea of a will with heteronomy, rather than autonomy (G 110–12).

This point is lost, I think, when contemporary writers refer to conscientious action as "autonomous" and to desire-motivated action as "heteronomous." These are not Kant's expressions and they misleadingly suggest that those who act wrongly, or act to satisfy innocent desires, lack autonomy (at least at the moment). Kant's predominant view, I would argue, is rather that all have autonomy, that this implies commitment to certain rational constraints, and that some live up to these commitments while others do not. The former, unlike the latter, *express* their autonomy in action;[7] but the commitment implied by "autonomy" is something anyone must have to be a moral agent.

The next point to note is that any will with autonomy is necessarily "free in a negative sense," which Kant defines as "the property [the will] has of being able to work independently of alien causes" (G 114). Construed as a practical idea, the point is that, in deliberating and choosing to act, as a rational agent one must take oneself to be deciding between outcomes that are still open, that is, are not fixed by causes operating *independently* of one's deliberation and choice. Moreover, whatever the agent's *beliefs* about metaphysical determinism, one must *when deliberating* take the attitude that the choice itself is still "up to oneself." If the agent knew of a particular prospective "choice" that it is already determined by prior conditions to be the outcome of one's current reflections, then the agent would not be deliberating, and the bare knowledge, or belief, that *something* will determine one's choice, whatever that may be, would be of no use in deciding what to do.

The previous point captures one sense in which agents see themselves as able to act "independently of desire": that is, they see their desires not as determining causes of what they will choose but rather as considerations about which a choice has to be made. But Kant implies, I think, that negatively free agents can "act independently of desire" in a further sense, not concerned with causes.

[7]This distinction between having and expressing autonomy I take from John Rawls.

Suppose we distinguish between being caused to act by a desire and choosing to act for the sake of satisfying a desire. In the first case, the desire figures as a prior causal condition; in the second, the desire is mentioned in a description of the agent's objective or end in acting. One who denied that acts are *caused* by desires might still maintain that acts are always *motivated* by desire, in the sense that they have satisfaction of desire as their intended object. By attributing "negative freedom" to rational agents, Kant in effect denies both claims, for "practical" purposes. This means at least that, in rational deliberation, one must not only take oneself to be able to choose and act without the choice having been causally determined by desire (or anything else), one must also take oneself to be able to act for the sake of ends other than the satisfaction of desire. In rational deliberation one cannot assume that what one will or must do is among those things for which one feels an antecedent desire.

A few words of caution may be helpful here. First, to say that in deliberation one "takes oneself" to be free (in the senses above) does not strictly imply that one denies that causal determinism is true or even that one disbelieves it while deliberating. Though Kant at times seems to argue (on moral grounds) for a belief in metaphysical freedom, his point that we can *act* only "under the Idea of freedom" is more limited and less controversial (G 115). This idea, which I have paraphrased as "taking oneself to be free," is less concerned with which propositions about the world one affirms or denies than with which working framework one must adopt in order to take seriously the question "What should I do?" The practical import of conceiving ourselves as negatively free is at least that, in seeking answers to *this* question, we are not looking for a causal basis to predict what we will do and we do not count our current and anticipated desires as finally settling what our aims and options are to be.

Also we should note that negative freedom for Kant is not an experienced "feeling of freedom" found to accompany all deliberations; nor is it any other psychological trait inductively inferred from repeated observations. The claim that in deliberating we must take ourselves to be free, then, is not meant as an empirical report that we constantly feel that our options are open whenever we raise practical questions. The point is quite different from my observation that whenever I play the piano from memory I must feel confident that I know the notes (even fleeting doubts disrupt the effort), for I can imagine what it would be like to play despite doubts (some do). By contrast, Kant is attempting to make a deep a priori point about what it is to engage in rational deliberation and action: we cannot even "think" what it would be for one who did not presuppose negative freedom.

Autonomy is not only negative freedom, Kant says, but is also freedom "positively conceived." This is characterized as the property a will has of being "a law unto itself . . . independently of every property belonging to the objects of volition".[8] No single paraphrase, however, adequately captures the idea, which gets its sense from a variety of contexts. Without going into textual details, let me just summarize the main features I think are contained in the complex Kantian idea of positive freedom.

To conceive a person as having positive freedom is to think of the person as having, (1) in addition to negative freedom, (2) a deep rational commitment to some principle(s) of conduct as (rationally) binding but (3) not adopted for the sake of satisfying desires, (4) not just prescribing means to rationally contingent ends, and yet (5) in some sense necessarily imposed on oneself by oneself as a rational agent. Further, though one may not always live up to it, (6) the commitment is seen by the agent as rationally overriding other sorts of principles and aims, in case of conflict. Finally, setting aside cognitive requirements and formal principles such as "Take the means or abandon the end," the *only* action-guiding principles that are rationally "authoritative" for the agent with autonomy are principles that satisfy these conditions; and so (7) no principle to which one is committed because of contingent features of one's human or individual makeup has this sort of necessary reason-giving force.

The basic idea is that, despite all the negative claims about what does *not* necessarily move the agent or provide reasons, there is still some rational standard of conduct, commitment to which is inherent in the point of view of agents who try to deliberate and choose rationally. This is later identified with the (supposedly) formal expressions of the supreme principle of morality, but the

[8]G 108; see also G 114.

claim that wills with autonomy must adopt the supreme moral principle is not part of the idea of autonomy but rather something Kant sees a need to argue. The sense in which the principles of autonomy are "imposed on oneself by oneself" is puzzling, but at least it is clear that Kant did not see this as an arbitrary, optional choice but as a commitment that clear thinking reveals, implicit in all efforts to will rationally, the way one may think that commitment to basic principles of logic is implicit in all efforts to think and understand. Rational principles of conduct do not "exist" independently of agents the way a Platonist might think of them; but neither are they "inventions" of God, as Ockham and Descartes thought, or "natural laws" discovered empirically, as some other philosophers seem to have believed.

III. Some Normative Implications

The most famous, and controversial, use Kant made of his idea of autonomy was his attempt to derive from it his special conception of the supreme moral principle. That is, Kant argues that the one and only principle that satisfies the conditions for being a necessary rational commitment of all agents with autonomy is the so-called Categorical Imperative, to act only on maxims that one can will as universal laws (G 108, 114). If true, this would imply that every minimally rational agent, in deliberating and acting, is actually committed to this principle, as an overriding rational constraint, and so can violate it only on pain of inconsistency. Like many others, I have doubts about this part of Kant's theory; but I think that such doubts should not prevent us from seeing some striking implications of the idea of autonomy that are independent of this strong claim about its connection with morality. Thus my focus in this section will be on the normative significance of Kantian autonomy aside from its alleged role in providing a basis for morality.

The first consequence to note is a broad negative thesis. In Kantian language, this is that *material* principles of conduct are never *necessary* principles of practical reason. In more familiar terms, this means that it is not a necessary rational requirement that we try to maximize desire-satisfaction, the balance of pleasure/pain, or any other substantive value that, as human beings or as individuals, we happen to care about. Power, fame, knowledge, and even Stoic peace of mind are at best contingently rational ends, rational to pursue only because chosen by rational agents and only when their pursuit satisfies more formal requirements of reason. The point, I take it, is not merely that rational principles are not "maximizing" principles; for it also implies that substantive values, such as desire and pleasure, do not *necessarily* provide even prima facie reasons for action. Their status as reasons depends upon their endorsement by the individual agent, subject to certain constraints; and there is nothing in our *rational* nature that prevents us from refusing to count any given desire or pleasure as a justifying reason for acting.

The idea is a radical one, which Hume and many modern preference theorists might applaud, but it should not be misunderstood. Of course, we normally count the fact that we desire something, especially after due reflection, as a good prima facie reason to pursue it, and there may be some values, such as avoidance of severe physical pain, that human beings, thinking clearly, will *always* endorse as ends. Kantian autonomy does not deny *this* but only certain philosophical accounts of *why* desires, pleasure, and so forth give us reasons. In particular it denies accounts that give these values necessary and unconstrained reason-giving force. Consider, for example, the view, held by Moore and more recently by Thomas Nagel, that pain has the objective property of being "bad in itself."[9] In this view, the intrinsic badness of pain by itself explains the rationality of choosing to avoid it, other things being equal. In Kant's view, by contrast, the claim that pain is bad is explained by the fact that, seeing pain for what it is and reflecting rationally, we choose to avoid it. No doubt the very concept of "pain" implies a *disposition* to avoid it, just as the concept of "desire" implies a tendency to seek objects of desire. But in the Kantian view dispositions to act are not necessarily reasons to act; they are considerations for deliberative agents to endorse or reject upon rational reflection. Substantive values do not exist independently of rational willing but are, as it were, created by it.

9G. E. Moore, *Principia Ethica* (Cambridge: Cambridge University Press, 1903), and Thomas Nagel, *The View from Nowhere* (Oxford: Oxford University Press, 1986).

Another point emerges when we consider the Kantian claim that wills with autonomy, though "free," cannot be "lawless" (G 114). This implies, I take it, that the idea of a Sartrean "radical choice," utterly unconstrained by rational principles, has no place in Kantian theory. Even when someone wills to do what is irrational, according to Kant, we can attribute the act to him or her as an agent only by understanding it as being done for a reason (in this case an insufficient reason) by someone committed to rational standards. Similar considerations lead Kant to reject the "libertarian" view, ridiculed by Hume, that free acts are random uncaused mental events ("acts of will"), not explicable in terms of the character and policies of the agent.[10] A will with autonomy is not to be pictured as "lawless" in this sense, even if the agent, in deliberating and acting, must ignore thoughts of the causal determinants of his or her choice. The "laws," however, that must be introduced to make sense of free choices are not causal laws but policies and rational commitments of the agent.

A further implication of Kantian autonomy is that, whether or not moral requirements prove to be always rational, there must be some necessary action-guiding constraints on rational choice beyond cognitive standards (regarding how to establish background beliefs and make valid inferences) and beyond the Hypothetical Imperative "to take the means or abandon the end." Kant argues this anti-Humean point, I think, quite independently of his efforts to prove the rationality of moral conduct. The idea is that in rational deliberation we presuppose at least some formal or procedural standards other than merely understanding what we are up to and adjusting our means to our ends.

Kant's own suggestions for what these could be, besides his famous (or notorious) "universal law" formula, include the idea that rational deliberative agents are committed to both a principle of self-respect and an extension of this that includes respect for other rational agents. The former requires that one's choices be justifiable to oneself not merely *at the moment*, but over *time*, and not merely as one reflects on the *products* of one's choices but also as one reflects on *the sort of person one makes of oneself* by these choices.

[10]David Hume, *A Treatise of Human Nature* (Oxford: Clarendon, 1955), bk. II, section III.

The more controversial requirement to respect other rational agents (as such) would have us confine our deliberations to what we could in principle justify to others who were willing to accept similar constraints. These suggestions, I take it, are part of Kant's idea of "rational nature" as an "end in itself."[11] Though controversial, these proposals are significantly different from the "material" principles Kant so vigorously opposes. For, though they purport to constrain what we may rationally choose, they do so not by prescribing any particular value to promote, such as knowledge, peace of mind, pleasure, or desire-satisfaction, but rather by insisting that we constrain our current self-interested deliberations by giving weight to whatever other reflective agents, and we ourselves later, would choose. Even if the idea of autonomy does not, by itself, require these particular principles, it sets limits to the sort of principles that moral theory of a Kantian sort should be looking for.

IV. Objections: Is It Obvious That We Lack Kantian Autonomy?

My remarks so far have been sketchy and leave us with only a promissory note that they can be supported by detailed examination of Kant's texts. But before closing, I want to address briefly a few further questions that most of us are inclined to ask, in exasperation, long before scholarly investigations are done. That is, does all this have any point in the modern world? Does it really make sense?

More specifically, aren't there familiar objections that are obviously decisive against the thesis that we have Kantian autonomy, as presented here? While I am not convinced that the difficulties can be satisfactorily resolved, the matter seems far from obvious to me. Some objections, I suspect, rest on misunderstanding, and in any case, it is so difficult to get a solid grasp on these issues that confidence one way or the other seems premature. My brief comments on the objections, then, should be taken not so much as

[11] G 95–103. I discuss some implications of this idea in "Humanity as an End in Itself," reprinted in this volume.

defense of Kantian autonomy as preliminary remarks designed to keep the questions open.

(A) First, isn't autonomy incompatible with a belief in determinism in physical science? Even if quantum mechanics leaves room for a degree of indeterminism at the subatomic level, most seem to agree that this makes little practical difference when we turn to the explanation and prediction of large-scale objects, such as human bodies. So doesn't this rule out autonomy? Kant, of course, *believed* that universal causation among phenomenal events was compatible with reasonable ascription of autonomy to human agents, but he seemed willing to pay a heroic price to sustain this belief when he referred to the will as not in space and time and thereby admitted the "incomprehensibility" of human agency. If we are unwilling to pay that price, do we not need to give up autonomy as an outmoded and useless concept?

Before we answer, we need to keep in mind the context in which the idea of autonomy is meant to be used. The context is not that of scientific, or even common sense, explanation but rather the context of practical deliberation. This alone does not make autonomy immune from criticism, of course, for one could not make the idea of ghosts respectable just be restricting one's thoughts of ghosts to occasions of deliberation. But there may be a difference. In deliberation the issue is "what should I do?"; and this, for Kant, amounts to "what is rational to do?" "what is there reason to do?" Now some beliefs about causes are highly relevant in this context, for example, the beliefs that smoking causes cancer and cancer causes pain. But what of the belief that, whatever I decide to do, there will have been some physical cause of my bodily movements and all the phenomena of decision making and, moreover, causes of those causes, and so forth? This is a disturbing thought to many, which no doubt prompts the desire, which Kant shared, to insist that the true decision, or act of will, cannot be explained in this way, that it cannot be "reduced" to physical or even introspectible phenomena. But stopping short of this, we may still ask, how is the belief that all the phenomena, and even the "decision," are caused supposed to be relevant to the problem at hand, namely, finding the rational thing to do? If the belief were true, it would not follow that the rational thing to do is to sit still or to do as one pleases. Nor would it follow that there is no solution, that there is nothing rational to do. Determinism raises questions about how to understand rational deliberation, but it offers no guidelines to those who attempt to deliberate rationally.

The point, of course, is not new: it is just that rational deliberation is the sort of activity in which conjectural, or even confident, belief in physical determinism is irrelevant. This is not because we are built to have some inescapable "feeling of freedom" but because of the sort of question we are asking. Thus in its proper place there may still be a use for at least one aspect of the idea of autonomy, namely, the idea of rational agents as deliberating among options not causally determined independently of the agent's choice and as having a decision to make for which it is irrelevant whether or not one believes that the final decision will have had causes.

The idea of autonomy, however, includes more than this notion of independence of causes; in particular, it includes the idea that rational agents have reasons not based on their desires, that practical rationality is not exhausted by hypothetical imperatives. Is this further idea undermined by determinism in physical science? Again, it is hard to see how it could be. The determinism in question, remember, is not a particular psychological thesis that human beings can act only for the sake of satisfaction of desire; it is rather that there are some physical causes for all phenomena. This does not tell us, one way or the other, what sort of reasons have weight in rational deliberation about what to do. "Why will it occur, if or when it does?" and "Why should I try to bring it about?" are different sorts of questions, and it is far from obvious how a general thesis about the former is relevant to the latter.

(B) But isn't autonomy incompatible with the explanation of human action in terms of beliefs and desires? The real problem, the critic might continue, does not come from determinism in physical science but rather from the way we explain human action in everyday life and in much of psychology. That is, what people do is seen as a function of their beliefs about their situation and their desires (broadly construed). The desires in question, it might be added, need not be selfish, urgently felt, or momentary so long as they are empirically discernible. We do not deny that people act from respect for moral principle, says the critic; we only insist that respect is an empirical motive, a sort of desire to be moral or (as Richard Brandt has suggested) an aversion to being immoral.[12] The problem with the idea of autonomy, then, is not that it is disproved by scientific evidence but that it pictures human beings as capable of acting without any understandable motivation. The charge is not that autonomy is falsified by physical science so much as that it is rendered incoherent by its supposition that human beings can act when stripped of the motivational features that make human acts, as opposed to mere bodily movements, understandable.

The Kantian might reply by noting, first, that Kant does not deny that all observable human acts, even acts from duty, can be understood and explained by reference to empirical feelings and dispositions. The claims about autonomy are somehow *supposed* to be compatible with this admission, but how? One move, of course, is to say that what we observe is mere appearance whereas "will" and "reason" are admittedly incomprehensible noumenal entities. But for most of us this will not do. Is there anything left to autonomy without this? Again, I think, we must return to the primary context in which the idea of autonomy is to be applied: the point of view of agents deliberating about what they have reason to do. Here, as I have suggested, to attribute autonomy to oneself amounts to at least two things: seeing oneself as causally undetermined in the process and acknowledging that one is committed to rational standards of choice other than desire-satisfaction. This does not imply that anyone, including the agent in deliberation, must cease to believe that the act he chooses will be understandable in terms of desires (in the broad sense). Agents ask, "What should I do?" and so long as they take this question seriously they will find that it is neither a help nor a hindrance to believe that the outcome will be understandable in terms of empirical dispositions. If agents conceive themselves, practically, as having autonomy, then they will not assume that every disposition they find themselves to have is a reason for action, nor will they assume that failure to feel or observe a disposition means that they have no reason to act. Their search for reasons will not be just a survey of present and predicted future dispositions and the

<hr />

[12]As I recall, Brandt made this suggestion in conversation at Oxford in 1973.

means to realize them. But, again, this is not to deny that when they act there will have been a disposition in terms of which their acts can be explained.

The point, it should be noted, is just that the mere fact that there are always explanatory empirical dispositions is not something that enters into the solution of a deliberative problem. This is not to say that the knowledge that one has particular empirical dispositions (e.g., those of a compulsive gambler) cannot render deliberation pointless. Compulsions, addictions, and the like can (perhaps contrary to Kant) render rational deliberation useless, and if the agent is aware of this, genuine deliberation becomes impossible. But to grant that certain desires render practical reasoning ineffective is not the same as granting that these desires determine the rational course of action. The idea of autonomy has its use, if at all, within practical deliberation, not as a general descriptive characterization of human powers.

(C) Finally, I imagine our exasperated critic to object as follows: "Suppose I grant that the idea of Kantian autonomy, or some residue you have distilled, is not shown useless or incoherent in the ways I had first thought. But have you, or Kant, given me any reason to accept it? You *say* that rational agents deliberate with the idea of autonomy, which implies commitment to rational standards independent of desires. But have you shown me even one such principle? Or demonstrated that there is one? Isn't the bottom line simply the old *assumption* that morality is rational whether it serves one's desires or not?"

Here, as a beginning, the Kantian would do well to invite the critic to examine again Kant's argument for autonomy in the third chapter of the *Groundwork*. There, as I have argued elsewhere, we find Kant's most tortured effort to avoid *assuming* that morality is necessarily rational and to give independent considerations for the belief that all reasons are not based on desires.[13] His strategy is easy to miss because it is so indirect: rather than trying to exhibit an example of a desire-independent rational standard and show its connection with the concept of rational choice, he tries to argue from claims about how we must see ourselves in deliberation to

---

[13]My attempt to reconstruct Kant's argument is in "Kant's Argument for the Rationality of Moral Conduct," reprinted in this volume.

the conclusion that we must acknowledge that there are such desire-independent standards, whatever they turn out to be. But whether, after all, there is any merit in the argument, and indeed whether my views of these matters are really Kant's, I must leave as open questions, along with many others.

6

Kant's Argument for the Rationality of Moral Conduct

Kant is known as a champion of the idea that moral conduct is demanded by reason; but, despite a remarkable revival of interest in Kant's ethics, surprisingly little attention has been paid to Kant's explicit argument for the idea.[1] This neglect is understandable but unfortunate. The misfortune is not that we have overlooked a sound and lucid proof which could have effectively settled all contemporary controversies about whether it is rational to be moral; it is rather that we have missed, or misread, a text which is crucially important for understanding Kant's *Groundwork of the Metaphysics of Morals* and which contains ideas worth considering in their own right. The argument in question is what is

This paper is a compressed version of ideas presented at a conference on Kant's ethics at Johns Hopkins in the summer of 1983, and an earlier version was also presented at the A.P.A., Pacific Division, meetings and at a meeting of the Triangle Ethics Group in Chapel Hill in the spring of 1985. Thanks are due to the participants at those meetings and also to Tyler Burge, Stephen Darwall, Gregory Kavka, William Lycan, Christopher Morris, and others for their helpful comments. A special thanks is due to Burge for constructive help and encouragement in long discussions on these matters.

[1] There are exceptions, e.g., Dieter Henrich's "Die Deduktion des Sittengesetzes" in *Denken im Schatten des Nihilismus*, ed. Alexander Schwan (Darmstadt: Wissenschaftliche Buchgesellschaft, 1975), pp. 55–112; Karl Ameriks's *Kant's Theory of Mind*, chap. 6; and Bruce Aune's *Kant's Theory of Morals* (Princeton: Princeton University Press, 1979). Two recent important books, published after this essay, are Henry Allison's *Kant's Theory of Freedom* (Cambridge: Cambridge University Press, 1990), and Rüdiger Bittner's *What Reason Demands*, trans. Theodore Talbot (Cambridge: Cambridge University Press, 1989).

summarized in the opening paragraphs of the notorious third chapter of the *Groundwork*. The usual reading not only makes Kant appear careless and unbelievably confused; it reinforces an interpretation which has Kant holding the outrageous view that immoral acts are unfree and not even willed. Moreover, common readings of the argument have Kant arguing from a forbidden empirical premise (regarding a feeling of freedom), confusing natural laws and laws of conduct, and committing an obvious non sequitur by overlooking the fact that he can only prove freedom "from a practical point of view."

In what follows I will sketch a reconstruction of the main features of Kant's argument, a reconstruction which I believe avoids these gross difficulties and yet remains (largely) faithful to the text. My discussion, however, will concentrate more heavily on the earlier stages of the argument, for two reasons. First, these early stages, in which Kant argues that rational wills have autonomy, offer an intriguing proof that Humeans and Hobbesians are mistaken about the nature of practical reason, and the proof is quite independent of Kant's belief that he has identified the supreme moral principle. Second, though the earlier stages have drawn the heaviest ridicule, I think they are both more crucial to the interpretation of the *Groundwork* and more promising than the later stages. Though focusing upon the earlier parts of Kant's argument, I will however comment briefly on a step at the end where I believe Kant goes wrong.

I. Aims of the Argument and Possible Reasons for Its Neglect

The task Kant undertakes in chapter 3 of the *Groundwork* is nothing less than proving that moral constraints are requirements of reason. His argument, then, amounts to an answer to the contemporary question "Why be moral?" But Kant's aim is easily obscured by the fact that his imagined audience is not the sort of moral skeptic with which we are most familiar today. Kant does not see himself as addressing, for example, those who are indifferent to morality and demand that philosophy supply them with a motive to be moral; for Kant's own theory denies that anyone rational enough to ask the question could really be so indifferent.[2] Nor, I think, is Kant addressing an audience that doubts that common sense duties, as opposed to some revisionary standards, are genuinely moral (G 71–72 [403–4]). He does not imagine that anyone who clearly understood his supreme moral principle would need to wait for a proof before he felt its rational force. The intended audience, I think, is rather those whose moral commitment is liable to be called into question by philosophical accounts of practical reason which imply that morality could not be grounded in reason. To these Kant argues, first, that their theories of practical reason must be mistaken and, second, that the only alternative shows moral requirements to be rational. The argument, if sound, has important implications for contemporary moral skeptics; but its focus, its style, and perhaps even the degree of care devoted to its parts are influenced by Kant's own conception of his audience. That audience may have picked up ideas of Epicurus, Hobbes, and Hume; Nietzsche comes later.

The aim of the third chapter, in Kant's terms, is to *establish* the supreme moral principle. This is the second of two main aims stated in the preface of the *Groundwork,* namely, "to seek out and establish the supreme principle of morality" (G 60 [391–92]). Seeking out, or identifying the principle, is accomplished in the first two chapters, which also analyze the principle, reformulate it in various ways, and relate it to ideas of moral worth, dignity, etc. In the second chapter, using a so-called "analytical" method, Kant also argues that the concept of moral duty *presupposes* unconditional commands of reason not based on desires and hypothetical imperatives; but this only raises the stakes for the third chapter and leaves us with the possibility that there may be no genuine moral duties. That is, the argument purports to show that if there are moral duties then there must be non–desire-based requirements of practical reason (G 92 [425]); but whether or not there are such

[2] I assume that the person who seriously asks "Why be moral?" judges that he morally ought to do certain things but still has some sort of question. But on Kant's view, to judge that one morally ought to do something is, in part, to believe that the conduct in question is required by an unconditional "command of reason"; and surely any (even minimally) rational person who believed this could not be indifferent to the conduct. This fits with Kant's repeated suggestions that respect for moral law is, as it were, forced from us, that even murderers acknowledge the justice of their (death) sentences, etc.

rational requirements is left an open question. As Kant says, for all that has been shown, morality may be "a phantom of the brain" (G 112 [445]), that is, a set of constraints falsely believed to be rational but actually having their source in imagination rather than reason. In chapter 2 the various formulations of the supreme moral principle are *labeled* "the Categorical Imperative" (G 88 [421], 96 [428–29], 108 [440]), but it is admitted that no proof has yet been given that they *are* categorical imperatives or indeed that a categorical imperative is possible (G 92 [425], 108 [440], 112 [445]). That task is left for chapter 3.

If my reading is right, the argument of the third chapter is obviously important; why, then, has it been so often overlooked or maligned? The most obvious explanation lies in the fact that the argument is extremely compact, unclearly stated, and deeply entangled with aspects of Kant's metaphysics that have little appeal today. A further obstacle is that Kant himself suggests that he may have been reasoning in a circle (G 117 [440–41]), and though he claims to have found a way out of the circle this turns on an introduction of the "intelligible world" that is not obviously helpful (G 120–21 [453]). One is discouraged from trying to unravel all this by the fact that in the *Critique of Practical Reason* Kant seems to abandon the project of establishing the rationality of morals. There moral obligation is simply declared a "fact of reason" and used to establish that rational wills are free (which is a crucial *premise* in the argument of the *Groundwork*).[3] Another obstacle is the fact that Kant spends so much of the third chapter of the *Groundwork* stressing the compatibility of phenomenal determinism and noumenal freedom that one is tempted to see the point of the chapter as a defense of morality against determinism. Finally, I suspect that Kant's argument has been underrated because many sympathetic commentators believe that, on Kant's own principles, it is unnecessary and perhaps even morally corrupt to ask seriously, "Why be moral?"[4] To read the third chapter of the *Groundwork* as an attempt to answer this question, then, would be to see it as misguided and bound to fail.

[3]*Critique of Practical Reason*, trans. L. W. Beck (New York: Liberal Arts Press, 1956), pp. 28–31[29–32].

[4]H. J. Paton is an example; see *The Categorical Imperative* (London: Hutchinson, 1965), p. 221.

Although these considerations help to make the neglect of Kant's argument understandable, they are not, I think, adequate to justify it. One can make some headway despite the obscurities and heavy metaphysics; the reversal of premises and conclusion in the *Critique of Practical Reason* can be explained by the different nature of its project;[5] and, despite Kant's dramatic rhetoric about circular reasoning, the argument of the third chapter is not in fact a circular one.[6] The long discussion of the compatibility of freedom and determinism (in chapter 3) cannot be the main point, because this was supposedly demonstrated earlier in the *Critique of Pure Reason*

[5]In *Critique of Practical Reason*, esp. pp. 29–31[30–31], Kant again argues for the mutual entailment of (a) rational beings are free and (b) rational beings are under moral law, but he says that consciousness of (b) is the grounds for knowing (a) and not the reverse. This is clearly a reversal of the order of argument in G, and probably represents an abandonment of that argument. But, whether Kant would want it or not, there does seem to be a way of reconciling the positions in the two works. That is, take the *Groundwork* as addressing doubts of agents deliberating about what to do, whereas the *Critique* is concerned more with completing a project on the nature of reason and which among traditional metaphysical beliefs one can reasonably accept (despite the arguments of the first *Critique*). The first, then, belongs to moral philosophy, traditionally conceived; the second to the special epistemological/metaphysical/moral undertaking involved in the new critical philosophy. Since the audience of G is raising a practical question, it can be presumed willing to accept for those practical purposes anything implied by what it must assume in asking the question. Thus it need not demand any theoretical demonstration or intuition ("intellectual" or otherwise) of freedom if it is made clear that freedom is presupposed in its questioning. The audience of the *Critique*, on the other hand, may be thought more concerned with the justifiability of certain metaphysical beliefs, not from sheer speculative curiosity of course but also not from a practical need to satisfy the doubts about the rationality of morals (expressed at the end of the second chapter of G). If so, this audience is prepared to accept what the other audience was ready to entertain doubts about (namely, that as rational agents we are really under moral obligations). And, if the *Critique*'s audience is not seen as engaged primarily in deliberation about what it ought to do, the argument of G from the implications of deliberation is less appropriate. In any case, it is worth noting that the argument of G does not commit any of the mistakes in arguing for freedom that the *Critique* condemns (e.g., supposing there is an intuition of freedom).

[6]This should be clear at least in my reconstruction of the argument, for none of the premises presuppose moral obligation. As Karl Ameriks helped me to see, the suspicion of circular reasoning may arise from worry that the first premise in the argument for negative freedom (i.e., rational wills cannot act except under the Idea of freedom) might seem convincing only because it is most evident in conflicts of duty and inclination. If so, the "solution" (which emphasizes that in *all* uses of reason we view ourselves as members of an "intelligible world") would have a point without admitting that the original argument ever actually presupposed moral obligation. More needs to be said about the supposed circle and its solution, but this goes beyond the main argument I try to reconstruct here.

and it would not answer the question so provocatively declared open at the end of chapter 2, namely, whether alleged duties are, as they purport to be, genuine unconditional commands of reason. Again, while Kant thought it a mistake to try to give reasons for being moral in terms of desired ends contingently served by morality, this does not mean that he failed to recognize a need to demonstrate that moral requirements are rooted in reason.[7]

II. The Structure of the Argument

The most crucial passages are the following:

Will is a kind of causality belonging to living beings so far as they are rational. *Freedom* would then be the property this causality has of being able to work independently of *determination* by alien causes. . . .

The above definition of freedom is *negative* and consequently unfruitful as a way of grasping its essence; but there springs from it a more *positive* concept, which, as positive, is richer and more fruitful. The concept of causality carries with it that of *laws (Gesetze)* in accordance with which, because of something we call a cause, something else—namely, its effect—must be posited *(gesetz)*. Hence freedom of the will, although it is not the property of conforming to laws of nature, is not for this reason lawless: it must rather be a causality conforming to immutable laws, though of a special kind; for otherwise a free will would be self-contradictory. . . . What else then can freedom of the will be but autonomy—that is, the property which the will has of being a law to itself? The proposition 'Will is in all its actions a law to itself' expresses, however, only the principle of acting on no maxim other than one which can have for its object itself as at the same time a universal law. This is precisely the formula of the Categorical Imperative and the principle of morality. Thus a free will and a will under moral laws are one and the same. (G 114 [446–47])

This passage argues in effect that, if free in a negative sense, every rational will is committed to morality. The following passage

[7]The argument reconstructed in this paper is an argument that morality is rational but it does not rely on the forbidden means–ends reasoning.

contains the nub of the rest of the argument, which is to show that every rational will is free (in a negative sense).

> Now I assert that every being who cannot act except under the *Idea of freedom* is by this alone—from a practical point of view—really free; that is to say, for him all the laws inseparably bound up with freedom are valid just as much as if his will could be pronounced free in itself on grounds valid for theoretical philosophy. And I maintain that to every rational being possessed of a will we must also lend the Idea of freedom as the only one under which he can act.[8]

The main outline of the argument is clear enough. Reordering the parts, we have (1) an argument that any rational will is free in at least a negative sense, (2) an argument, turning on definitions of negative freedom and autonomy, that any will free in the negative sense has the property autonomy (G 114 [446]), (3) an assertion, relying on earlier arguments, that any rational will with autonomy is committed to the principle "Act only on maxims you can will as universal laws,"[9] (4) an assertion, again relying on earlier arguments, that this last principle is the supreme principle of morality.[10] From all this it follows that any rational will is committed to the supreme principle of morality. Thus we can conclude that anyone who acts immorally is acting contrary to a principle which he himself accepts. If we assume that the principle in question is an unconditional and not merely prima facie one,[11] then

---

[8] G 115–16 [448]. This is the heart of (1) in the summary of my next paragraph.

[9] G 114 [447]. I assume that the strange formula in this passage, "the principle of acting on no maxim other than one which can have for its object itself as at the same time a universal law," is meant to be the first formulation of the Categorical Imperative, and so have reformulated it.

[10] G 114 [447]. "This is precisely the formula of the Categorical Imperative and the principle of morality." This is argued twice, at G 69–70 [402] and G 88 [420–21].

[11] Kant clearly intended the principle to be unconditional and overriding, rather than prima facie, but one may question whether the argument supports this. In fact the sort of argument he gives seems unlikely to support an overriding principle; for the idea is to show that free rational agents unmotivated by desire must nevertheless have some rational principle to follow. Why would a principle that says what one prima facie ought to do not suffice? If this is all the argument supports, then the conclusion must be more modest, i.e., that every rational agent has some reason to be moral or immorality is always opposed to some prima facie principle of the agent. I will pass over this problem here, not only from lack of time, but also because the problem concerns later stages of the argument which are not my main concern.

such immoral acts must be irrational because contrary to an unconditional commitment of the agent. If we assume further that
the argument shows that rational autonomous agents are committed to the supreme moral principle *qua* rational and autonomous,
then immoral acts will be irrational not only because they are contrary to the agent's commitments but also because they are contrary to a principle the agent acknowledges to be rational.[12]

Each of the major steps, of course, depends upon subsidiary arguments, some of which I shall consider shortly. But before that,
a few preliminary remarks may be helpful.

First, in steps (1) and (2) Kant aims to show that any rational
will has autonomy, and these stages presuppose nothing about
morality. Now though these stages are parts of a larger argument
that it is rational to be moral, they are of interest independently of
that larger project. They are concerned not merely to affirm a
freedom unthreatened by causal determinism but to argue the necessity of acknowledging rational principles of conduct other than
those which prescribe efficiency in satisfying our desires or in co-
ordinating our means and ends. The conclusion, even at this earlier stage, is that anyone who acts for reasons must acknowledge at
least some reasons other than facts about what is needed to achieve
his ends and to satisfy his desires. If so, then regardless of what we
think of morality there must be practical reasons which are not hypothetical imperatives. Hobbesians will be wrong to construe all
rational principles as rules of rational self-interest; modern decision theorists will be wrong if they suppose that all rational choice
principles are relative to intrinsic preferences themselves uncriti-
cizable by reason; and Humeans will be wrong to suppose that
reason merely calculates and discovers facts rather than prescribing

---

[12]The idea here is that there are two routes to show the rationality of moral conduct.
One is to show that immorality conflicts with a commitment of the agent, whether or
not that commitment was independently demanded by reason. The other is to show
that rational agents, as such, necessarily are committed to a principle. I suspect that
Kant intended both; for he argues that all minimally rational agents have autonomy and
so are committed to the supreme moral principle, and he argues that necessarily, *qua*
rational and free, they must accept the supreme moral principle. It is worth noting,
though, that if the argument failed for the second, stronger claim, the first, weaker
claim still would need to be considered. That strategy fits with the often repeated point
that immorality involves conflict of will.

conduct. The conclusion is a strong and controversial one: a striking feature of the *Groundwork* is that Kant's argument for it does not depend upon claims about morality.

As a final preliminary, I must say a few words about the interpretation which I shall try to avoid.[13] According to this, the will is practical reason and so cannot will anything contrary to reason; morality is prescribed by reason and so no one wills to be immoral; the will, which is thus always good, is free negatively and wills unequivocally perfect conformity to the laws of autonomy. Thus, on this view, one who acts to satisfy desire contrary to morality, and perhaps even one who acts to satisfy a morally neutral desire, does not really will so to act and does not act freely in any sense. His behavior is a product of natural forces, like that of animals or, better, animals with complex built-in computers for calculating the best means to satisfaction. We are strange hybrids sometimes governed by freely acknowledged rational moral principles and sometimes in the grip of natural forces beyond rational control; and what switches us from the one mode to the other is inexplicable. It could not be a free choice because to be capable of free choice is to be in one mode rather than the other. When we act from desires we act heteronomously, which is to say unfreely and nonrationally; when we act from moral principle, we act autonomously, which is to say freely and rationally. And there can be no free choice between the two, for free choice is always for the rational and moral.

Kant does say things in the *Groundwork* which suggest this strange picture, but I am convinced that the textual evidence, on the whole, is opposed to it. However, in order to lay out my reconstruction of the argument under consideration even in the present sketchy form, I must leave detailed examination of particular passages for another occasion. For now I must be content to offer an alternative reading which, I hope, makes more sense of the compressed and puzzling argument in the third chapter and to call attention to the disparity between the interpretation I reject and the views Kant makes more evident in his later ethical

[13]This account is most evident in R. P. Wolff's *The Autonomy of Reason* (New York: Harper and Row, 1973).

writings. These later works,[14] with the explicit distinction between *Wille* and *Willkur,* make clear that Kant then thought the
adoption of ends in general and certainly the adoption of immoral
maxims were free choices of a rational agent, even though not
maximally rational choices. To understand the *Groundwork* in the
context of Kant's work as a whole without regarding it as a radical
deviation, we must see if we can understand his argument without
having to attribute to him the bizarre picture I have sketched with
its consequence that immorality is unfree and unwilling.

III. From Negative Freedom to Autonomy

Conceptual analysis, Kant suggests, should suffice to show
that any rational will which is free in a negative sense is also free
in the positive sense (autonomy). The crucial definitions are those
of *will, negative freedom,* and *autonomy.*

Will is a "kind of causality," distinct from causation by prior
events and natural laws, a sort of ability to make things happen
peculiar to rational agents (G 114 [446]). Elsewhere, importantly,
Kant characterizes the will as a power to act "in accordance
with (his) idea of laws—that is, in accordance with principles" (G
80 [412], 95 [427]). The idea is that to be an agent, or a rational
being with a will, one must be able to make things happen in such
a way that the appropriate explanation is reference to the principles, laws, or reasons on which the person acted. Principles, even
laws, enter into the explanation of why a rational agent did something (as distinct from merely why the body moved) as the agent's
guiding "ideas" or rationale, not as empirically observable regu-
larities among types of events. In fact the will for Kant (in contrast, say, to Hobbes and Hume) is not an event, a mental episode

---

[14]The two views of *will* are discussed in John Silber's introduction to *Religion within
the Limits of Reason Alone* (R). Silber thinks that Kant was ambivalent at least in the
Groundwork between the later view and the dualistic picture presented by Wolff. Beck's
commentary on the second *Critique* also makes much of the *Wille* vs. *Willkur* distinction. Rawls, I am told, distinguishes in lectures between the "Manichean" view and the
"Augustinian" view of *will,* finding Kant ambivalent in the *Groundwork.* My concern
here is not so much to deny the ambivalence, or confusion, as to see how the argument
of the *Groundwork* does not rest on the more simplistic picture.

occurring prior to action, which explains that action in the ordinary empirical way.[15] Kant believed, of course, that explanations of an act by reference to the agent's reasons (and so his will) were compatible with accepting deterministic explanations of the corresponding behavior by empirical laws; but that belief is not essential to the important distinction between the two types of explanation.

This conception of the will has several important implications. First, Hume's famous *reductio ad absurdum* of indeterminism does not apply to Kant.[16] Hume, assuming that an indeterminist's "free will" was an uncaused event prior to an agent's act, argued that such an event, unconnected with the agent's character, was not something for which a person could be held morally responsible. Kant undercuts the objection by denying that "willing" is a prior event. His own metaphysical account of the will has problems enough of its own, but he may be right to suspect that, in its classic form, the dispute between determinists and indeterminists rests on a shared model of rational action that is inadequate. As many since Kant have acknowledged, those who are troubled by the picture of *desire, act of will,* and *bodily movement* as discrete physical events in a causal sequence, like falling dominos, do not obviously render responsibility less puzzling simply by denying the causal connection between the first two items (desire and will) and/or by assigning these items to an introspectible mental realm. Second, since an act of will for Kant is not an introspectible phenomenon, it is no reply to Kant's argument that the will is committed to a certain principle (e.g., the Categorical Imperative) to say, "But I don't remember deciding to follow that." An argument that the will of every rational agent is committed to morality need not be based on observations of their life histories. In at least this respect moral commitment is supposed to be like rational commitment to basic principles of logic and empirical

[15]Strictly, the will is not even a hidden, unobservable event in time; to ascribe a will to a person is not to refer to a mysterious event or thing but merely to say, without further explanation, that the person has a capacity to make things happen in a way that makes appropriate the explanation "His reason . . . ," "He was guided by the principle . . . ," etc.

[16]See the section entitled "Of Liberty and Necessity" in David Hume's *A Treatise of Human Nature,* ed. L. A. Selby-Bigge (Oxford: Clarendon, 1955), bk. II, part III, pp. 399–412.

understanding. Third, behavior cannot be attributed to the will of an agent, not even to the "free will" of an agent, unless it is supposed that the agent was acting for a reason, or guided by "the idea of a principle (or law)." Thus it is part of the concept of a will that it cannot be "lawless."[7]

Next we need to look at the *negative concept of freedom,* which is "the property (the will) has of being able to work independently of *determination* by alien causes." It is clear enough that Kant means at least to deny that there is an empirical causal account for why free wills act for the reasons they do. To attribute an act to the free will of a rational agent is not to cite its empirical causes or to refer to an empirical mechanism or power, caused or uncaused, which explains how an observed behavior came about. The *Critique of Pure Reason* is supposed to have established the *possibility* that such a will is in some sense responsible for what we do despite Kant's insistence, and supposed proof, that empirical science can in principle give causal explanations of all phenomena, mental as well as physical. The first *Critique* also makes clear the price Kant is willing to pay for this compatibility, namely, conceiving the will as something apart from the spatiotemporal order which we can "comprehend"; but that full price, I think, is not essential to the main thrust of our argument.

The preceding remarks reflect the usual (though still vague) understanding of a will's capacity "to work independently of determination by alien causes." But, importantly, there must be more than this to Kant's conception of negative freedom if the step from negative freedom to autonomy is at all plausible. For even if we conceive a negatively free will as somehow independent of causal

[7]Kant suggests that it is because the will is a kind of cause that it cannot be "lawless," but I take it that the point follows as well from the definition of will as acting in accord with the idea of principles or laws. There is no doubt a play on different senses of lawful and lawless, but the main point seems clear enough, namely, that to attribute an event to a person, thing, or prior happening as its cause (source, or author) we need some appropriate connection between the event and the alleged source, something to warrant saying the event occurred in some sense because of the source. Often the connection is an observable regularity between types of events, and then the "because" is an empirical causal one; but in the case of human action, on Kant's view, the connection is between the event and a person's beliefs and policy commitments, and then the "because" must be of a different type. This leaves much unexplained, of course, but the minimal point is just that some connection must be made, that this can be of two kinds, and that both involve "laws" in some sense or other.

determinism, we could still regard such wills as (causally inexplicable) capacities to act for the sake of satisfying desires and inclinations. In other words, though acting for reasons is not to be understood as being causally determined by one's given desires, nevertheless one's capacity to act for reasons might be limited, perhaps even by the concept of reasons, to policies aimed at satisfaction of some of the desires and inclinations one happens to have. We might speak of such a will as incapable of *motivation* by anything but inclination and desire, where "motivation" refers not to what causes the willing but rather to the range of things the will can count as reasons or rational objectives of its policies. Though again I must forgo detailed textual argument, I think it is evident once the distinction is made that Kant regarded a negatively free will as also capable of acting independently of motivation by desires and inclinations. There is a sense, perhaps unfortunate, in which Kant regarded even the agent's own desires as "alien," and "determination" of the will, even by "alien" factors, does not refer exclusively to having a place in a deterministic nexus of causes. On the contrary, when Kant writes of a will "determined" by reason, this is not to cite a prior event and a causal law but rather to say that the guiding idea on which the agent acted was a rational one; and, similarly, when a will is "determined" by inclination in a standard case (not a knee jerk, reflexive scratching, etc.), this means the agent's policy or guiding idea was some hypothetical imperative concerning the means to satisfy the inclination. In the latter case there is a (misleading) sense in which "alien causes" determine the will; it is not that the agent's inclination deterministically causes the agent to will what he does, but rather that the agent's chosen policy makes a certain causal connection, or strictly his belief in a certain causal connection, be a decisive (or "determining") factor for what he does. His full rationale (not a causal event) is: "I shall do whatever is necessary as a means to satisfy my inclination *B; A* is a necessary means to satisfy *B;* hence I shall do *A.*" The agent has let the causal law, or strictly his idea of the causal law, between that sort of means and end be the dominant or "determining" factor in his choice; but this does not mean that the willing itself was subject to causal explanation.

Notice that the interpretation I have pledged to avoid does not make this distinction between being caused to act by one's inclinations and choosing to act on policies which make satisfaction of inclination the rationale for acting. Once it is made, however, it seems clear that Kant's conception of freedom, even negatively defined, encompasses not only capacity to will without the willing being explainable by causal laws and prior events; crucially, freedom also includes the ability to will, or act for reasons, where the agent's rationale is not a hypothetical imperative indicating the means to satisfy an inclination. Without this stipulation the argument that negatively free wills necessarily have autonomy would fall flat: for autonomy, as we shall see, implies a capacity/disposition to follow principles other than desire-based hypothetical imperatives.

The most difficult definition in the argument is that of *autonomy* (or freedom positively conceived). Part of the difficulty in understanding this stems from the fact that the misguided picture I am trying to avoid is rather deeply entrenched in commentaries and is encouraged both by ambiguities in Kant and by everyday (non-Kantian) talk about autonomy. On that picture autonomy is an ideal achieved by some and not others, or perhaps by some people some of the time but not always. Rather than a property of all human wills, it is seen as a property of purely conscientious wills when willing out of respect for the moral law. The misleading picture is reinforced by a facile use of the expressions, which are not Kant's, of "acting autonomously" for free/morally inspired conduct and "acting heteronomously" for causally determined or at least desire-motivated conduct.

To the contrary, Kant's view, I think, was that autonomy is a property of the will of every minimally rational agent, which includes virtually all adult sane human beings, no matter how wicked. Heteronomy is a possible property of wills which misguided moral philosophers have mistakenly attributed to human beings.[18] All rational agents, Kant argues, have negative freedom, and to have negative freedom is to have autonomy as well. This is

---

[18]See G 111–12 [443–44]. Note that we have *heteronomy* as (mistakenly) regarded as the "basis of morality," as a characterization of a rule or (would be) law, or as "the result" if one tries to make hypothetical imperatives the basis of morality (G 108[441]), etc. It is significant that Kant's discussion of heteronomy concerns not the ordinary following of prudential maxims and rules of skill but wrong-headed philosophical attempts to base morality in various ways on hypothetical imperatives.

not to say that everyone chooses to fulfill the commitments he has by virtue of having autonomy of will. The immoralist is not one who has a will characterized by heteronomy but rather one who acts as if the human will were such, i.e., one who in practice ignores the implications of having a will with autonomy and acts as if the only authoritative rational principles were hypothetical imperatives.

Kant's most explicit definition of autonomy is that it is a will's property of "being a law to itself (independently of every property belonging to the objects of volition)" (G 108 [440]). Though by itself this is not so illuminating, what is meant, I think, can be plausibly reconstructed as follows: a will with autonomy is not only negatively free but is committed to at least one principle acknowledged as rational to follow but such that (a) one is not causally determined to accept or follow it, (b) it does not merely prescribe taking the necessary (or best) means to one's desired ends, (c) the rationality of accepting it does not depend upon contingent facts about what means will serve one's ends or about what ends one happens to desire, and (d) the principle is "one's own" or "given to oneself by oneself," i.e., it expresses a deep commitment from one's "true" nature as a rational and (negatively) free agent rather than, say, expressing respect for an external authority, tradition, conventions, etc. All this is simply a long way of saying what is (more vaguely) summarized by saying that a will with autonomy accepts for itself rational constraints independently of any desires and other "alien" influences.

With these preliminaries and definition in hand, we can see how that argument from negative freedom to autonomy must go. Negatively free rational wills can act for reasons without being motivated by desires and hypothetical imperatives. But, as they are not "lawless," when they so act they must be following some principle (or principles) which allows us to attribute the act to a rational agent, acting for reasons, as opposed to whimsical behavior, knee-jerk reactions, etc. So the agent must have, or be committed to, principles he acknowledges as rational even though they are not of the hypothetical imperative sort. Because the agent is negatively free, acceptance of such principles cannot be causally determined. Since principles adopted because of external authorities (e.g., God), tradition, convention, etc., would be based on hypothetical imperatives, these cannot be the rational principles in question. The only alternative, it seems, is that the principles reflect some necessary features of rational agency itself independently of its special contexts. If we assume (with Kant) that one's nature as a rational will is in some sense one's "true" self in contrast to passively "given" phenomenal desires, then we could conclude further that the rational principles in question are "one's own" or "given to oneself by oneself" in a way that desire-based principles are not.

The last step raises deep questions about personal identity which need not cloud the main point, namely, that if one can act rationally without causal determination and without following desire-based principles, then one must have some principle or principles which are rational and yet not hypothetical imperatives. If rational agents are negatively free, then, they must acknowledge rational principles of conduct beyond those recognized by followers of Hume and Hobbes. This conclusion is reached not by exhibiting an example of such a nonhypothetical rational principle but by indirect argument that there must be such if there is rational free agency.

Since the argument turns on the *capacity* to act without motivation by desire, the conclusion is not that free agents invariably follow nonhypothetical rational principles but only that they must have or acknowledge them. If they had no such commitments, they would lack the ability to act rationally without following hypothetical imperatives; but having the capacity does not mean that they will follow the principles whenever they can (or even whenever the principles prescribe for them). Thus, when later stages of the argument identify the laws of autonomy with moral constraints, it will not follow that free rational agents invariably act morally but only that they can (and must to avoid irrational conflict of will).

It may be useful to consider two objections. First, does it make sense to say (with Kant) that rational agents can act independently of desires and inclinations? This depends upon how these are conceived. Kant's idea of desires and inclinations, at least in the context of our argument, is narrower than some conceptions and wider than others. If it is confused with the narrower conceptions, Kant's idea of freedom will seem less controversial (and interesting) than it is; and if Kant's idea of desires and inclinations is confused with the wider conceptions, then his idea of freedom will seem absurd. To begin with the wider conception, there seems to be a use of "desire" and related words which refers to whatever motivates an agent, whether empirically discernable independently of his act or not. That an agent "desired" (or, better, "wanted") to do something in this sense is simply inferred from the fact that he did it, given options. Since there are no independent grounds for attributing the "desire," obviously mentioning it does not explain what was done but only characterizes it as voluntary, unlike knee jerks, etc. To say that we can freely will to act independently of desire, in this sense, is obviously absurd; and Kant did not mean this, for he held that even the purest moral acts are motivated, in some sense, by an inexplicable "interest" in the commands of reason.

Sometimes "desire" (and related words) seem to be used quite narrowly, referring to dispositions that are noticeably (and often urgently) *felt* by the agent prior to acting, involving pleasant anticipation, painful fear of loss, tendencies to search for means of fulfillment, to experience frustration when thwarted and joy when fulfilled, etc. It is tempting to suppose that this is what Kant had in mind, for it is not very controversial that we can act for reasons without being motivated by desires in this narrow sense.[19] We seem to do so often when we go about our routine business, forgo minor pleasures for health reasons, and so on. Kant does at times seem to have in mind this narrow sense, especially when dramatically depicting struggles between duty and inclination; but the argument needs more than this and Kant clearly intended more than this in his discussions of freedom. We would still be acting independently of desire in this narrow sense whenever our reasons were based simply on Hume's "calm passions," or mild preferences unaccompanied by pleasures of anticipation, or aversions we attribute to ourselves more from inference than from feeling. But, however rational, such acts would not have the independence of empirical motivation Kant attributes to acts which manifest freedom.

[19]I owe a thanks to Gregory Kavka for alerting me when, in an earlier version, I was yielding to this temptation.

What, then, is the relevant sense of "desire" and "inclination"? Fine points aside, these are virtually any empirically discernible motivations that one may happen to have so long as they are not concerns essential to all rational agents as such. They include desires in the narrow sense but also Hume's "calm passions" and any other preference, liking, aversion, love, hate, etc. which rational agents might lack and which is not attributed solely because they acted voluntarily. Negative freedom and autonomy imply capacity for rational action in which the agent's reason is not to achieve or do something desired in this intermediate sense. Since Kant repeatedly grants that any behavior may also be empirically explained (e.g., by desires, by the feelings associated with "respect," or by physical science), his point is not to deny this but to say something about reasons: namely, that the status of the rational agent's end as a reason for the agent does not always depend upon the agent having towards it an empirical disposition of the sort rational agents might or might not have. The thesis that we are free agents in this sense is controversial, of course, but not obviously absurd (as on the wide conception of desire) or uninterestingly true (as on the narrow conception of desire).

A second objection should be mentioned.[20] For all that has been said, is it not possible that a will with autonomy has for its one and only rational principle the pure Hypothetical Imperative? This is the principle that it is rational to take the necessary and available means to one's ends or else abandon those ends. I call this "the Hypothetical Imperative" because it is a version of the principle behind Kant's particular hypothetical imperatives, and I call it "pure" because it does not specify that the ends are willed because desired, or for some other reason, or indeed for any reason. It might seem that my characterization of autonomy leaves open that this is the only non–desire-based rational principle.

One problem with this suggestion is that the principle in question (as the name suggests) does not unequivocally prescribe any act even given full information about the situation, one's preferences, etc. It says only, "Take the means or drop the end," giving no standards for the rational assessment of ends. Now conceivably

---

[20]This objection comes from Stephen Darwall, who may still be dissatisfied with my sketchy reply.

this principle (in a more carefully stated version) is the only necessary principle of rational agency; but then agents who followed it, selecting their ends according to their inclinations or for no reason at all, would never act for sufficient reasons, as (I believe) Kant thought a rational free will could do. Admittedly, in a sense such a will would not be "lawless," for it would have the pure Hypothetical Imperative as a necessary rational principle; but, unless we assume something further, reason would at best prescribe an option rather than a course of action.[21] Though Kant does not raise the issue explicitly, I take it that he conceived rational free wills as sometimes more definitely constrained than this.

If we could assume (as many do) that all preferences, or all preferences that survive a process of informed reflection, have some weight as reasons, then ends could be rationally assessed by the likelihood and costs of achieving coherent sets of preferences. But this would presuppose a putative principle of rationality beyond the pure Hypothetical Imperative, which is the only principle of practical reason Kant recognizes as analytic. Since that further principle assigning prima facie rational force to our empirically given preferences (or informed preferences) is nonanalytic, unless it could be given a "synthetic a priori" justification Kant would deny it status as a necessary principle of reason just as he denies this status to the substantive principles "Satisfy the promptings of your (supposed) moral sense" and "Do all you can to satisfy your desire to be happy." Assuming, then, that such principles are not necessarily rational and also that free wills independently of their given desires and inclinations can nonetheless have sufficient determinate reasons to act, one whose "reasons" were fixed solely by the pure Hypothetical Imperative and de facto preferences (or informed preferences) would not have a will with autonomy.

These remarks reveal a heavy burden left for the next stage of the argument, i.e., the attempt to show that rational wills necessarily have negative freedom (and so autonomy), but we should perhaps not expect the conditions for freedom to be so easily

---

[21]There is a sense, of course, in which even the non-conditional "Always pay your debts" prescribes options, for one may pay in coins or in bills, in cash or by check, etc. I trust, however, that patience could make clear how the relevant sense differs from this.

satisfied that the concept is of little use in Kant's ultimate project of showing that the basic standards of morality are necessarily rational.

IV. From Rational Agency to Negative Freedom

Now, more briefly, we need to consider the notoriously compact argument that every rational will is (negatively) free.

First some preliminary comments. Though Kant does not explicitly refer to freedom *negatively conceived* in presenting the argument, this is what the argument requires (given that the transition from negative freedom to autonomy is argued separately). Further, we should not think of the argument as concerned with some new *sense* of freedom ("practical freedom"), as some have suggested; the qualification "from a practical point of view" which Kant attaches to the argument refers not to a new sense of freedom but to the type of argument given and a restriction on the legitimate use of its conclusion. Again, we should note that the argument, strictly speaking, is not that we, or any particular individuals, are free; it is that every rational agent, as such, must be free. Later, after raising the objection that his reasoning may have been circular, Kant supplements the basic argument under consideration with the contention that even in our theoretical judgments, apart from practical questions, we must take ourselves to be members of an "intelligible world," in some sense independent of given sensuous inclinations (G 116–21 [448–53]). This further argument seems relevant to residual doubts that *we* are rational free agents (as defined); but this goes beyond the project at hand. Finally, the standards for rational agency must not be too high. Since any being not rational in this sense will not be under moral obligation, the criteria of rationality here must be satisfied not only by the perfectly rational but also by the imperfectly rational wills that Kant thought virtually all human beings to be.

The outline of the argument for negative freedom is as follows:

(1) A rational will cannot act except under the Idea of freedom.
(2) Any being that cannot act except under the Idea of freedom is free from a practical point of view.
(3) Therefore, rational wills are free from a practical point of view.

Implicitly the argument continues:

(4) "Free from a practical point of view" is sufficient for purposes of the rest of the argument for the rationality of moral conduct; and so for the purposes of that argument the qualification can be dropped.

In order to avoid reducing the argument to obvious silliness, we need to guard against several temptations. First, the first premise cannot be read as saying that we "feel free." Whether true or not, this would be a contingent empirical premise about us incompatible with Kant's insistence on an a priori method; what is needed is rather a necessary truth about rational agency. It would not follow from the fact that one could not act without feeling free that one was free even for practical purposes; just as it would not follow from the fact that a professor could not lecture without feeling brilliant that he was brilliant for practical purposes. What is so "for practical purposes" is at least a reasonable assumption to make in deliberating and deciding what to do, and neither assumption is reasonable to act on just because it is an unavoidable feeling associated with the activity in question.

Second, the first premise should not be read as saying that those who sincerely believe in thorough-going determinism cannot act or, conversely, that no one who acts ever believes sincerely in thorough-going determinism. Surely many philosophers and scientists have believed in complete determinism, and it is too much to suppose that they lose that belief whenever they do anything. "Acting under the idea of freedom," then, is more plausibly construed as "seeing oneself as free" or perhaps "taking oneself to be free" for certain purposes. The point of the first premise, then, would be that rational agents, in deliberating and deciding what to do, necessarily see themselves as free, regardless of their standing convictions on the metaphysical status of determinism. It is, one might say, a necessary condition of playing the game of deliberation.

Third, an important background of the argument is Kant's belief, which he thought he had proved, that the idea of free agency is such that there can be no empirical evidence or sound metaphysical ("speculative") argument that rational agents are unfree. If there were strong reasons for believing that rational agents are not free, then one could not so convincingly argue that it is reasonable to assume the opposite for practical purposes just because that is how rational agents must see themselves in acting. By analogy, suppose (implausibly) that in acting rational agents necessarily see themselves as indestructible Cartesian souls but that there are good empirical and/or philosophical arguments that this is an illusion. Then we would naturally be reluctant to conclude that for all practical purposes they are reasonable to assume that they are indestructible Cartesian souls, for *practical purposes* include deliberation about life-risking activities and their assumption has implications for this which they should reject no matter how they unavoidably "see themselves."

Finally, we must not construe the conclusion that rational wills are free from a practical point of view as merely a repetition of the first premise that in acting rational wills necessarily see themselves as free. If construed that way, the argument would go nowhere. The conclusion is that for all purposes of deliberation and decision it is reasonable to accept all implications of the assumption that one is free and unreasonable to let one's deliberations be influenced by the contrary idea that one is, or might be, unfree.[22] We need here a distinction between merely seeing oneself as free, which is (by the first premise) unavoidable in rational deliberation, and taking full account in one's deliberation of all the implications of the assumption that one is free. This is important because, by the rest of Kant's argument, the implication of the assumption that rational wills are free is nothing less than that they are rationally bound to morality. The inevitability of rational agency (expressed in the first premise) is taking oneself to be free when deliberating and acting; the resulting prescription for all ra-

---

[22]Strictly speaking, I suppose, the claim that, from a practical perspective, rational wills are free implies not only (a) that one should, for purposes of deliberation, accept all the implications of assuming that one is oneself free but also (b) that one should, for purposes of deliberation, accept the implications of assuming that others one takes to be rational are also free. The latter would be of practical importance when trying to decide whether execution for murder is justified. Unfortunately, the argument for (b) has to be more complicated and raises special problems. So I shall ignore it here. Implication (a) should suffice for most practical purposes, e.g., to dispel the doubts about one's own rationality in being moral which are raised by either determinism or the thesis that all rationality is means-end calculation to maximum desire-satisfaction.

tional agents (expressed in the conclusion that we are free from a practical point of view) is that it is only rational to act on the full implications of the assumption that we are free. The latter is not inevitable but is what, according to the argument, we rationally should do.

Putting the pieces together, then, the argument runs as follows: Rational agents necessarily see themselves as (negatively) free when deliberating and acting; this means not only that they look upon themselves as choosing among options the outcome of which is not determined by prior empirical causes, but also that they see themselves as capable of reaching a decision in a way that is not a function of their given desires and their beliefs about the means to satisfy them. As in theoretical judgments guided by reason, rational agents deliberate with the view of themselves as able to reach reasoned conclusions which do not fit, or well serve, what they feel most inclined to. Given the impossibility of proof or even evidence that this view of themselves is illusory, they should accept, for all practical purposes, the idea that they are free in this sense. That is, they should accept any implication of the idea that "as a rational agent I am (negatively) free" as a reasonable assumption in all their deliberations about what to do.

This conclusion, we should note, is all that the remaining argument needs. For the argument as a whole is a practical one, addressed as it were to those deliberating about what it is rational to do and, in particular, to those wondering whether philosophical arguments concerning practical reason should be allowed to undermine their confidence that it is rational to be moral. To this audience the argument for negative freedom says, in effect, it is perfectly rational for your deliberative purposes to assume that, as a rational agent, you are negatively free: that is, you should assume that any account of practical reason is mistaken if it denies your ability to choose independently of determining causes or your ability to act for reasons other than desire-based hypothetical imperatives.

The preceding remarks are intended to reveal, or reconstruct, the initial argument for negative freedom as more coherent and plausible than it may at first appear; but two residual doubts should at least be raised. First, now that so much seems built into the first premise, what reason do we have to accept it? In particular, why suppose that rational agents must see themselves in deliberation as capable of being guided by rational standards other than maximum preference satisfaction? Kant believed that the latter standard could not be established as necessary by either the analytic or synthetic a prior methods he acknowledged; but has this been shown? Second, even if the sort of rational wills Kant had in mind necessarily see themselves as Kant says, why believe that *we* have rational wills of this sort? Perhaps we can form an idea of such rational agency but have to content ourselves with more mundane standards.

The argument we have been considering seems to rest the case on a thought experiment, or (more grandly) a phenomenological test: "Just try to see yourself (in acting) as lacking negative freedom and you will discover that you cannot." But this reply, as Kant apparently realized, may be unconvincing by itself. Even if we discover what Kant expects, how do we know that the test reveals anything more than a universal but contingent feature of human nature? Also since the cases in which we are most convinced of our capacity to act rationally independently of given preferences are likely to be cases of duty versus inclination, might not our conviction be due to the fact that we have presupposed the rationality of moral conduct (which is what was to be established)? These worries would lead naturally to Kant's discussion of the possibility of circular reasoning and his introduction of the "intelligible world" as the "third term" between reason and freedom. The latter idea, I suspect, stems not so much from obsessive concern with an otherworldly metaphysics as from the thought that even theoretical judgments, in science and everyday life, presuppose that we are guided (or guidable) by standards of rationality which, though applicable to experience, are not derived from experience and which are importantly different from "Find the conclusion that best suits your given preferences." That we are the sort of beings capable of being guided by such standards is supposed to be evident not only in cases of moral conflict or other practical choices but also in theoretical judgments. The reply assumes Kant's idea of the unity of theoretical and practical reason, which Kant does not try to defend in the *Groundwork;* and it raises deep questions beyond the immediate aim of this paper.

V. From Autonomy to Morality

The preceding steps leave us with the striking conclusion that any rational agent is, as such, committed to at least some principle of conduct acknowledged as rational but not based on his desires and the imperative to take the necessary means to them. The underlying idea is that practical reason, like theoretical reason, enables us to reach conclusions on some basis other than that they get us what we most want. The next step, of course, is to identify the rational principles acknowledged by wills with autonomy as moral principles, the supreme moral principle and (perhaps) its derivatives. Kant attempts to do this in the first and second chapters of the *Groundwork* by (a) arguing that the supreme moral principle is "Act only on maxims which you can will as universal law" and (b) arguing through successive reformulations of this principle that it is "the principle of autonomy," i.e., equivalent to saying, "follow the laws of a rational will with autonomy."[23]

Though I believe these steps to be fundamentally flawed, I must postpone the attempt to argue the point and to explore a more promising route to a later formulation of the supreme moral principle. Nevertheless I will venture one general comment on this final stage of the argument. The main problem, I suspect, is that Kant switched illegitimately between two quite different readings of his famous first formulation of the supreme moral principle. The first reading is what naturally emerges from the argument we have been considering. Ask what principle, if any, must a rational will with autonomy accept, and an obvious, though rather unhelpful, answer will be "Act in such a way that you conform to laws, or rational principles of conduct, you (or any rational being) accept independently of desire." Assuming that all morally relevant acts can be construed in terms of their maxims, this can also be expressed "Act so that your maxims can be willed consistently with whatever rational constraints you (and others) are committed to as wills with autonomy." Now in his transitions to the first formula of the supreme moral principle, Kant seems to be assuming

[23]This culminates at G 108 [440].

that this is just what the formula says. What it declares, he says, is "conform to universal law as such," where "universal law" has been defined to exclude rational considerations based on desires (G 69–70 [402], 88 [420–21]). So far, so good: that is, the formula is readily seen as one that any rational will with autonomy must accept. But now the trouble begins when Kant treats the same first formula as identical with, or as entailing, a principle that one must act only on maxims which one can will as universal laws *in the sense* that it is (rationally) acceptable that everyone act on the maxim. This moves from an undeniable formal principle to a dubious substantive principle; and despite all the brilliant aid Kant has received from sympathetic commentators, I fail to see how this transition can be made legitimately.

I conclude, however, with a more modest point. If I am right that Kant's transition to a substantive supreme moral principle is illegitimate, this would be quite in line with my main reading of his argument. For my hypothesis has been that the task which Kant saw as most difficult and most sorely needed was not to convince anyone to accept his supreme moral principle or even to believe that if there are laws of autonomy they must be the familiar moral constraints. These matters, I suspect, he considered relatively easy, and perhaps for this reason he did not bother much about his argument for them. The harder task, and what was most needed, was what he thought he had accomplished in the earlier stages we have considered above: namely, to show that, despite philosophers' arguments to the contrary, there must be principles of rational conduct other than desire-based hypothetical imperatives. That too may be an error, but Kant's argument for it deserves more attention.

7

Kant's Theory of
Practical Reason

Contemporary discussions of practical reason often refer vaguely to the Kantian conception of reasons as an alternative to various means-ends theories, but it is rarely clear what this is supposed to be, except that somehow moral concerns are supposed to fare better under the Kantian conception. The theories of Nagel, Gewirth, Darwall, and Donagan have been labeled "Kantian" because they deviate strikingly from standard preference models, but their roots in Kant have not been traced in detail and important differences may go unnoticed. All this is not surprising, of course, because Kant's conception of practical reason is inseparable from his ideas of freedom, which are notoriously difficult and controversial. It is hard enough to characterize these ideas accurately in Kantian terminology, harder still to explain them in terms of contemporary debates about reasons for action.

Though well aware of these obstacles, I want to present here a summary of some main features of Kant's theory of practical reason, as I have come to see this, indicating along the way how Kant's theory differs from some familiar alternatives. My focus will be primarily on the *Groundwork,* but, unlike some, I do not see the basic theory of the *Groundwork* as radically different from Kant's later writings. What I have to say here is part of a larger project in which, I hope, there will be enough detailed textual analysis to make convincing what I will now present as more or less unargued conclusions. For present purposes, detail will be

sacrificed for scope. The main aim is to give a coherent characterization of Kant's idea of practical reason rather than to defend it
either on textual grounds or as a tenable theory; but, of course, if
as a result the text seems clearer or the Kantian perspective more
plausible, I will not be disappointed.

I. Reasoning with Hypothetical Imperatives

Practical reasoning, in general, is reasoning about what I
ought to do. This, for Kant, is the same as reasoning about what is
good for me to do except that "ought" conveys the sense that, as
imperfectly rational and liable to contrary inclinations, I might not
do what is good even though I can (G 80-81 [413-14]). The word
"ought" [*Sollen*], like "must" and other ways of expressing Kant's
imperatives, is supposed to express the sense that something is
"necessary," whether to achieve an end or to satisfy morality; but
the necessity is a practical one posed by "compelling" reasons, not
a logical necessity or a causal or metaphysical inevitability.

The connection between "ought" and "good" should not be
misunderstood. Kant accepts the traditional equivalence between
what one rationally ought to do and what is good to do; but
rational choice is prior to goodness.[1] That is, goodness is not a
property of acts, experiences, or ends which can be discerned independently of the reasons, or rational considerations, for acting.
Thus, though Kant agrees with the tradition that an act is rational
if and only if it is good to do (or promotes what is best), he does
not hold that an act is rational *because* it is (or promotes) good, but
rather an act is counted as good (or good producing) *because* rational considerations favor it. What is *good* to do and what one
ought to do are both determined by what reason prescribes; the difference in the expressions lies in the sense of practical necessity
conveyed by the word "ought."

The capacity to engage in practical reasoning is a feature of beings with a *will,* and only such beings (G 80 [412], 114 [446]. At
times Kant announces grandly that practical reason *is* the will, but

---

[1] See *Critique of Practical Reason,* trans. L. W. Beck (New York: Liberal Arts Press,
1956), "The Concept of an Object of Pure Practical Reason," pp. 59ff. [58ff.].

subsequent discussion quickly reveals that the concepts are too complex to maintain the identification (G 80 [412-13]). Reason, Kant implies, sometimes "determines" the will, but sometimes does not. Relations between "reason" and "will" are complex and puzzling, but several preliminary points seem clear. First, Kant did not conceive of the reasoning relevant to practical affairs in the way that Hume did: that is, as merely a capacity to discern "matters of [empirical] fact" and "relations of ideas."² Hume's picture is that reason is essentially theoretical, a fact-finding and analyzing power which may serve to present background information for agents who are then moved to act by their desires. It is this picture that led Hume to deny that there are rational principles of conduct, even governing prudential choices. The only Humean offenses against reason, strictly speaking, are in the formation of beliefs. Kant's attempt to make an essential connection between reason and will represents an important departure from Hume's picture. To have a will is to acknowledge the force of certain rational constraints, even if one's final choice does not always conform to them. And if one engages in the reasoning relevant to practical concerns one could not have a will indifferent to its conclusions. Kant is an "internalist" about reasons: there are, in addition to reasons for *believing,* reasons for *acting,* and to acknowledge these is (in part) to be disposed to follow them.

A second point stems from Kant's repeated definitions of *will* as a causal power that works in accord with the agent's *idea* of principles or laws (G 80 [412], 95 [427]. When a being with a will "makes things happen," we attribute this to his acceptance of a reason; and this can be partially expressed as his policy, maxim, or principle. We understand the act not merely by reference to a prior cause, e.g., an inner impulse, but by constructing a rationale for it. The rationale, if fully stated, would refer to the agent's ideas about the effects of his act, his goals, his attitude regarding similar cases, and, ultimately, the principle of reason that (we suppose) guided and constrained his choice. Acts are judged rational or not according to how this *rationale* measures up to the standards of rationality

²David Hume, *A Treatise of Human Nature,* ed. L. A. Selby-Bigge (Oxford: Clarendon, 1955), esp. pp. 458, 463.

and not by trying to see whether the right metaphysical faculty ("Reason" and not "Sensibility") was operative.[3]

Nonmoral practical reasoning is supposed to be guided by hypothetical imperatives.[4] Though the term "hypothetical imperative" derives from a classification of forms of judgment, it is widely conceded that Kant's basic idea cannot be adequately captured by focus on linguistic form alone. Moral imperatives, supposedly categorical, can be expressed in hypothetical form: for example, "If you plan to judge a man in law, you ought not to engage in business with him." And nonmoral imperatives, supposedly hypothetical, can be expressed in categorical form: for example, "You ought to take an aspirin." Kant's idea of hypothetical imperatives is best understood, I think, when they are seen as "oughts" which have their rational force entirely from their place in a complex rationale which has the following structure:

(1) Any fully rational agent (necessarily) wills the necessary (and available) means to his ends.

(2) So one ought to will the necessary (and available) means to one's ends. (The Hypothetical Imperative)

(3) *M* is a necessary (and available) means to *E*.

(4) So if one wills *E*, one ought to will *M*.

(5) *P* (a person) wills *E*.

(6) So *P* ought to will *M*.

The first premise is, for Kant, an analytic truth about rational agency, and the second simply reexpresses the idea with the word "ought" (according to Kant's view that "ought" is merely a way of expressing rational requirements especially appropriate to "imperfect wills"). The third and fifth premises express beliefs about relevant facts: causal connections and the ends to which the agent is committed. The conclusion is "hypothetical" in that its rational force is entirely dependent on the facts presupposed in the argument and, further, because one can rationally escape the conclu-

---

[3]This is especially clear in the primary context of practical reasoning, which is not third-person judgments but first-person deliberation in which the yet undecided agent tries to find the most rational option. In this context, practical reason searches for the best rationale, which is obviously different from trying to find an elusive inner something that will have moved one when one acts.

[4]The ideas in this paragraph are spelled out more fully in my paper "The Hypothetical Imperative," reprinted in this volume.

sion by choosing to give up an end to which one was committed. In effect, the rational requirement is always an option: take the means or abandon your end.

This interpretation of Kant on nonmoral reasoning is controversial in at least one important respect. I have assumed that human wills can fail to live up to the basic standard of nonmoral practical reason, just as they can fail to live up to the rational standards of morality. This is what most of us think, and it is implied in Kant's calling even the nonmoral rational standards (hypothetical) *imperatives*. But some construe Kant's remarks about the analyticity of "Who wills the end wills the means" as a denial that anyone can will an end and fail to will the necessary means. This view fits with, and perhaps reinforces, an all-or-nothing view of the will in moral cases, according to which one cannot will contrary to rational moral standards.[5] In both cases, this all-or-nothing account says that one always wills what is rational by the standards in question, and so one's acts (or bodily movements) are either attributed to the agent's will, in which case they are rational, or they are seen as mere products of natural causes, in which case they are nonrational. *Irrational* willing becomes impossible.

The question whether one can (irrationally) fail to will the necessary means to one's ends is more complex than it may seem. Consider first the situation when one initially comes to will an end. What seems obvious, and may count as analytic, is that when one wills an end one intends to take *some* means to achieve it, even if one may not know what means will be necessary. But does one in willing an end, say to win an election, thereby intend (or will) to take *whatever* means prove to be necessary? Ends need not be willed so unrevisably. I may will to win the election, for example, thereby intending to take the necessary means unless those means prove unacceptable, in which case I intend to abandon my end. In effect, I will to take the necessary means or else revise my ends.

Now consider the common situation in which time lapses between an initial decision to pursue an end and the occasions for taking the means. One can know, I think, that certain means (e.g., lighter meals) are necessary to achieve a goal (e.g., to lose weight)

[5]The clearest case of this is Robert Paul Wolff's commentary, *The Autonomy of Reason* (New York: Harper & Row, 1973).

and yet neither take the necessary means nor abandon the goal. This is the pattern, if any, which hypothetical imperatives would condemn as irrational willing: one wills something incompatible with the means known to be necessary to an end, thereby failing to will the means, but one also fails to take the only rational alternative, i.e., to reassess one's ends. It is arguable, of course, that this is impossible *if* the agent is fully and vividly focused upon his end and the immediate urgency of taking the means. To borrow Philippa Foot's example, if you intended to go to London tonight and you stand on the Oxford platform fully aware that the last train, your only means to London, is starting to pull away, then unless you step on that train you *have* in fact given up your end.[6] What follows, however, is just that the irrationalities falling under hypothetical reasoning always involve some failure of attention, careful reflection, or willingness to face up to one's options, and that when the necessary means are immediate, urgent, and obvious the failure may be impossible for anyone still rational enough to be an agent. But this concession does not deny my main point, which is that even Kant's hypothetical imperatives refer to a standard of rational choice which we can sometimes, by willing irrationally, fail to satisfy. When we fail, revealing that we are not perfectly rational, it is not that we do not will to act but rather move as mere products of natural forces; we will to act, but in this case "reason" does not fully "determine the will." As Kant says, what is analytic is not simply that "whoever wills the end, wills the (necessary) means" but that this is so "so far as reason has decisive influence on his actions" (G 84-85 [417-18]).

This means–end principle is in fact the only principle of rational choice that Kant explicitly acknowledges as analytic of rationality. One can easily imagine that Kant would have accepted certain other formal principles as analytic of means–ends reasoning: for example, Rawls's principle of inclusion and principle of greater likelihood. But it is significant that he did not recognize as analytic of rational choice any of the *substantive* or *maximizing* principles which philosophers have often accepted for nonmoral practical reasoning. By "substantive" principles I mean principles which declare certain ends, such as pleasure, as intrinsically worth pur-

---

[6]From a seminar at the University of California, Los Angeles, about 1975.

suing or which specify certain particular sorts of acts, such as promise-keeping, as rationally required. Kant was well aware that previous rationalistic philosophers had simply declared their favorite moral principles to be rational without much argument, and, with his analytic/synthetic distinction in hand as a critical tool, he could see that a successful argument for the rationality of these principles could not be a simple inference from the familiar concept of rational choice. Similarly, he saw that there is no contradiction in supposing a rational agent might lack the particular ends of wealth, power, honor, and even pleasure. The point is not just that there are contexts in which a rational person might forgo these ends; it is also that our disposition to pursue these ends is not a consequence of our having reason but rather of other aspects of our human nature. Even the universal human inclination to pleasure is not by its nature a reason to act; it becomes so when, with appropriate reflection, a rational agent chooses to include it in the system of ends he wills to pursue.[7] The same would be true, on

---

[7]This point may be controversial and certainly needs more discussion, with specific reference to the texts; but I think it is the most plausible reconstruction of Kant's view into the contemporary terminology of "reasons for action" (which is not Kant's). The idea is not, of course, that we view the choice to indulge a (harmless) pleasure or not with the same detached indifference as we might view the choice between two equally nourishing but tasteless foods; we care, and set our ends accordingly, thereby acquiring a reason (relative to the end). Also, especially when there is no reason not to indulge the pleasure, the agent's awareness of it will no doubt figure into the *explanation* or "reason why" the agent acted. But when the issue is what counts as a good reason in *deliberation*, for the agent who has not yet formed his ends, the alternative view (that inclination per se gives at least prima facie reason to act) has implications I think Kant would not accept. For example, one who decides not to indulge an inclination (say, for pleasure) in the absence of reasons to the contrary would be thereby choosing irrationally, not merely in a strange manner hard to comprehend. And, more seriously, the prima facie force of many intense inclinations would have to be weighed against moral considerations to determine what is rational to do, thus generating potential conflicts between moral and nonmoral reasoning. Some specify that inclinations must be "informed," or capable of surviving appropriate reflection, in order for them to have prima facie rational force; but, unless the reflective process includes the Kantian "setting oneself an end," I doubt that Kant would count even reflection-surviving inclinations as necessarily providing the deliberator with normative reasons for acting.

To be sure, inclinations may explain why the agent sets the end, and the description of the end, or object of acting, may refer to the inclination (as in "my end was to get pleasure"); but the choice of an end is not rationally required by an inclination, even in the absence of contrary inclinations. Oddly enough, despite the frequent claim that desires are reasons for Hume, I think that Hume would agree on the point: for, on Hume's view, desires motivate but do not generate requirements of reason. A consequence of

Kant's view, of any natural altruistic disposition we may have to promote the pleasure of others.

It is significant, too, that Kant does not count as analytic of rationality any *maximizing* principle such as "Maximize your expected utility over time" or "Act in such a way that you maximally satisfy your current preferences (or the preferences you would have if fully informed)."[8] Such principles differ from Kant's Hypothetical Imperative in that they do not always leave an agent an option, whatever his preferences may be. Thus, if there are categorical moral imperatives, such maximizing principles could be in irreconcilable conflict with them: a categorical imperative might forbid X even though, given one's (informed) preferences, the maximizing principle demands X. Kant's Hypothetical Imperative, by contrast, can always be fully satisfied no matter what moral imperatives demand; for whenever it prescribes a means on the basis of one's end, it leaves the rational option of giving up the end.

Prudential hypothetical imperatives might seem to be an exception, for Kant says happiness is necessarily an end for all human beings. When morality conflicts with my happiness, how can I abandon my end of happiness? This raises an interesting problem, but I think it is more a problem in Kant's exposition than a deep inconsistency in his theory. The inclination to happiness may be irrepressible or, as Kant says, a "natural necessity" (G 83 [415]), but hypothetical imperatives refer to *ends* which we will and nothing becomes this except by choice of a rational agent (MPV 38-39 [381-82], 42 [384-85], 50 [392]). Kant concedes at least that most people, most of the time, will happiness as a higher-order end, i.e., the goal of fulfilling all of their specific (desire-based) ends or

---

my interpretation, incidentally, is that reason does not always dictate what we should do: for when moral principles are silent and one had not yet chosen one's ends, no rational requirement follows from a full understanding of one's inclinations. And even after one chooses one's ends, if moral principles remain irrelevant, one always has a rational option of revising or abandoning the ends.

[8]For sophisticated theories of this type see, for example, Richard Brandt's "The Concept of Rational Action" and John C. Harsanyi's "Basic Moral Decisions and Alternative Concepts of Rationality" in *Social Theory and Practice 9*, nos. 2-3 (1983); 143-64, 231-44.

of satisfying all their desires.[9] But since the set of all a person's desires, or desire-based ends, over time is an amorphous, vaguely conceived, and usually incoherent set, there is little that can be declared unequivocally both a means to happiness and inescapably necessary for happiness (G 85–86 [418–19]). Even if there were, Kant clearly thought that when morality demands we can suspend, qualify, or abandon happiness as the end we will to pursue on the occasion. Thus, despite the universality of the inclination to happiness and its typical place in our rational deliberations, even the prudential imperatives to achieve happiness must be understood to leave the same option as all other hypothetical imperatives: take the means or (at least temporarily) abandon the end. Given the qualification, nonmoral imperatives do not, strictly speaking, conflict with categorical imperatives: both can be satisfied.[10]

The point might be summarized by saying, darkly, that Kant's theory of nonmoral practical reason "makes room for freedom" even though it is not "derived from freedom." That is, the rational constraints on nonmoral choice are not derived from the idea of a rational agent with freedom (autonomy) in the way moral constraints are supposed to be; but these nonmoral rational constraints always leave us the rational option to do whatever is demanded by moral reasoning based on the idea of freedom.

II. Reasoning with Autonomy: Negative Aspects of Freedom

Kant held, of course, that the Hypothetical Imperative is not the only necessary principle of rational conduct, even though

[9]Kant works with different notions of "happiness" at different points, but the dominant idea in the *Groundwork* is the idea of the satisfaction of all one's inclinations. See G 67 [399], 73 [405], 85 [418]; MPV 45 [388], 149 [480]; and *Critique of Pure Reason*, trans. Norman Kemp Smith (New York: St. Martin's, 1965), p. 632 [A800/B828].

[10]This is not to deny, of course, that the pursuit of happiness often conflicts with morality and, even in the best persons, must be constrained by moral principles. The point is that, when it conflicts with morality, the pursuit of happiness is not prescribed by reason.

it is the only analytic one. This means that there is another sort of practical reasoning not captured by the pattern of argument we have been considering. Such reasoning is guided by principles which are acknowledged by every rational will with the property *autonomy* but which would be irrelevant to any "will" without this property. Kant believed these further principles to be identical with the highest principles of morality, but this is a conclusion rather than a defining feature of rational autonomy.

In the *Groundwork* there are several ways Kant tries to show that common morality presupposes rational principles beyond hypothetical imperatives. The first, in chapter 1, aims to show that ordinary judgments that certain acts are morally commendable are based on our attributing to the agent a motive, respect for moral law, which does not fit the hypothetical imperative pattern. Then, in chapter 2, Kant argues that the concept of a moral duty is such that, if there are duties, then there must be principles which are rationally compelling even if following them fails to serve our ends. Reasoning with hypothetical imperatives, in the pattern we have considered, might often prescribe the sort of acts commonly regarded as duties, but it obviously could not account for their being duties, i.e., rationally required independently of their serving our ends.[11]

Kant also argues, apart from moral assumptions, that the way we view ourselves in practical deliberation presupposes a capacity to reason independently of hypothetical imperatives. Even would-be moral skeptics, questioning whether there are really any duties, inevitably take themselves in deliberation to be capable of acting for reasons that inclinations together with the Hypothetical Imperative cannot provide.[12] A central feature of this self-concept is affirmed, Kant thinks, even when we make theoretical judgments, as in science; for here too we see ourselves as surveying and as-

[11] "Another, more obscure line of argument in chap. 2 consists of a series of illuminating reformulations of the principle initially identified as the "supreme principle of morality," a procedure which supposedly enables us to see that this principle is "the principle of autonomy," i.e., a constraint on rational willing independent of the concern to do what serves one's ends. See G 89-108 [421-41].

[12] See G 114-18ff. [446-51]. A reconstruction of this argument is attempted in my paper "Kant's Argument for the Rationality of Moral Conduct," reprinted in this volume.

sessing reasons from a point of view where the question is not what do we want and what is needed to achieve some revisable personal goal. [13]

These arguments are open to all sorts of questions, of course; but my present task is not to defend them but rather to draw out some main features of the idea of practical reason which the arguments claim to be so deeply embedded in our thought. I begin with some negative features.

(1) The first point is that immoral persons do not differ from the morally best persons in the standards of rational choice to which they are committed. They differ in what they do, and in the priorities represented in their deepest policies, but as human beings they both have wills with the property of autonomy, which implies an acknowledgment of the nonhypothetical standards of rationality with which we are now concerned. [14]

In this respect, I think, Kant's view is unlike that of some contemporary philosophers who also distinguish means–end reasoning from a richer conception ("the reasonable") which is at work in moral discussions. For the contemporary philosophers generally treat the commitment to the wider (more "impartial") sort of reasoning as in a sense optional: a necessary part of thinking morally, perhaps, but not something one needs to be a fully consistent, informed rational agent. For example, in Rawls's terminology it is "reasonable" to respect the principles of justice because it is (in a narrower sense) "rational" for anyone who takes a certain impartial perspective to choose these principles for the basic structure of societies. [15] But Rawls admits that not everyone is committed to the (impartial) standards built into this idea of the "reasonable." One may ask, "Why be reasonable?" or, in other words, "Why is it rational for me to respect what rational persons *would* choose *if* impartial?" For the amoralist who rejects the moral perspective there may be no adequate answer. Kant's view, I think, is different,

---

[13] I take this to be at least part of Kant's point in saying that even in theoretical judgments we see ourselves as members of an "intelligible world." See G 116 [448], 118–19 [451–52].

[14] This is discussed more fully in "Kant's Argument for the Rationality of Moral Conduct," reprinted in this volume.

[15] John Rawls, "Kantian Constructivism in Moral Theory: The Dewey Lectures 1980," *Journal of Philosophy* 77, no. 9 (1980): 515–72.

though of course it raises problems of its own. The wider conception of practical reason, i.e., rational autonomy, is thought to be an inescapable feature of rational agency, revealed in moral thinking but not an optional form of reasoning one takes on with a voluntary commitment to the moral point of view. Thus when Kant argues that an act is demanded by a principle that rational agents with autonomy would adopt, he considers one's rational options to be closed; for the perspective of rational autonomy is one, he thought, inherent in all rational human wills.[16] It is rational to do what rational agents with autonomy *would* prescribe because we are such agents and, as such, we *do* so prescribe to ourselves.

(2) The next feature of rational autonomy to consider is its alleged independence from natural causes. Something of this sort is entailed by Kant's identification of autonomy with negatively conceived freedom, together with the definition of the latter as a "capacity to work independently of determination by alien causes" (G 114 [446]). But the problem is to be clear about what sort of independence is in question. The point cannot be that the behavior we attribute to rational wills cannot be explained and predicted by causal laws in physical science or psychology: for Kant repeatedly insists that any observed phenomena, regarding human behavior or anything else, can in principle be comprehended under natural

---

[16]The point that all human beings are committed to the standards of rational autonomy is so deep and pervasive in Kant's thought that no one would overlook it if it were not for certain confusing matters of terminology. Unfortunately the word "autonomy" is not always understood, even by Kant himself, in exactly the same sense. The primary use, for example in the central arguments of chap. 2 and 3 of the *Groundwork*, refers to a property we attribute to all rational wills, and this is said to be the same property, differently conceived, as negative freedom. It implies a capacity to deliberate and act independently, in some sense, from natural causes and from motivation by inclinations; and, crucially, it entails commitment to rational standards of conduct beyond the means-end standards underlying hypothetical imperatives. All wills with autonomy of this primary sort "make universal laws" in the metaphorical sense of "legislators" in the "kingdom of ends"; but they are not all so perfectly conscientious that they act only on maxims which they, in another sense, "can will as universal laws." Unfortunately, the words "autonomy" and especially "autonomous" have come to be used more narrowly to refer to persons, motives, and acts that fully exemplify Kant's moral ideals or, in other words, to refer only to what fully lives up to the rational commitments we all have as agents with autonomy in the primary sense. There is some ambivalence in Kant's usage, I think, which perpetuates the problem. But the underlying points seem clear enough: the commitment to rational standards beyond means-ends reasoning is inherent in all rational wills, but only the morally best, if any, manifest, express, or live up to these standards consistently.

causal laws. Nor, I think, can his point be that we can equally well describe and explain human behavior from another metaphysical perspective compatible with the scientific one; for Kant repeats that the attribution of behavior to wills is warranted only for practical purposes and, in any case, it leaves us with unanswerable questions rather than any comprehensible account of how the will results in behavior.

The main point, instead, seems to be an idea about the task of practical deliberation, about what the deliberator is looking for. He is looking for reasons for choosing to act one way rather than another, which is not the same as looking for the causes, if any, which will have moved him to act when he does. In deliberation, one sees oneself as having options, some of which may be supported by better (practical) reasons than others. One cannot know prior to choosing what the causes are, if any, in terms of which one's choice can be explained or could have been predicted. But even if one knew all that is conceptually and empirically possible to know about oneself and the situation prior to choice, that still would not give the deliberator what he is looking for, namely, better reasons for choosing one option over the other.

We can imagine, perhaps, that one might learn on an occasion that he is so "wired" that he will behave in a certain way no matter how he should deliberate, reflect on reasons, and "choose"; but to imagine this is to imagine that, unless he forgets what he has learned, he has had to abandon the point of view of deliberation, for he no longer sees himself as having options. Causal determinism does not, of course, imply that this is a common occurrence; for causal determinism does not imply that the phenomena corresponding to reflection on reason are causally inefficacious. And even supposing we could have evidence that this is a common, even universal, occurrence, the conclusion to draw would be that deliberation presupposes an illusion and becomes impossible once one is enlightened. However, shocking as this (fantastically implausible) conclusion would be, even this would not deny Kant's main point about practical reasoning which, once understood, seems hard to deny: that is, when one deliberates, one is engaged in the task of assessing the reasons for choosing among alternative outcomes one presumes will be influenced by one's reflection and choice, and whether one's reflection and choice are themselves causally determined, even whether the agent believes this as a metaphysical thesis, is irrelevant to his deliberative task.

A similar point, as Kant suggests, can be made about theoretical judgment in science: whether or not one's weighing of the evidence by rational standards is causally determined, even whether the scientist believes this, is irrelevant to a scientist's task of finding the conclusion best supported by the evidence.

(3) Practical reasoning with autonomy is, in some sense, independent of inclination; but in what sense? Sometimes Kant's expressions suggest a picture, or rather featureless idea, of a "self" without desires, body, or even spatiotemporal location, and this mysterious "self" is somehow giving abstract orders to a corrupt, embodied, lusty, earthbound being, and, oddly enough, *I* am both the mysterious giver and the embodied receiver of the orders. Kant also, of course, issues warnings against taking such a picture, or non-picture, too seriously or out of context; and I think the main force of his remarks about practical reasoning's being independent of inclination does not presuppose metaphysical (or metaphorical) ideas of this sort.

Part of the idea of independence from inclination is no doubt connected with the point of the previous section: that is, the point of view of a deliberator engaged in practical reasoning is one from which it is irrelevant whether or not scientific explanation of behavior proceeds by showing law-like connections between antecedent psychological states, such as inclinations, and consequent behavior. Just as the abstract thesis of causal determinism is irrelevant to the deliberator's task, so is the more specific psychological determinism that insists that there are always lawful correlations between behavior and prior observable psychological states. The deliberator asks whether having a certain inclination is a good reason for doing what he proposes, and this question is not resolved by believing or even knowing that some conjunction of psychological states, including that inclination, will correlate lawfully with his subsequent behavior. The deliberator sees himself as capable of squelching the inclination, no matter how urgent it feels, if there is sufficient reason to do so; but this is not a belief about *how* the resistance is to be explained, and it is not incompatible with any but the crudest psychological determinism (e.g., one which held that the most urgently felt desires determine behavior irrespective of reflection).

But the main point, I think, lies elsewhere, and is more interesting. The idea is that, for a rational agent with autonomy, the reasons for acting are not settled by knowing all one's current and future inclinations and how most effectively to satisfy them. There may be reasons for acting which do not correspond to one's felt inclinations, and there may be inclinations one has sufficient reason to suppress and not just for the sake of satisfying other inclinations. The point of view of the rational agent in deliberation, then, is that of one who presumes not only that he can act against, or without, inclination but also that he may have good reason to. He may grant, with Kant, that once he acts (even "against inclination"), a scientist can in principle "explain" his behavior by reference to his psychological states. But, as deliberator, he faced the different task of finding the best reasons for acting, and even the liveliest awareness of what he feels inclined to do would not settle this issue for him.

To say that the deliberator presumes that he can act "against or without inclination" is perhaps misleading, in a way that makes the point seem less plausible than it is. If one acts against inclination, or in the absence of inclination, in the relevant sense, this need not mean that the best phenomenological explanation is that "he did it though all the while he felt neither disposition to do so nor aversion to not doing so." That would be puzzling, and would also run counter to what Kant says about the feeling of "respect" for law.[17] The basic idea might be put this way: in acting for good reason but against or without inclination, one of course feels disposed to act as one does; but one does not acknowledge that there is good reason to act because one has such a disposition or because of any other inclination. Rather, when one acts against (or in the absence of) inclination, the felt disposition is seen as an acknowledgment of the reasons, not the basis for the reasons. When, for example, I forgo the temptation to eat the piece of pie which someone else has been saving, I do feel averse to eating it but the reason I acknowledge is not that I have a feeling of aversion but

[17]G 68 [400]; *Critique of Practical Reason*, pp. 74ff. [72ff.].

that the pie belongs to someone else. I make sense of my aversion by reference to my judgment that my eating the pie would be unreasonable; and I do not justify the judgment that taking the pie is unreasonable by saying that the aversion felt stronger than the temptation.

Kant's position here runs counter to many familiar contemporary accounts of practical reason, but I suspect it is deeply rooted in common sense thinking. In the *Groundwork* the idea is pervasive, and in particular it is implicit in the argument that rational wills have negative freedom. This is said to be a capacity of rational agents to will independently of "alien causes," but the structure of the argument makes clear that the point is not merely the irrelevance of determinism but the capacity to will without the rationale being to satisfy inclination. In other words, it is not just that we treat our choices as not causally determined; it is that we treat the task of rational deliberation as not always settled by information about our inclinations.

III. Reasoning with Autonomy: Positive Aspects of Freedom

Two related features of the wider notion of practical reason are inherent in the claims (1) that a rational will cannot be "lawless," (2) that it has laws that are self-imposed but also rooted in its rational nature. Here interpretation is more difficult, and the viewpoint more controversial.

(1) The remark that the will cannot be lawless is made in the context of the argument to show that any negatively free rational will must have autonomy.[18] A negatively free will is conceived as one independent from causal determinism and from motivation by inclination, in the senses we have considered. The question then arises: how are we to understand attributions of behavior to a will, given that we have set aside both causal explanations and the rationale to satisfy inclinations? In saying that the agent willed the behavior, rather than merely that it occurred, we must have in mind some other sort of rationale we attribute to the agent. That

---

[18]G 114 [446]; *Critique of Practical Reason*, p. 28 [29].

is, the agent must be acting for reasons, even though the reason is not to satisfy inclinations. Suppose a particular reason is given, e.g., "to keep my word" or "to save a person's life." If this really is a reason, there must be some general rational principle supporting the conclusion that one ought to keep one's word, or save a life, in the circumstances. When we cite the facts of the situation as "reasons," this is at best a partial statement of the rationale; we need also the principle of rationality according to which it follows that, given those facts, one has a reason.

The one general principle of practical reason we have considered so far, the Hypothetical Imperative, will not suffice here: for, by hypothesis, our agent's rationale is not to satisfy an inclination. The Hypothetical Imperative says, "If you will an end for which your act is a necessary means, then you ought to do the act (or give up the end)"; but without inclination, or *some other sort of reason,* to will the end, the Hypothetical Imperative is inapplicable. There must be, then, some other sort of reason, independent of inclination and the Hypothetical Imperative, if (as we have supposed) rational wills can exercise the independence defined as negative freedom. And a full statement of that reason, or rationale, must include the principle of practical reason which justifies the conclusion about the particular case. Such a principle would be a "law" in Kant's sense, i.e., a principle that any rational agent necessarily accepts (and, if fully rational, follows).

Note that the will is "lawful," on this account, not by virtue of being controlled by some mysterious noumenal "causes" instead of natural causes. Rather, it is lawful in the sense that there are practical laws, or rational principles of conduct, to guide its choices. At least sometimes we can act from inclination or not; but when we choose not to, the choice is not thereby without reason. It is based on reasons of a different kind.

(2) Kant concludes from the above that, if they have negative freedom, rational wills have *autonomy.*[19] This is said to be the property of "being a law unto itself," a phrase that suggests arbitrary, unconstrained choice, but one which must be understood along with Kant's repeated insistence that the laws come from one's "rational nature." The background, of course, is Kant's view

[19]Ibid.

that we, as human beings, have both a rational and a sensible nature and that, in some sense, the rational is more truly ourselves while the inclinations of sensibility are "alien" (G 125-26 [457-58]). This raises deep questions about personal identity which I set aside here; but we may be able nonetheless to discern some of the practical implications.

The metaphor of "governing oneself," by having one's reason "legislate" laws to one's lower nature, is one that Kant obviously found captivating. Its roots, of course, can be traced back through a tradition to Plato. In Kant the picture appears in a bewildering variety of contexts: (a) the conscientious agent checking his maxims by trying to "will" them as "universal laws" (G 89ff. [421ff.]), (b) the "legislator" in the "kingdom of ends" making laws for himself (and other rational agents) as "subjects" (G 100ff. [433ff.]), (c) the ideal "social contract" underlying principles of the *Metaphysical Elements of Justice* (MEJ 80-81 [315-16]), and finally (d) the general idea of rational "autonomy" as "being a law unto oneself" (G 108 [440], 114 [446-47]). Though related, these various uses of the metaphor need to be cashed out in somewhat different ways, and it is important to keep in mind that here our concern is with the last, most general use.

Because the law-giving in question is attributed to our "rational nature," the point is obviously not the "existentialist" idea that individuals must simply choose, or make up, what is to be a basic reason for them. Kant's view of the commands of a will with autonomy is no doubt modeled on traditional views of the commands of God, with the innovation that now the legislative will is attributed to each rational agent and not exclusively to an external being. But the model is more nearly Aquinas's God than Ockham's or Descartes's: that is, it is a will that acknowledges what is rational and commands accordingly (with sanctions), rather than a "voluntarist's" will that "invents" the standards, making the nonrational rational by choice alone. Autonomy means identifying with rational constraints, not seeing them as imposed by others or as something we could give up without ceasing to be ourselves; but it does not mean we "voluntarily" choose to commit ourselves to them in the way we might choose to accept the rules of a club, a church, or a private code.

The best clue to what Kant means by "being a law unto one-self" is perhaps the list of moral theories which he declares to be based on the notion that the human will is heteronomous: perfectionism, divine command theories, hedonism, and moral sense theories.[20] In each case, Kant charges, something "alien" to our rational wills is treated as the ground of moral obligation. In divine command theories, this is most obvious: we are under obligation because someone else, God, so commands. In hedonistic theories, of both egoistic and universalistic varieties, the basic principles are derived from common human dispositions but not from our rationality. The objection at this point is not that "Always maximize pleasure (your own or everyone's)" is *incompatible* with morality or rationality; it is that the principle is not itself a (necessary) principle of rational choice and that discovery of a universal human inclination to follow it would not make it so. In discussing the Hypothetical Imperative, Kant has already implied that "Maximize satisfaction of inclination" is not a principle of rationality; and so, even if it is a fact (as Epicurus and later utilitarians say) that all human beings are disposed to promote pleasure (their own or everyone's), this by itself would not show that it was rational to follow the hedonistic principles. Whether or not their conclusions are warranted, the arguments of hedonistic moral theories start from an unwarranted assumption: that we can determine what is rational to do by simple inference from generalizations about our nonrational dispositions.

The same objection, I take it, applies to any "moral sense" theory which tries to derive the truth (and so, for Kant, the rational force) of moral judgments entirely from empirical facts about how human beings are disposed to feel when facing a moral problem. The objection, oddly enough, is one in which Hume would concur, for Hume agrees that moral judgments get neither truth nor *rational* force from moral sentiment.

The upshot is that, even in the moral sphere, Kant refuses to recognize as inherently rational any of the familiar substantive principles which philosophers labeled "Kantian" sometimes offer to counteract egoistic reasoning. The fact that an act would cause

---

[20]G 110ff. [443ff.]; *Critique of Practical Reason*, pp. 41–42 [39–40].

another pleasure, or prevent him pain, is not by itself a reason for doing it. There are no objective "intrinsic values" which rational agents necessarily aim to maximize; and, contrary to Nagel, the bare fact that I could prevent someone pain by warning him that there is a bee on his hamburger is not, without further argument, a reason to warn him.[21] Similarly, "perfectionist" principles that urge the realization of various (nonrational) human capacities have no force unless willed by rational agents with autonomy.

There is one further feature of rational autonomy that is presupposed in Kant's arguments and so must be understood as part of the idea that its laws have their source in our common nature as rational beings. This is the notion that the standards, or ends, of rational autonomous wills are not relative to individuals in a certain sense. The sense, however, is not merely weak universalizability: that is, that a reason for one person is a reason for anyone exactly (or relevantly) like that person in exactly (or relevantly) similar circumstances. Nor is this the extreme impartialist thesis that rational agents count the *welfare* of each person as of equal weight in their deliberations as their own. The point, I think, is more limited than the latter and more substantial than the former: namely, there is something about our common rational nature, no matter who possesses it, that provides special reasons to all rational agents with autonomy. Thus principles which state the reasons for an agent need not be relativized to features of that individual agent, as in "One has a reason to promote *one's own* pleasure (self-realization, knowledge, etc.)."[22]

The claim here is a strong and controversial one, imputing to all rational agents a limited rational concern that is not self-regarding; but it is important that the claim not be confused with the more familiar contemporary impartialism that gives equal prima facie

[21]See Thomas Nagel, *The Possibility of Altruism,* (Princeton: Princeton University Press, 1970).

[22]Like the extreme impartialist position, this implies that what is important to one person (by virtue of rational autonomy) is important to any other (by virtue of his rational autonomy); but this thing of importance is not welfare or any "intrinsic value" that exists independently of rational agency. And, crucially, this important common concern is not describable in self-referential terms. Thus, for example, the basic principle of rational autonomy cannot even be "Do what most enhances your own rational agency," even though this cites a value that we have as rational agents rather than one (like pleasure or welfare) which we have as human beings with desires.

weight to the (equally intense, etc.) desires or satisfactions of all persons. Like that more extreme impartialism, Kant holds that what is a reason for an agent is not always relativized to the agent, as in "*A* has a reason to *X* because *X* does . . . for *A*, gets *A* . . . , or promotes *A*'s. . . . " But the reasons in question are not, ultimately and without further argument, the fact that a pleasure will be promoted, a pain averted, civilization advanced, or any purported "intrinsic value" other than what is inherently a concern to all rational agents as such.

IV. Transition to Morality: Identifying the Principles of Rational Autonomy

So far our account of rational autonomy may seem disappointingly abstract, negative, and "formal," though those familiar with the *Groundwork* (and Kant's other works) should not be surprised. The large question remains: how from these bare beginnings can one derive any substantive guidance in deciding what to do? The answer, if there is one, must lie in Kant's attempt to show that the various formulations of the Categorical Imperative express the sort of reasons, or guiding principles, that any rational agent with autonomy, as such, must acknowledge. Since I believe that Kant's attempt to prove this for his famous first formulation is a failure, resting on a deep confusion, I will conclude with some brief remarks on one of two other formulations that may be more promising.

One formula states that "humanity," or our rational nature, is an end in itself (G 95ff. [427ff.]). I take this to mean that rational agency itself is something of "unconditional and incomparable worth," which implies that each has a reason to preserve, develop, exercise, and "honor" rational capacities in himself and others.[23] *The Metaphysics of Morals* is filled with examples of how Kant thought this principle yields practical guidelines, and the *Groundwork* offers some sketchy arguments for thinking that the principle is one to which any rational agent with autonomy is committed.

---

[23]The interpretation is developed in my "Humanity as an End in Itself," reprinted in this volume.

We might paraphrase one of these arguments as follows (G 96 [428-29]): A value (or "end") that any rational agent (with autonomy) would acknowledge, whatever his or her desires, is living as a rational agent. We recognize this first and most obviously in thinking of our own agency, but on reflection we see that what we value, by virtue of our rational nature rather than self-love, is the rational agency rather than the fact that it is our own. Because our particular ends are chosen by us, as rational agents, we count these particular ends as having at least some impersonal (though for Kant still "relative") value, i.e., as worthy of consideration in others' deliberations as well as our own. This reflects an attitude, or point of view, which sees each rational agent as a source of value which other rational agents must take into account, not because of *what* is valued but because it is valued by a rational agent like ourselves. Moreover, in valuing rational agency in ourselves we attribute a special (impersonal) importance to our existence, development, and opportunities to pursue the system of ends we choose; we do not simply count these as important *to us* but see them as worthy of the concern of any rational agent. But in acknowledging this impersonal worth of rational agency in our own case, because of what it is and not because it is ours, we can see that we are committed to the worth of rational agency in others as well. Thus we cannot be indifferent to anything that affects the existence and development of other rational agents and their opportunities to pursue the system of ends they choose.

This argument does not imply that we value the happiness or the particular ends of others in *just the same way* we value our own; for even in valuing our own rational agency, as rational agents, we are not claiming that others should give equal regard to our happiness or our particular ends. Because we are rational agents, and not just because we want happiness or particular ends, we (supposedly) see our own rational agency as an "end in itself," i.e., as something worthy of respect and concern by all rational agents. But this valuing of rational agency in ourselves (where it first and most obviously invokes our respect) is not the same as valuing our happiness, or the satisfaction of our particular ends; it is the more limited attribution of an (impersonal) worth to our living as rational agents, and so primarily to our existence, rational development, and opportunities to exercise our rational agency. We do value our own happiness and particular projects, of course, but this is not the primary value we claim and acknowledge by virtue of being rational agents. Thus when we acknowledge, as we must, the same value of rational agency in others, what we grant as important per se is not their happiness or particular projects but their existence, development, and opportunity to live as rational agents. The happiness and projects of others get whatever importance they have to the rational agent derivatively: they are important in some cases because the agent happens to care for others but, even when this is absent, they are important because we cannot show respect for the rational agency of others without giving some weight to the projects they choose to pursue.

The contention that rational agents with autonomy necessarily value rational agency per se is a controversial one, of course; but at least it should not be confused with the even stronger claim that preserving and developing rational agency is a value to all rational agents no matter how rational agents are conceived. The argument sketched above presupposes we are addressing rational *agents with autonomy;* that is, rational agents which have *some* reasons, or rational commitments, not tied to inclinations or agent-relative concerns. To such agents (assuming we all so conceive ourselves) Kant in effect argues by elimination: assume that there are such (impersonal) reasons for all rational agents; we have seen that they are not the supposed "intrinsic values" of pleasure, etc.; so what else could they be but concern for rational agency itself?

This can hardly convince anyone who professes to use narrower means-end practical reasoning exclusively; nor, I think, is it meant to. To convince those instrumentalists Kant needs to show that the point of view of rational autonomy is, for all practical purposes, inescapable. Kant has arguments to this effect in the *Groundwork,* though in the second *Critique* he is content to rest the case on the unargued "fact" of moral consciousness. But, on either approach, the task of showing that every deliberator must accept the point of view of rational autonomy is distinct from the Kantian project which has been our concern here: namely, to illuminate and draw the practical consequences from that rich but limited conception of rational autonomy which Kant thought we all share.

To summarize: I have sketched some main features of Kant's theory of practical reason, as I reconstruct it primarily from the

Groundwork but not, I think, as radically different from Kant's later ethical writings. My aim has not been to defend the theory, or even to establish it as an interpretation; but I have made several main interpretative suggestions. Among these are: (1) Nonmoral practical reasoning is governed by the Hypothetical Imperative, a principle which is analytic of ideal rationality but is often violated. (2) The Hypothetical Imperative, as a non-substantive and non-maximizing principle, is always compatible with categorical moral principles, if there are any, and so nonmoral and moral reasoning do not conflict. (3) Kant argues that there is a form of practical reasoning beyond hypothetical imperatives, and the negative claim that this is independent of causes and inclinations does not imply radical metaphysical views but rather expresses a widely held view of what is relevant to practical deliberation. (4) Kant's positive account of practical reasoning beyond hypothetical imperatives is again not a metaphysical story about non-natural laws that explain (moral) behavior but rather a claim about a special sort of practical reasons we acknowledge. (5) These reasons are in a sense impersonal, or not relativized to the agent in the manner of familiar means–ends principles, but they imply a more limited impersonal regard for others than many contemporary theories of impartial reason.[24] (6) The rational standards are "self-imposed" but not in a sense that implies that we arbitrarily or even "voluntarily" commit ourselves to them. (7) One principle which is supposed to express these special reasons is the formula that one ought to treat humanity as an end in itself, and this conveys the idea that the existence of rational agency in anyone gives us special reasons which are not self-regarding but also not primarily concerned with the happiness of others.

To many this will not be a congenial theory, but it represents Kant's deep struggle to avoid what he regarded as two major temptations for theories of reason: first, treating reason as essentially self-regarding and, second, calling substantive values "principles of reason" without reason.

---

[24]For example, Nagel's *The Possibility of Altruism,* Alan Gewirth's *Reason and Morality* (Chicago: University of Chicago Press, 1977), Kurt Baier's *The Moral Point of View* (Ithaca: Cornell University Press, 1958), and R. M. Hare's *Moral Thinking* (Oxford: Clarendon, 1981), though important qualifications need to be noted. Donagan, Darwell, and Rawls, I think, have more limited impartialist theories.

8

Kant on Imperfect Duty
and Supererogation

In *The Metaphysics of Morals* Kant presents the outlines of
a system of moral principles. The Categorical Imperative is still
the supreme principle of morality, but it is seen as guiding conduct only by means of intermediate principles. These principles
are divided into several types, and how a given principle can be
justified and applied depends upon which type of principle it is.
In discussing these divisions, I have a general aim and a special
one. The general aim is to clarify and reconstruct some of Kant's
main distinctions among the types of duty and to show how, on
Kant's view, the moral worth of actions varies accordingly. What
Kant says on these matters is often unclear, but the attempt to reconstruct the main lines of his thought uncovers a set of distinctions more complex and coherent than commentaries typically
lead one to expect. The special aim is to show, on the basis of these
distinctions, that Kant has a place in his moral scheme for supererogatory actions. Several philosophers have recently criticized
Kant's ethics for not allowing for supererogation. Some believe
that for Kant all actions are either forbidden or obligatory.[1] Another allows that Kant has a place for the morally indifferent
and even for acts which are somewhat bad though not forbidden,

[1] See R. M. Chisholm, "Supererogation and Offense," *Ratio* 5 (1963): 13.

but not for the supererogatory.[2] I shall argue that these interpretations, though suggested by some of Kant's remarks, are mistaken. If I am right, Kant's ethics is less rigoristic than commonly thought. There is more room for choice in pursuing moral ideals, and not everything good is required.

My remarks are divided as follows. First, I give an account of Kant's distinction between perfect and imperfect duty. This is the most controversial of Kant's divisions of moral principles and the most important one for my purposes. Second, I discuss more briefly juridical duty, ethical duty, and some subdivisions of the latter. The main elements of all these concepts are then represented in a more systematic, though somewhat simplified, manner. Third, I attempt to clarify the complex way in which Kant attributes moral worth to actions according to the types of principles they satisfy or fail to satisfy. Finally, I argue that Kant's scheme does allow for supererogatory actions, if these are understood more or less in the ways recently proposed by Roderick Chisholm and Joel Feinberg.

I

In the *Groundwork* Kant divides the duties in his examples into perfect and imperfect duties, but he adds that this division is "put forward as arbitrary" and that he reserves his classification of duties for "a future *Metaphysics of Morals*" (G 89n [422]). He does go on to remark that a perfect duty is "one which allows no exception in the interests of inclination," leaving us to infer that imperfect duties allow some such exception. What this means, however, does not become clear until the distinction is explained more fully in *The Metaphysics of Morals*.

In this work Kant distinguishes between the kind of duty and the manner and degree in which it obligates a person. Thus while every duty is either perfect (narrow) or imperfect (wide), some im-

[2]See Paul Eisenberg, "Basic Ethical Categories in Kant's *Tugendlehre*," *American Philosophical Quarterly* 3 (1966): 255–69. That Kant excludes the supererogatory is also suggested by J. O. Urmson in "Saints and Heroes" in *Essays in Moral Philosophy*, ed. A. I. Melden (Seattle: University of Washington Press, 1958).

perfect duties are of wider obligation than others. The distinguishing feature of imperfect duties seems at first to be that they allow a latitude for choice not permitted by perfect duties. In giving us imperfect duties, Kant says, the moral law "leaves a play-room (*latitudo*) for free choice in following (observing) the law" (DV 49 [390]). Our imperfect duty to develop our natural talents, for example, "determines nothing about the kind and extent of the actions themselves but leaves a play-room for free choice" (DV 112 [446]). Again, Kant says of the imperfect duty of beneficence,

> . . . this duty is only a wide one: since no determinate limits can be assigned to what should be done, the duty has in it a play-room for doing more or less. (DV 54 [393])

Unlike the Doctrine of Law, ethics (which prescribes imperfect duties) does not "determine duties strictly (precisely)" and so leads to questions of casuistry (DV 73-74 [411]).

These passages suggest that principles of imperfect duty can be expressed in the form "One ought to do (or avoid) x sometimes, to some extent" whereas principles of perfect duty must be expressed in the form "One ought always (or never) to do x." The word "sometimes" here would not mean "at least two times" but something less definite. Principles of imperfect duty would be indefinite prescriptions of the sort intended, for example, when a person moralizes to his children, with no immediate problem in mind, "You ought to help the less fortunate (give to worthy causes, learn about political matters, etc.)."

The suggestion needs to be qualified, however, for the play-room for choice permitted by principles of imperfect duty is restricted by the principles of perfect duty. In prescribing imperfect duties, Kant says, the moral law is requiring the adoption of general maxims to promote certain ends; and "maxims" in this context are defined as subjective principles which already qualify for universal law, that is, principles not contrary to perfect duty (DV 48 [389]). Thus in promoting an end prescribed by an imperfect duty, one must not do anything prohibited by a perfect duty. Although one should promote the happiness of others, one may not steal, lie, or murder in doing so. Accordingly, we can think of principles of imperfect duty, fully stated, as principles of the form

"One ought to do (or avoid) x sometimes, to some extent, but never when or to a degree contrary to principles of perfect duty."[3]

So far my account suggests that, in distinguishing perfect and imperfect duties, Kant is simply marking off two sorts of principles derivable from the supreme principle of morality, one indefinite ("Sometimes . . . ") and one definite ("Always. . . . " or "Never . . . "), but both prescribing actions to be done or avoided. In fact, when he presents his various principles of imperfect duty (beneficence, development of talents, and so on), he seems to treat them in this way, as principles prescribing actions of certain sorts, though not specifying when, how often, or precisely how they are to be done. Strictly speaking, however, his position is somewhat different from this, though not in serious conflict with it. In giving us imperfect duties, he says, the moral law "can prescribe only the maxim of actions, not actions themselves (DV 49 [390]). That is, what the moral law prescribes in addition to the actions demanded or prohibited by principles of perfect duty is that each person adopts certain maxims for guiding his other actions. What is required, at least directly, is that we take to heart certain principles, not that we act in certain ways. For example, what we can directly infer from the moral law is that one ought to adopt the maxim to promote the happiness of others, not that *this* or *that* beneficent act is obligatory and not even that one ought sometimes to promote the happiness of others.

This way of putting the matter is not incompatible with the previous suggestion that we distinguish principles of perfect and imperfect duty by their form, though it does add something important. In giving us imperfect duties, what the moral law directly requires of us is that we adopt certain guiding principles. These, in contrast to the principles of perfect duty ("Always . . . " or "Never . . . "), are indefinite principles ("Sometimes, to some extent . . . "), typically indicating some general end to be promoted. Anyone, however, who sincerely adopts such a principle will act accordingly, at least sometimes, if he gets a chance. For

[3]Principles of imperfect duty are understood to be qualified in this way from now on. This qualification, incidentally, gives an importance to Kant's distinction between perfect and imperfect duties independently of any further content which that distinction may have; for it tells us that whatever principles are labeled "perfect duty" are always to take precedence to those labeled "imperfect duty."

example, if a person with the usual abilities and opportunities did nothing to promote the happiness of others, he would thereby show that he did not really adopt a maxim of beneficence. He cannot fulfill his duty to adopt such a maxim without also satisfying the principle. "One ought sometimes, to some extent, to promote the happiness of others." There is still a point, however, in Kant's claim that the duty of beneficence is strictly speaking, a duty *to adopt a maxim* rather than *to act* sometimes in ways that promote others' happiness; for one can do what in fact brings happiness to others without ever making it one's principle to do so. Kant's point is that both are required.

While the preceding account of perfect and imperfect duty fits most of what Kant says about the distinction, it may seem to conflict with other passages. For example, Kant writes,

> But a wide duty is not to be taken as a permission to make exceptions to the maxim of actions, but only as a permission to limit one maxim of duty by another (e.g. love of one's neighbor in general by love of one's parents). (DV 49 [390])

One might take this to mean that although we have a free choice on those occasions when we could be guided by any of several principles of imperfect duty, we have no choice when only one such principle is relevant to our situation. In other words, if two actions, x and y, are each possible in given circumstances but not both possible and x is a kind of act prescribed by a principle of imperfect duty and y is not, then it is obligatory to do x rather than y. Thus, for example, if at any time I can do something to promote the happiness of another, then I am not permitted to do something else that I prefer, no matter how much I want to, unless this alternative also is commended by principles of imperfect duty (e.g., to develop one's talents). If this interpretation is correct, then principles of imperfect duty cannot be expressed "One ought to do x sometimes, to some extent" but are of the form "One ought to do x whenever one can, unless one chooses to follow instead some other principle of imperfect duty." Understood in this way, Kant's belief that we have an imperfect duty of beneficence is similar to Ross's belief that we have a prima facie obligation of beneficence.

There are, however, a number of reasons for rejecting this rigoristic interpretation. As Mary Gregor points out, the context of the controversial passage indicates that to make an "exception to the maxim of actions" would be to refuse to adopt some principle of imperfect duty as one's own guiding maxim.[4] The point of Kant's remark, then, is that what has been said about the latitude of imperfect duties is not to be construed as implying that a person has a free choice to adopt some of the maxims prescribed by moral law but to reject others. Whenever we adopt an indefinite maxim, we "limit" the range of application of previously adopted maxims. That is, we restrict somewhat the number of occasions on which we will act on those maxims. Thus what Kant seems to be saying is that, whereas we may (and indeed must) restrict the number of times we are prepared to act on one maxim (e.g., to develop our talents) by adopting another maxim (e.g., to promote the happiness of others), we may not let our concern for one maxim keep us from also adopting the other.

Another consideration against the rigoristic interpretation of imperfect duties is that Kant disassociates himself from the "fantastically virtuous" man, "who admits *nothing* morally *indifferent (adiaphora)* and strews all his steps with duties, as with man-traps" (DV 71 [409]). If we interpret Kant rigoristically, however, we impute to him the view that a person is never free from obligation unless it is impossible for him to do something for the happiness of others or towards the development of his own talents. He may be able to fulfill his obligation in any of several ways, but his acts will not be morally indifferent unless this condition is satisfied. Since it is virtually always possible to do something for others' happiness or to develop one's talents, the rigoristic interpretation leads to the conclusion that there is virtually nothing morally indifferent, contrary to what Kant says. Again, according to the *Groundwork,* the distinguishing mark of imperfect duties is that they allow some "exception in the interests of inclination" (G 89n [422]). This apparently means that imperfect duties allow us to do what we please on some occasions even if this is not an act of a kind prescribed by moral principles and even if we could on those occasions do something of a kind that is prescribed. For example,

---

[4]Mary Gregor, *Laws of Freedom* (New York: Barnes & Noble, 1963), p. 105.

though we have an imperfect duty of beneficence we may sometimes pass over an opportunity to make others happy simply
because we would rather do something else. This position, suggested in the *Groundwork,* is reaffirmed in *The Metaphysics of
Morals,* when Kant writes,

> . . . it is rather that legislative reason, which includes the whole spe-
> cies (and so myself with it) in its Idea of humanity as such (not of
> men), includes me, when it gives universal law, in the duty of be-
> nevolence, according to the principle that I am equal with all others
> besides me, and *permits* you to be benevolent to *yourself* under the
> condition of your being benevolent to every other man as well. (DV
> 118 [451])

Here Kant is not making the familiar point that we have an "indirect" duty to look after our own happiness in order to make ourselves less liable to temptation (see DV 47 [388]). The point is that,
since my own happiness counts morally as much as anyone else's
and might even be an obligatory end for me if I were not so ready
to pursue it, the principle of beneficence is to be construed as allowing me considerable freedom to pursue my own happiness
provided that I adopt and act on a maxim to promote the happiness of others also. This is incompatible with the rigoristic account of imperfect duties, which would allow me freedom to
pursue my own happiness only when I cannot do anything for the
happiness of others (or fulfill some other duty).[5]

Another obstacle to my interpretation is that there are passages
which raise doubts whether any clear-cut distinction between perfect and imperfect duty can be made. Kant says, for example, that
ethical duty must be conceived as wide (imperfect) duty and yet he
includes "perfect duties to oneself" among ethical duties. Since
this implies that the same duties are both perfect and imperfect, it

---

[5]The principle of beneficence, at least in *The Metaphysics of Morals,* is the very general
principle to promote the happiness of others. If this is an imperfect duty on the non-
rigoristic interpretation I have been defending, what follows is that it is not my duty to
promote the happiness of others on every occasion that I can without conflicting with
other principles. It does not follow, however, that I am perfectly free to refuse to help
a person in distress when only I can help and I can do so at little cost to myself; for this
may be (and surely should be) prohibited by other principles.

invites the suggestion that Kant uses the labels "perfect" and "imperfect" only to indicate the degree of latitude that a principle allows relative to certain others.[6] Thus "perfect" and "imperfect" do not place duties into exclusive categories: the so-called "perfect duties to oneself" are perfect relative to duties of love but imperfect relative to juridical duties. Though it explains the apparent contradiction, this proposal will not do as an account of Kant's intentions: for, while he speaks of imperfect duties as more or less wide, he clearly treats the division of duties into perfect and imperfect as exhaustive and exclusive. There are, however, other ways of explaining the apparent contradiction about perfect duties to oneself. Mary Gregor suggests that Kant regarded these as sharing some but not all of the features of ethical duties (DV xxix). That is, though they "arise in ethical legislation," they are not derived from "the first principle of ethics." Thus, though Kant had some reason to place them among ethical duties, he did not have these in mind when making his general, introductory comments about ethical duty. The same could be said about "indirectly ethical" duties, which are perfect duties though also ethical. This reply admits the contradiction but regards Kant's considered position to be that only the paradigm ethical duties ("duties of virtue" as opposed to the "indirectly ethical" and "perfect duties to oneself") are imperfect duties. Another explanation of the apparent contradiction might be the following. As I shall explain later, a principle of ethical duty, if fully stated, is always complex: it is, in effect, a conjunction of two principles, one prescribing actions of certain sorts and the other prescribing a moral motive. Our duty to act from moral motives, according to Kant, is always a wide or imperfect one. Thus every ethical duty is imperfect in at least one component. The other component may be a principle of the "Always . . . " or "Never . . . " sort and so may express a perfect duty.

A more serious problem arises when we consider the status of duties of respect to others. Kant classifies these as imperfect duties but calls them "narrow in comparison with duties of love" (DV 117 [449-50]). In general, the duty of respect to others is a duty to adopt "a maxim of limiting our self-esteem by the dignity of hu-

---

[6]See Eisenberg, "Basic Ethical Categories in Kant's *Tugendlehre*."

manity in another person"; more specifically, it consists in avoiding the vices of pride, calumny, and mockery (DV 135ff. [465ff.]). Here the principles we infer from the duty to adopt the general maxim of respect are obviously not expressible in the form "One ought to do (or avoid) *x* sometimes, to some extent." Why, then, are they called imperfect duties? As ethical duties, they (in part) prescribe a moral motive and this component is an imperfect duty; but the same can be said for the *perfect* ethical duties. Nor can the prohibitions of pride, calumny, and mockery be imperfect duties because they fail to specify "precisely" what actions are to be avoided; for this is also true of the *perfect* duties to avoid suicide, lying, self-stupefaction, and servility.

Duties of respect can be "imperfect duties" only in a broader sense than the one considered so far. The reason that they are regarded as imperfect duties is apparently that, like the other imperfect duties, they derive from a primary duty to adopt a very general maxim. This maxim ("to limit our self-esteem by the dignity of humanity in another person") is vague enough to allow considerable latitude of certain sorts. The principles of beneficence and self-improvement, however, allow a latitude of a different kind. The principles of respect, and to varying degrees every principle, allow latitude in the senses: (a) room for judgment in deciding whether or not a given principle is relevant to a particular situation, and (b) freedom to choose various ways of satisfying a principle in a particular situation once we decide that the principle applies. The principles of respect, however, are unlike the principles of beneficence and self-improvement in that they do not allow latitude in the sense (c) freedom to choose to do *x* or not on a given occasion, as one pleases, even though one knows that *x* is the sort of act that falls under the principle, provided that one is ready to perform acts of that sort on some other occasions.

This last kind of latitude, (c), is allowed by principles of the form "One ought to do (or avoid) *x* sometimes, to some extent," but not by principles of the form "Always (never) do *x*," regardless of how vaguely or precisely the relevant act is defined. Principles of both kinds, however, vary in (a) the amount of judgment required to apply the principle and (b) how much choice they leave us among various ways of doing what the principle requires of us on a given occasion. For example, it requires more judgment to decide whether an act violates the principle "Never act disrespect-fully" than it does if the principle is "Never say 'You fool!' " Sim-ilarly, there is more room for debate whether a given act is the sort commended by a principle if the principle is "Sometimes give a person what he most wants" than if it is "Sometimes give a teacher an apple." Again, "Always pay your taxes" leaves more choice among various ways to do what is required than does "Always pay your taxes in new one–dollar bills," and there are more ways to fulfill "Sometimes give to charity" than "Sometimes give clothes to the Salvation Army." Every principle will allow some latitude of the sorts (a) and (b), but some principles (namely, the "Always" and "Never" types) allow no latitude in the third sense, (c).

The inclusion of duties of respect among imperfect duties, then, requires us to broaden our initial account of this concept. An im-perfect duty, we must now say, is a duty to adopt a maxim which is so unspecific about what one is to do that the only principles of action that we can draw from this duty allow considerable latitude in senses (a) and (b). These principles may be of the "Never" or "Always" type, as are the principles of respect for others, but they will prescribe in relatively general terms, leaving a wide area for judgment in deciding when they apply and a substantial freedom of choice among specific actions which will satisfy them. A per-fect duty, by contrast, will be, not a duty to adopt a maxim, but a duty always (or never) to act in certain ways; and this duty may be stated either generally or specifically. This enables us to say that no duty can be both perfect and imperfect but also to admit that the principles of imperfect duty (principles of action inferred from the duty to adopt a maxim) may have the same form as principles of perfect duty. Thus, for example, both Kant's principle that one ought never to act in a servile way (perfect duty) and his principle that one ought never to mock others (imperfect duty) are relatively unspecific and of the "Never . . . " sort.

There is a sharper distinction, however, between perfect duties and the paradigms of imperfect duty, the duties of beneficence and the development of talents. These duties, as imperfect duties, are at first duties to adopt a very general maxim; but they differ from the duty of respect to others in that the only principles of action that we can infer from them (Kant believes) are indefinite princi-ples of the form "Sometimes, to some extent, one ought to x."

This is a form which principles of perfect duty never take. These widest principles of imperfect duty leave a latitude of a sort (namely, (c) above) that principles of perfect duty do not. Once we decide that a principle of perfect duty applies to our situation, we have no choice but to do what it prescribes, though there may be many ways of doing this. However, even if we know that one of the widest principles of imperfect duty applies, we may still do something we would rather do which is not commended by a principle of duty, provided that we stand ready to do acts of the prescribed sort on some other occasions.

Several noted philosophers have criticized Kant's attempt to divide duties into perfect and imperfect, but, if we interpret Kant as suggested above, some of the objections lose their force. Consider, for example, an argument well expressed by Roderick Chisholm, which, though not explicitly directed to Kant's distinction, has been adopted for this purpose by others.[7]

> The distinction has also been put more broadly: imperfect duties are said to be "indeterminate" in that we have latitude with respect to the manner in which we fulfill them, whereas perfect duties are not thus "indeterminate." But if the distinction amounted only to this, then, surely, it would require us to say that *no* duties are perfect. If it is my duty to pay you ten dollars then I have latitude in that I may pay by cash, check, or money order; or if it is my duty to pay you in cash, then I may pay by giving you a ten, or fives, or ones; or if it is my duty to give you a ten, then I may give you this one, that one, or the other one; or if it is my duty to give you this one, then I may hand it to you with the face looking up, or down, or right, or left; and so on, *ad infinitum*.

Clearly the sort of latitude Chisholm is thinking of here is what I labeled type (b), that is, choice among different ways of fulfilling a requirement. If the distinction between perfect and imperfect duties were simply a distinction between principles which allow this sort of latitude and those which do not, then there would indeed be no perfect duties. This, however, is not Kant's distinction.

[7]Chisholm, "Supererogation and Offense," p. 4. See also Eisenberg, "Basic Ethical Categories," p. 262.

Imperfect duties, at least in part, are duties to adopt a maxim, whereas perfect duties are not. One could fulfill a perfect duty by doing the right sort of act without having adopted any principles relevant to the case; but one could not fulfill an imperfect duty in this manner. Also, there is the important distinction untouched by Chisholm's argument, between perfect duties and the widest imperfect duties; and this is concerned with whether or not the principles allow a latitude of a certain kind (c). The principles of widest imperfect duty (beneficence, self-improvement) allow latitude in this sense whereas principles of perfect duty do not. It is not that perfect duties allow a lesser degree of latitude along a scale without end points. The distinction is as clear-cut as the difference between principles of the forms "Always do x" and "Sometimes do x."

Another objection is raised by W. D. Ross, in his commentary on the *Groundwork*.

[Kant's distinction between perfect and imperfect duties] is, in his own words, a distinction between duties that admit of no exception in favor of inclination, and those that do admit of such exception. That is, of course, an inadmissable distinction; what sort of duty would that be, which we are free to do or not to do as we feel inclined?[8]

There is, unfortunately, an ambiguity concerning "duty" which is apt to affect any discussion of these matters, and Ross's is no exception. In saying "You have a duty to . . . ," we may intend either to state a general principle or to declare that a person is required to do something on a particular occasion. Consider, for example, "It is your duty (here and now) to help that man" and "It is your duty to help others (sometimes)." Now suppose that Ross is speaking of particular duties in the passage quoted above. His point in this case would be that it is impossible for a person to have a duty to do something on a given occasion and yet be free to do it or not as he feels inclined. This is surely correct; but Kant does not deny it. When a person has an imperfect duty of beneficence, we may infer both (i) that it is his duty to adopt a maxim to promote the happiness of others sometimes and (ii) that it is his duty to promote the happiness of others sometimes but not that (iii) he has a duty on a given occasion to do a certain beneficent act. Thus Kant does not maintain that we have a duty to do a particular act which nevertheless we are free to do or not as we feel inclined.

Suppose, on the contrary, that Ross's argument is concerned with general principles of duty rather than requirements that a person has on a particular occasion. Then his point must be that it is inconsistent to assert both that it is a principle of duty, say, to promote happiness in others sometimes and that one may avoid doing so whenever (i.e., at all times) one wants to. Again, this is beyond doubt but is not an objection to Kant. What Kant maintains, in saying that we have an imperfect duty of beneficence, is not the inconsistent proposition just mentioned but rather that it is a principle of duty to promote the happiness of others sometimes and that, accordingly, one may avoid doing so at *any* time (though not at all times) that one feels inclined.

This way of putting Kant's position shows that an imperfect duty of beneficence is, in part, a duty to do this or that or the other beneficent act. Ross considers this possibility but says that it "is not the line which Kant actually takes."[9] His only reasons for believing this, apparently, are that Kant's examples of imperfect duties in the *Groundwork* are not stated in disjunctive form and, unlike perfect duties, are expressed as positive prescriptions rather than prohibitions. This leads Ross to conclude that the distinction between perfect and imperfect duties is simply a division between positive and negative duties, or "duties of abstinence and duties of performance." Ross's reasons, however, are not very persuasive. Imperfect duties are often expressed negatively in *The Metaphysics of Morals;* and even if they were all expressed as positive prescriptions, they could still be duties to do this or that or another beneficent act. Moreover, even though Kant's most general statements of the imperfect duties of beneficence and self-improvement are not explicitly in disjunctive form (or in the form "Sometimes . . . do *x*"), this way of expressing them may capture his meaning perfectly well. It is in fact reasonable to understand them

[9]Ibid., p. 45.

in this way, given the evidence in *The Metaphysics of Morals* against the more rigoristic interpretation.

II

Before we can proceed, we must sketch some of Kant's other moral categories. First, he distinguishes *juridical* and *ethical* duties. All duties included in Kant's system of principles belong to morality in a broad sense; hence juridical duties are not to be identified with requirements imposed by actual political authorities. They are distinguished from ethical duties by the fact that a juridical duty "implies corresponding *rights* of other people to exercise *compulsion*" whereas an ethical duty does not (DV 40–41 [383]). If I have a juridical duty to do something, someone has a right to compel me to do it; but this is not always (or usually) true for ethical duties. Moreover, ethical duties are the result of "ethical" or "inner" legislation whereas juridical duties are the result of "juridical" or "external" legislation. Ethical legislation "makes an action a duty and also makes duty the motive" (DV 16 [219]). Juridical legislation, in contrast, "does not include the motive in the law and so permits a motive other than the Idea of duty itself" (DV 16 [219]). Principles of ethical duty, then, tell us to do (or avoid) some act or to adopt some general maxim *and* to do so from a "motive of duty." Principles of juridical duty, however, prescribe no special motive.

For every juridical duty to do *x* there is also an ethical duty to do *x* from a motive of duty. There are more ethical duties than juridical ones, however, for ethics contains some special duties also: that is, some ethical duties tell us to do *x* from a motive of duty even though *x* is not prescribed by a juridical duty. An ethical duty corresponding to a juridical duty would be "Pay your debts from a sense of duty"; a special ethical duty would be "Promote the happiness of others from a sense of duty." The former is called an *indirectly* ethical duty; the latter, a *directly* ethical duty.

Directly ethical duties that enjoin us to pursue certain general ends are called *duties of virtue*. In discussing certain duties, Kant also distinguishes between *positive* and *negative* duties. Positive duties are duties of commission; negative duties are duties of omission. Duties are further divided according to the object to which the duty is owed. Since there are no duties to subhuman and superhuman creatures, according to Kant, there are only duties to oneself and duties to other men.

Kant does not hold that there are actually duties of every type that can be generated from these divisions. In fact only principles of the following kinds are proposed in *The Metaphysics of Morals*.

Juridical duty: to others; perfect; e.g., a duty to obey the state.
Ethical duty:[10]
    Indirectly ethical: to others; perfect; e.g., a duty to obey the state
           from a motive of duty.
    Directly ethical: (All prescribe also a motive of duty)
      To oneself
        Perfect; negative; e.g., a duty to avoid suicide.
        Imperfect; positive; e.g., duties of self-improvement.
      To others
        Imperfect
          narrower; negative, e.g., duties of respect.
          wider; negative or positive; e.g., duties of love.

It may be useful to present the main distinctions in a somewhat simplified manner. For this purpose let us overlook the fact that imperfect duties are initially duties to adopt certain maxims rather than to do this or that. What we shall consider, instead, are the principles of action that can be inferred from the duties to adopt the maxims. Accordingly, we should not try to reflect the general distinction between perfect duties and imperfect duties but only the difference between perfect duties and the widest imperfect duties. Also, since ethical duties "arise in ethical legislation" which "makes duty the motive," we may, somewhat artificially, add the prescription of a moral motive to every principle of ethical duty. The result is a division of principles into types which correspond, more or less, to Kant's categories of *perfect* duty, the *widest imperfect* duty, *ethical* duty, and *juridical* duty.

[10]In classifying these duties as "perfect" or "imperfect," we think only of that component which enjoins action (in contrast to the component which enjoins a motive of duty).

(1) *P* principles are principles of the form "Whenever *C*, one ought to do (or avoid) *x*" or "One ought never to do (or avoid) *x* when *C*."

(2) *WIP* principles are principles of the form "Sometimes when *C* one ought to do (or avoid) *x*." (*x* might be "something which promotes the end *e*.")

(3) *E* principles are principles of this form " . . . , and sometimes one ought to do (or avoid) this from a motive of duty," where the blank is filled with some *P* or *WIP* principle.

(4) *J* principles are *P* principles such that someone has a right to compel persons to comply with the principle. That is, the principle is the sort of principle which a person could be compelled to follow, someone *A* is not prohibited by valid *P* principles from coercing a person to comply, and when *A* attempts to compel a person to comply then everyone else is required by valid *P* principles not to interfere.

Kant's ideal, apparently, was a system of valid moral principles that satisfies these conditions:

(5) A principle is a morally valid principle if and only if it is derivable from, or is warranted in some way by, a supreme moral principle, the Categorical Imperative.

(6) The system of valid principles will be consistent in the following senses. First, the principles will be formally consistent. For example, "Whenever *A*, do *B*" and "Sometimes when *A*, do not do *B*" cannot both be valid. Second, valid *P* principles will not give conflicting directions for a particular situation. That is, for any particular situation, it must be in fact possible for a person to satisfy all valid *P* principles which are relevant to it. Third, *WIP* principles must satisfy the condition that no valid principle will ever commend what is prohibited by valid *P* principles or discourage what is required by valid *P* principles. Thus, in effect, every valid *WIP* principle will include in its conditions, *C*, the rider "(when) not contrary to valid *P* principles."

Notice that (6) has the effect of making all *P* principles take precedence over *WIP* principles but it does not imply that valid *WIP* principles never give conflicting advice. One valid *WIP* principle might commend something (e.g., an act of beneficence) for a given situation even though this is incompatible with something (e.g., developing talents) commended by another valid *WIP* principle.

This way of representing Kant's types of duty preserves the important relations he attributes to them. For example, every *J* principle will be a *P* principle, but not conversely. No *J* principle will be an *E* principle or a *WIP* principle. No principle will be both *P* and *WIP*, but all principles will be either *P* or *WIP* or a conjunction of principles of these types. At least one part of every *E* principle ("and do [or avoid] this from a motive of duty") is a *WIP* principle. The other part of *E* principles may be either a *P* principle (as in "indirectly ethical" duties) or *WIP* principles (as in most directly ethical duties). If one assumes, as Kant did, that one has a duty to fulfill moral requirements from a motive of duty, then every valid principle will be either an *E* principle or included as part of a valid *E* principle. Thus "all duties . . . belong to ethics."

III

In *The Metaphysics of Morals* Kant implies that some acts have positive moral worth, some have negative moral worth, and some have no moral worth at all. In order to determine the moral worth of a given act, we must know the kinds of moral principles relevant to it.

The pattern by which moral worth is attributed to actions is suggested by the following passage.

> If someone does *more* in the way of duty than the law can compel him to do, his action is *meritorious (meritum)*. If he does only the *exact* thing required by the law, he does what is *due (debitum)*. Finally, if he does less than the law requires, this is moral guilt *(demeritum)*. (DV 27 [227])

This tells us that an action is *meritorious* (of positive moral worth) if it "does more in the way of duty" than juridical duty; for "what the law can compel" is, as we have seen, simply juridical duty. Doing more in the way of duty can only be something which fulfills an ethical duty, that is, either fulfills a perfect (e.g., juridical) duty from a motive of duty or conscientiously promotes an end prescribed by a principle of imperfect duty. An action is *due* (or neutral in moral worth) if it conforms to juridical duty but is not motivated by a sense of duty; for this, in the context of laws that "can compel," is "the exact thing required by the law." Later Kant indicates that a person only renders what is due if, not motivated by duty, he avoids what is prohibited by perfect (ethical) duties to oneself and conforms to the duties of respect to others (DV 83ff. [420ff.], 138 [468]). Failure to conform to juridical duty involves *guilt* or demerit; for this is "doing less than the law requires." Also, Kant implies later that acts have this negative moral worth if they are contrary to perfect duties to oneself or duties of respect to others or if they result from the agent's refusal to adopt a principle of imperfect duty.

In another passage Kant represents merit and guilt as positive and negative quantities along the same scale of moral worth.

> To fulfill [duties of virtue] is *merit (meritum = +a)*; but to transgress them is not so much *guilt (demeritum = −a)* as rather *lack* of moral *worth* (=0), unless the agent makes it his principle not to submit to these duties. (DV 49 [390])

The concept of moral worth here is apparently the same as in the *Groundwork*. There Kant held that actions have moral worth only if done from a motive of duty, whereas actions merely in accord with duty have no moral worth. The account in *The Metaphysics of Morals* is not incompatible with this but presents a more complex picture. Consider, for example, the imperfect (ethical) duty of beneficence. Fully stated, this has two parts: (a) one ought to promote the happiness of others (sometimes) and (b) one ought to do so (sometimes) from a motive of duty. Now what sorts of acts will be "in accord with" this duty and what sort "contrary to" it? There are a number of cases, and moral worth varies accordingly. First, one might do something to promote the happiness of another from a sense of duty. Here the act has positive moral worth (+a). Second, one might do something to promote the happiness of another out of love, without a sense of duty. Here the act has no moral worth (0). Third, one might do nothing to promote the happiness of another but, instead, do something that promotes a different end prescribed by a principle of imperfect duty. This, if done conscientiously, has positive moral worth (+a). Fourth, one might refuse to do something for the happiness of another because one has a principle against helping others. Here the act has negative moral worth (−a). Finally, one might do something one wants to do rather than take an opportunity to make someone else happy. Provided that other moral principles are irrelevant and one still makes it his principle to help others sometimes, his act has no moral worth (o).

If we fail to keep in mind the differences between types of duty, we are tempted to attribute to Kant the following, appealingly simple, scheme for distributing moral worth.

Juridical duties (perfect):
    (1) Actions in accord with them are due   (o)
    (2) Actions not in accord with them bring guilt or demerit (−a)
Ethical duties (imperfect):
    (1) Actions in accord with them are meritorious   (+a)
    (2) Actions not in accord with them lack moral worth   (o)

This simple account is inadequate for a number of reasons. It does not reflect Kant's belief that one is guilty (−a) if one fails to avoid what is prohibited by special ethical duties, the perfect duties to oneself and duties of respect to others. More importantly, the scheme fails to allow for the variety of ways in which acts can be "in accord with" and "contrary to" the wider principles of imperfect duty, e.g., beneficence. This complexity is illustrated by the five cases distinguished in the preceding paragraph. Also the scheme above does not show how moral worth varies as the duty is positive or negative.

A more comprehensive representation of how the types of duty determine moral worth is given below. Let x stand for an "external" action, E for an end promoted by x, and M for a sense of duty. The symbols "+a," "−a," and "o" are meant to represent, respectively, positive moral worth, negative moral worth, and mere lack of moral worth. A question mark indicates that there is no clear evidence how Kant would attribute moral worth in that case. Since there is an "indirectly ethical" duty to conform to every juridical duty from a motive of duty, juridical duties are not listed separately. The negative duties of love, e.g., "Avoid envy," are not represented because they raise special problems. Again for simplicity, we presuppose that only one principle is relevant to the acts in question.

	Where there is no M		Where there is M	
	Doing x	Not doing x	Doing x	Not doing x
Indirectly ethical duty				
Positive: "Do x from M"	o	−a	+a	?
Negative: "Avoid x from M"	−a	o	?	+a
Directly ethical duty				
A. Perfect duties to oneself and duties of respect to others (all negative): "Avoid x from M"	−a	o	?	+a
B. Wider imperfect duties (e.g., self-improvement and beneficence), positive: "Promote E from M" or "Sometimes do x from M"	o	o (or −a)[11]	+a	?

The interesting distinction for present purposes is not that between perfect and imperfect duties but that between the wider imperfect duties (beneficence and self-improvement) and all other duties. The distinguishing feature of the former is this: when we do something in accord with the wider imperfect duties, our action may be either meritorious or neutral in moral worth but, except in the rare case of those who altogether reject the moral principle, failure to take an opportunity to act in accord with these duties brings no guilt or demerit. In other words, acting in accord with the principles of beneficence and self-improvement may be morally praiseworthy but, with one exception, not doing so even when one knows one has an opportunity is not blameworthy. By contrast, if we knowingly do not act in accord with other duties we are said to be guilty.

One should note that the moral worth in question here is not the same as the "intrinsic value" or "dignity" of persons. Kant ascribes to human personality a worth which is not diminished or

[11]The moral worth is negative (−a) only if the agent acts on a principle to refuse to promote E.

increased by what the person does. It depends not on his actions but upon his capacities. This is a man's "inner worth" as a person, based on the fact that he is a moral agent rather than upon his moral achievements. The moral worth which I have been discussing is, in contrast, the moral worth of a man's actions. This varies with what a man does, his motives, and the type of duties that apply.

It should be noted, also, that we cannot assume that the worth of a person's character can be determined by summing up, as it were, the positive and negative worth of his actions. One reason is that a person's motives, on which his moral worth depends, cannot be known with certainty. Also, it would be simple-minded to suppose that we could fairly assign numerical values to the worth of actions. However, in using the symbols "+a," "−a," and "o," Kant suggests that positive and negative moral worth are commensurate, that they are in principle measureable on the same scale. It follows that, if the worth of a person's character is fixed by the worth of his actions, then acts of conscientious generosity may compensate for acts of injustice. The man who is a liar and a thief but is generous on principle may be as worthy a person as the honest miser. This is a consequence that Kant could never accept. One cannot make up for violations of strict duty by doing more towards moral ends than is strictly required.

Again, it is important not to confuse the distinction between meritorious acts (of positive moral worth) and acts that involve guilt (or negative moral worth) with the overlapping distinction between virtuous and vicious action. At one point Kant invites confusion by using the same quantitative symbols when he contrasts virtue and vice.

> Virtue (= +a) is opposed to *negative lack of virtue* (moral weakness = o) as its logical opposite (*contradictorie oppositum*); but it is opposed to vice (= −a) as its *real opposite (contrarie s. realiter oppositum).* (DV 42 [384])

The point, however, is not that virtue is the same as merit but that virtue and vice, like merit and guilt, are "real opposites," not merely contraries. Virtue is the strength of one's will to fulfill one's duties in the face of obstacles. Vice is a bad disposition, i.e., a will not to do one's duty or to do wrong. A virtuous act (i.e., one that displays such strength of will) is meritorious, unless perhaps the agent is mistaken in thinking the act is a duty; but a meritorious act need not be virtuous. One might, for example, fulfill a duty from a motive of duty in the absence of obstacles and temptations that require strength of will. Again, acts that display vice will bring guilt, but one may incur guilt without acting with vice. For example, one might have guilt for violating a perfect duty through weakness without having a will to do wrong or to neglect one's duties.

IV

Where, then, in Kant's complex scheme should we look for supererogatory acts? Clearly they cannot be identified with acts that fulfill imperfect duties, for we have seen that duties of respect for others are imperfect. These are given in principles of the "Never . . . " variety, and to fail to satisfy them, except perhaps unintentionally, brings guilt upon the agent. Nor can we equate supererogatory acts with those that fulfill principles of wider imperfect duty, such as beneficence. For in some circumstances promoting the happiness of others will be obligatory; e.g., if one's only alternatives on that occasion are contrary to perfect duty or if one who has continually neglected to help others is faced with his last opportunity. In the first case the act is obligatory because it happens to be the only way to avoid other wrongs, and in the second case it is obligatory because it is the only way, given the agent's past record, to satisfy the limited demands of the principle, "Sometimes promote the happiness of others."

If Kant's scheme has a place for supererogatory acts, then, they will be found as a subclass of acts which fulfill principles of wider imperfect duty. The best candidate for a supererogatory act is an act which (a) is of a sort commended by a principle of wider imperfect duty, (b) is motivated by a sense of duty (or, perhaps, respect for moral reasons), (c) is neither forbidden nor required by another, more stringent duty (i.e., does not fall under valid P principles), (d) is in a context where no alternative is required by more stringent duty and there is at least one alternative that is neither forbidden by more stringent duty nor commended by other principles of wide duty, and (e) is done by an agent who has adopted the relevant principle of wider imperfect duty and has often and continually acted on that principle.

Consider an example. Suppose a man, who had conscientiously helped others and given to charities all his life, buys for a neighborhood child a treat that is neither needed nor solicited but is quite welcome. The giver, a naturally cold person, is not prompted by kindly or sympathetic feelings but a strong desire to do the sort of act commended by moral principles. Far from rejecting Kant's limited principle of beneficence, he is disposed out of a (perhaps misguided) respect for it to do more of the sort of act it directs than it strictly requires. Imagine, too, that other moral principles are irrelevant in this case. He is not, for example, contributing to the gluttony of a greedy and obese child, and there is nothing else he is obliged to do with the money.

What would Kant say of cases such as this? First, the act is not demanded by any principle of duty, perfect or imperfect, though it is the sort of act which an indefinite principle of imperfect duty requires us to do sometimes and which a good man, who has adopted the principle as his own, will do sometimes. Moreover, the act is meritorious, i.e., of positive moral worth, but its omission would not bring guilt, i.e., be of negative moral worth. In short, the act is neither obligatory nor forbidden but is rather a good and praiseworthy thing to do whereas its omission is neither forbidden nor required, neither praiseworthy nor blameworthy.

Supererogation has been variously defined, and the implications of the different conceptions have yet to be worked out in a fully satisfactory way. It is obvious, however, when we compare Kant's position with what recent philosophers call "supererogatory" that it is far less misleading to grant that Kant allows for supererogatory acts than to deny it. Although Kant's terminology cannot be matched perfectly with recent counterparts, there is enough affinity to show that it is a mistake to insist that Kant divided all actions, oversimply, into the forbidden, the obligatory, and the indifferent.

Consider, first, the account of supererogation given by Roderick Chisholm.[12] According to this, a supererogatory act is one that is neither forbidden nor obligatory but is still good to do. Alternatively, in Chisholm's terms, we may say that a supererogatory act is one that is good to do but neither good nor bad not to do. Now if we let "good to do" stand for positive moral worth and "bad to do" for negative moral worth, Kant's supererogation candidates are formally the same as Chisholm's supererogatory acts: good to do but neither good nor bad not to do. The difference is that for Kant "good" here has to do with the moral praiseworthiness of an act whereas for Chisholm it is defined in terms of "ought to exist." In each case, however, the good act in question is not required or obligatory and its omission is not wrong or forbidden. Moreover, Kant's conception of a non-obligatory but praiseworthy act has at least as much claim to the title of supererogation as Chisholm's acts that are non-obligatory but ought to exist; for the notion of supererogation has its roots in the official Church doctrine that saints can earn and store up credits with God by their unusually fine deeds. It was not simply that they did acts that ought to have existed but that they did what, from the divine point of view, was worthy of special praise and credit.

In his article "Supererogation and Rules" Joel Feinberg distinguishes two conceptions of "going beyond duty."[13] One is the idea of "duty-plus" or "institutional over-subscriptions." These are acts that do measurably more than is required by some law-like rule but are still acts of the same kind. Such acts are not necessarily praiseworthy and may have little to do with the overall worth of a man's character. They simply increase his balance on a quasi-institutional accounting of merits and demerits. The other idea of supererogation is that of acts which are commended by imprecise "maxims" or "counsels of wisdom" but are not duties or obligations. These include both small favors and praiseworthy, abnormally risky non-duties (e.g., the sacrifice of a doctor who volunteers for service in a foreign, plague-ridden city). The worth of such acts is not seen as merit points to offset definite demerits but rather as an important factor in the assessment of a man's

[12]Chisholm, "Supererogation and Offense."
[13]Joel Feinberg, "Supererogation and Rules," *Ethics* 71 (1961): 276–88.

worth "all things considered." Now, despite what Kant's symbols "+a," "−a," and "o" suggest, the acts which are Kant's best candidates to be called "supererogatory" are more like Feinberg's second type than his first. They are prompted by our adoption of indefinite maxims to promote certain general ends, and these do not specify exactly what or how much a good man will do. Thus they are not simply cases of doing the sort of thing a definite lawlike rule requires but more of it than the rule demands. Moreover, they are always of positive moral worth. That is, unlike "dutyplus," they are regarded as morally praiseworthy and thus always relevant, at least as evidence, in the overall assessment of the character of a person. Their worth is not a measurable quantity which Kant would balance against the demerits resulting from dereliction of (perfect) duty. Nevertheless, like Feinberg's second type of supererogatory acts, Kant's supererogation candidates are viewed as praiseworthy but not wrong to omit. Favors are good examples of both conceptions, and at least some instances of risky action for the common good would be examples too. There are differences, of course. For example, Kant attributes moral worth only to acts motivated by a sense of duty. Also for Kant the fact that an act involves sacrifice greater than normally required by duty is of no special significance in determining whether it is supererogatory or required, though it does affect the degree of moral worth which the act has.

There seems, then, to be good reason to grant that Kant has a place for supererogatory acts, though his conception of them differs in some ways from recent conceptions.[14] What remains now is to consider some natural objections to this position.

(1) One may sense an air of paradox about Kant's position, as I have stated it, because it implies that the only acts that are super-

---

[14] My support for this conclusion has been drawn from *The Metaphysics of Morals*, in which Kant discussed these matters most thoroughly. In *Religion within the Limits of Reason Alone* Kant seems to take a different position (R 44 [48–49], 18n [22–23]). His main point here, as in a pertinent passage in the *Critique of Practical Reason* (CPrR 158–59 [155–56]), is that one should not try to teach morality by encouraging a special awe for "supermeritorious" acts; but he also says "all the goodness [a man] can ever perform is still his simple duty." If this means that every particular good act is obligatory (hence wrong not to do), then it is incompatible with the position of *The Metaphysics of Morals*. If, however, it means only that every good act is the sort commended by some principle of duty (e.g., imperfect duty), then there is no incompatibility.

erogatory ("beyond duty") for Kant are acts motivated by a sense of duty. It seems, then, that one can do something supererogatory only if he mistakenly thinks that it is his duty. Though not inconsistent, this is peculiar. In reply, we might suggest that it is not an unreasonable extension of Kant's position to say that what is required for moral worth is not a motive to do one's *duty* but a motive to do what is demanded or encouraged by moral considerations. Kant was preoccupied with duty in much of his ethical thinking, but his main point, surely, was that moral worth depends upon one's disposition to live by whatever demands and ideals are implicit in a rational, moral life. If doing a certain favor for a person is not morally obligatory, then Kant would not want him to do it in the mistaken belief that it is. The most that he could expect of a moral-minded man is that he does the favor because he wants to do the sort of thing encouraged by moral principles even if on this occasion they do not demand it of him. We may doubt whether this is as worthy a motive as kindness, but that is another matter.

(2) Another source of dissatisfaction may be that the moral principle which one would be following in doing something supererogatory is still called a principle of *duty*, even if "imperfect" and "ethical." How, one may wonder, can I be going "beyond duty" if I am guided by a principle of duty? Kant's terminology of "imperfect" and "perfect" duty does confuse the issues. It is as if Kant started to work out a moral theory on the model of law-like strict duties, and then, discovering that there is more to morality than duty, still retained the old labels for types of duty rather than spoil the symmetry of his theory by changing to more natural expressions. For example, what Kant is concerned to say about beneficence is (i) it is a duty to adopt a maxim of beneficence, and therefore (ii) it is a duty to promote the happiness of others sometimes, but also (iii) when one has satisfied these minimum and rather indefinite requirements, one may promote their happiness or not, as one pleases, but to do so with the proper motive will always be of positive moral worth. Kant tried to say all of this with his restrictive terminology of duty when it could be put more simply by making an early distinction between what is obligatory and what is merely good to do. Nevertheless, though Kant's terms are confusing, there is nothing in what he says to imply that it

is a person's duty on a particular occasion to do an act if it has the features of those I have described as his best candidates for supererogation.

(3) Paul Eisenberg has argued that failure to take an opportunity to fulfill an imperfect duty is an offense, that is, something not strictly wrong but still somewhat bad.[15] If so, then the omission of an act of beneficence is never morally indifferent. This weakens the case for regarding some beneficent acts as supererogatory, for it implies that a thoroughly conscientious person would never willingly let an occasion pass for making others happy (unless required to do so by some other duty), and it seems odd to call an act supererogatory if it is what any thoroughly conscientious man would strive to do. The grounds for Eisenberg's position, however, are questionable. The main evidence cited is the following passage.

> To neglect mere duties of love is *lack of virtue (peccatum)*. But to neglect duty that proceeds from the *respect* due to every man as such is *vice (vitium)*. (DV 134 [464])

Eisenberg argues, quite rightly, that "neglect of duties of love" cannot mean either (a) rejection of the principle of beneficence or (b) not doing anything beneficent. He concludes that it means not doing all one could to promote the happiness of others. The inference, however, is unwarranted. Surely what is intended is just what "neglect" suggests, namely, being lax, letting one's actions fall short of one's commitments to the end. A man neglects the principle of beneficence if, though he accepts the principle and is occasionally guided by it, his pattern of action over a time shows him approaching all too close to the minimum amount of effort on behalf of others that would be exerted by a person who had normal opportunities and adopted the indefinite maxim of beneficence in good spirit. Thus, neglecting one's duties of love is not something one does on a particular occasion, still less on every occasion when one passes up an opportunity to make someone happy. Therefore, though Kant obviously thought such neglect bad in some way, there is no reason to suppose he thought of every

---

[15]Eisenberg, "Basic Ethical Categories," pp. 265–66.

omission of an act of beneficence (when other duties are irrelevant) as an "offense." It should be noted, too, that the defect associated with neglect of duties of love is "lack of virtue (*peccatum*)," not negative moral worth or even "somewhat bad" conduct. Virtue, or strength of one's will in following moral principles, is a character trait, not the value of a particular action; and *peccatum*, despite its original connotations, is Kant's most general term for any transgression, i.e., whatever falls off from what should be. This includes unintentional wrongs, and even poor judgment in working out the practical problems posed by two conflicting, indefinite principles (DV 50 [390], 23 [224], 98n (433n]). Thus Kant's point in the passage quoted above is not that one does something bad whenever one passes over a chance to make someone happy but that one who, having adopted the maxim of beneficence, continually lets these opportunities pass gives evidence at some point of the character defect of weakness of will.

(4) Paul Eisenberg places most of the weight of his contention that Kant has no place for supererogation upon the following passage.

> To fulfill the first [duties of love] is meritorious (in relation to the other person); but to fulfill the second [duties of respect] is to render the other only what is *due* to him.[16]

The parenthetical expression "in relation to the other person," Eisenberg believes, indicates that duties of love are meritorious only *in the opinion* of the other person. That is, fulfilling duties of love is actually obligatory but those who benefit from them view them, and should view them, as if they were meritorious. Eisenberg's reading of the quoted sentence, I think, is mistaken, or at least too dubious to override the other evidence. In other passages Kant clearly indicates that the fulfillment of an imperfect duty from the proper motive is meritorious. Even if "meritorious in relation to the other person" means "to be viewed as meritorious by the other," it does not follow that fulfilling a duty of love is not

---

[16]DV 115 [449]. Eisenberg's contention is that Kant denied supererogation in *The Metaphysics of Morals*. He cites evidence in the *Critique of Practical Reason* that earlier Kant acknowledged supererogatory acts.

really meritorious. Moreover, the context suggests a different reading. Just before the sentence quoted above Kant makes the point that when we do something for a person in accord with our duties of love that person is placed under an obligation (of gratitude) to us whereas the same is not true for duties of respect. In this context, then, the point of the quoted sentence seems to be to say why one who receives a favor (fulfillment of a duty of love) incurs an obligation of gratitude and one who is only accorded respect does not. The answer is that the favor, unlike respect, was not *due* to the recipient but was more than he could claim as his right. In saying that the particular beneficent act is "meritorious in relation to the other person," Kant is denying that it fulfills an *obligation to that person*. This leaves it open whether or not, considered simply as one of his acts, it is obligatory or meritorious.

9

Kant's Anti-Moralistic Strain

For many people Kant is the paradigm of a moralistic philosopher. He is famous for his rigorous standards, his eloquence on the importance of duty, and his insistence on refusing to make exceptions to moral principles in the interests of utility. He saw the moral life as an unending struggle between reason and desire, and yet he could hardly be regarded as sympathetic with liars, drunkards, and adulterers who, in his opinion, yield to natural temptation (MPV 85–93 [424–32]). Love and pity had no moral worth for him aside from an accompanying devotion to duty for duty's sake, and commitment to duty was, he believed, the only practical manifestation of the special metaphysical status that separates human beings from animals. But, surprisingly, there are aspects of Kant's views that are strongly opposed to moralism, at least so far as this concerns judgments about the moral deserts of others. Though he believed that our moral deserts vary with the extent of our commitment to duty, in several important ways he resisted the idea that the way we treat others should depend upon our judgments of their moral worth. Since Kant is famous for insisting that ethics is practical, or action-guiding, it is remarkable that to a large extent he regarded opinions about the variable merits of persons as impractical.

In what follows I first trace the several ways in which Kant is anti-moralistic with regard to judgments about others. Those familiar with *The Metaphysics of Morals* may find Kant's views on

punishment the least likely place to find this strain, but nevertheless I argue that Kant's official theory of punishment is less retrib-
utivistic than commonly supposed. Next I consider various
possible reasons why, despite his rigorism and the importance he
placed on morality, he should be, relatively speaking, so restrained
regarding the use of moral judgments about others.

I

It must be admitted that Kant often sounds moralistic when
writing about the immorality of others, in both his books and his
letters,[1] but the main principles he espoused do not urge us to treat
people in accord with our opinion of their moral merits or lack of
merit. Consider, for example, the various forms of the Categorical
Imperative (G 88ff. [420–25]). The first tells us to restrict our
maxims to what we could will for a world in which everyone follows suit. Whether others are in fact motivated to do so, or to restrict themselves by the same principle, is not considered relevant.
In using the test we are asked to consider everyone, not just the
morally deserving. And in his lectures Kant strongly urges us
against modifying our beliefs about what we ought to do from an
awareness that, due to human weakness, many will not conform
to our highest moral standards.[2] This desire to leave aside worries
about how many will in fact conform to a rule is, I think, a source
of problems in applying Kant's formula. For many of us believe
that what we would will if we could be assured that all would conform is often different from what we should will when we know
that, from weakness, meanness, or whatever, many will not in
fact follow our principles or any moral principles. Maxims never
to lie or to give only a calculated "fair share" to charity would be
more acceptable in a world where everyone adopted Kant's formula than in our world where lies are sometimes necessary to

---

[1] For a striking example, see the response to Maria von Herbert in *Kant: Philosophical
Correspondence, 1759–99,* ed. A. Zweig (Chicago: University of Chicago Press, 1967), p.
188 [331–34].

[2] "Moral Laws must never take human weakness into account, but must be enunci-
ated in their perfect holiness, purity and morality, without any regard to man's actual
constitution" (LE 66).

prevent murders and rich people often refuse to give anything to charity.[3] These problems may be solvable in Kant's theory, but the fact that they arise illustrates his reluctance to rely on judgments about the extent and depth of corruption in others.

Kant's second formula, which says to treat humanity as an end in itself, also prescribes ways of treating others independently of their moral merits. He does not say that morally upright people should never be used merely as means but that no one should be; and the principle is supposed to hold without exception. The dignity which Kant ascribes to all persons as "ends in themselves" is said to be grounded in their autonomy of will, and this is a property, he argues later, that must be attributed to every rational person with a will (G 103 [436], 115–16 [448]). The context makes clear that this does not mean only conscientious and dutiful persons, but virtually all adult human beings; for autonomy is a necessary condition of even having moral obligations. Thus all persons capable of having moral obligation are thought to have dignity, no matter how immoral they may be.

Kant's ideal of a "kingdom of ends," insofar as it is action-guiding at all, asks us to decide what laws we would legislate if members of an ideal community. We are then to follow those laws without exception, regardless of whether or not we believe that others will do so.

> Now a kingdom of ends would actually come into existence through maxims which the categorical imperative prescribes as a rule for all rational beings, *if these maxims were universally followed.* Yet even if a rational being were himself to follow such a maxim strictly, he cannot count on everybody else being faithful to it. . . . But in spite of this the law 'Act on the maxims of a member who makes universal laws for a merely possible kingdom of ends' remains in full force, since the command is categorical.[4]

Thus, at least at the highest level of moral deliberation, whether or not others are morally worthy, or even dutiful, is not to be taken into account.

---

[3]This problem is discussed in my paper "Kant's Utopianism," reprinted in this volume.

[4]G 106 [438]. An interpretation of this ideal as an action guide is given in my paper "The Kingdom of Ends," reprinted in this volume.

When we turn to the more specific ethical principles sketched in *The Metaphysics of Morals,* here too we find surprisingly little qualification concerning how to deal differently with those judged to be exceptionally meritorious or immoral. The principle of benevolence, for example, tells us simply to promote the happiness of others without expecting anything in return (MPV 117 [453]). The argument for the duty does not mention what people deserve but only what they want and need. Moreover, Kant explicitly notes that people do not have to be meritorious in order to be appropriate objects of benevolence.

> The maxim of benevolence (practical love of mankind) is a duty of all men toward one another. One may or may not find them worthy of love according to the ethical law of perfection. . . . (MPV 115 [450])

Kant does at one point add the qualification that one should promote only the "permissible" ends of others (MPV 46 [388]). And in his "fragments of a moral catechism" he has the teacher telling the pupil that, supposing he had the power to make everyone happy, he should first inquire to what extent each person is worthy of happiness (MPV 149 [480–81]). The context, however, makes it reasonably clear that the point is not that each should be made happy, or left unhappy, according to his deserts but rather that one should not make people happy by giving them the means to indulge their special vices: e.g., wine to the drunkard, soft pillows to the sluggard, and captivating manners to the deceiver. Thus the principle of benevolence is qualified by a principle that one should not encourage vice, but this does not mean that in general we should try to reward the worthy and deprive the unworthy.

Many would agree, perhaps, that benevolence should not be constrained by judgments of moral desert, but how about respect? The principles of respect for persons are the second major category of Kant's ethical principles regarding others. Rather than urging respect in accord with merit, Kant makes the basis of respect the "humanity" in each person, which is something no one loses, no matter how immoral he may be (MPV 127 [462]). Although one sometimes cannot help thinking little of some people as compared to others, one must nevertheless give each person respect as a human being (MPV 128 [463]). On this basis Kant condemns mockery, calumny, and pride which "demands from others a respect which it denies them" (MPV 131 [465]). The vicious person, Kant says, makes himself unworthy of respect, but despite that we should not deny him all respect (MPV 128 [463]). Thus, though Kant was not opposed to execution, he regarded certain punishments (such as drawing and quartering, cutting off an ear) as forbidden because of the disrespect they show.

It would be an exaggeration, of course, to suggest that Kant thought that we should be blind to apparent differences in moral worth. He grants that one cannot avoid thinking less of some people than others, and he was not altogether opposed to reproaching others in theory or in practice.[5] The amount of gratitude owed to a benefactor is said to vary with how disinterested we judge his motives in giving to be (MPV 120 [456]); and when a person becomes flagrantly vicious, we are urged to disassociate from him (MPV 140–41 [474]). What is remarkable, however, is that one so deeply committed to the view that people differ in their worthiness to be happy did not conclude, as did Ross, that we should try in general to see that happiness is distributed proportionately according to merit. The *Summum Bonum,* Kant tells us, is happiness combined with the worthiness to be happy, and yet our duty is to promote our own worthiness and other people's happiness (CPrR 115 [110]; MPV 44–46 [386–88]). No impartial spectator could look with approval, he says, on the uninterrupted prosperity of the thoroughly corrupt (G 61 [393]); but no conclusion is drawn that one should in general try to make the wicked suffer. The emphasis instead is on the duty to respect every human being and to make the (permissible) ends of others one's own ends.

II

When we turn to Kant's theory of punishment, we naturally expect to find the practical import of judgments of moral worth to be most evident. In fact Kant is often taken to be the par-

[5]See, for example, CPrR 103 [100–101] and the above-mentioned letter to Maria von Herbert.

adigm retributivist regarding punishment. There is no denying that he had some harsh and inflexible views on the subject, and one searches in vain for a tone of compassion or sympathetic understanding of criminals. A close examination of the theory, however, yields a more complex picture, at least of Kant's official views of punishment in *The Metaphysics of Morals*. The principles are stern but not in the fullest sense retributive; and their avowed purpose is not to see that happiness and misery are proportionate to moral desert but rather to secure a system of fair laws that maximize liberty.

Kant did accept four points which are commonly associated with a retributive theory of punishment (MEJ 99–108 [331–38]). First, he believed, as most of us do, that only the guilty should be punished. That is, the official coercive powers of the state exercised through fines, imprisonment, execution, etc. should be turned on an individual only when he has violated public laws, duly promulgated. Attempts to "punish" the innocent with imprisonment for arbitrary reasons of state, or for the sake of special utilitarian benefits, are out of the question. The authority for punishment comes from the general rationale for government coercion, which is just only when applied through general laws (MEJ 34ff. [230–33]). Second, Kant held, as fewer of us do, that all the guilty should be punished. Especially he thought it unjust to release criminals, or to waive standard penalties, in special circumstances because doing so might have better consequences.

> The law concerning punishment is a categorical imperative, and woe to him who rummages around in the winding paths of a theory of happiness looking for some advantage to be gained by releasing the criminal from punishment or by reducing the amount of it. . . . (MEJ 100 [331])

This means not only that threats should be ignored, as for example when a criminal has powerful friends demanding his release, but also that penalties should not be set aside for those who volunteer for dangerous medical experiments or for those who have families to support. Even if a society were to dissolve itself, its members to disperse to other communities, the last murderer should be executed (MEJ 102 [333]). To say that judges and juries should not refuse to invoke the penalties prescribed by law does not, of course, imply that legislators should not take utilitarian considerations into account in assigning penalties to different sorts of offenses; but, as we shall see, Kant was opposed to such flexibility on the legislative level as well. Third, Kant seems to hold that the severity of punishments should be proportionate to the seriousness of the crimes. Seriousness can be judged by several standards, but that he advocated proportionality of some sort is evident. Thus, for example, even if theft could be prevented by making it a capital crime, this would not be regarded as just. Fourth, the rule for determining the proper degree and kind of punishment is the *jus talionis:* an eye for an eye, and anyone who commits murder must die (MEJ 101 [332]). All other standards, Kant says, are variable and fluctuating. The *jus talionis* apparently appealed to Kant not only because he thought it offered a fixed and rigorous standard but because it guaranteed the sort of proportionality he thought important and suggested types of punishment intuitively appropriate to each crime.

Most people, I suspect, will find some of these views (e.g., the second and fourth) unreasonably harsh; and at least the last one raises notorious problems of interpretation (e.g., about how to repay in kind the drunk driver, the blackmailer, and the rapist). But, however harsh and troublesome they may be, these points do not yet constitute the most extreme form of retributivism. A utilitarian in fact could accept all of them if he had the appropriate beliefs about the world, e.g., that punishing all and only the guilty in accord with *jus talionis* would maximize happiness in the long run. The thoroughgoing retributivist will distinguish himself from such a hypothetical utilitarian by two further beliefs. The first is that the standard of the seriousness of crimes which legislators, and judges exercising discretion, should take into account is the moral worth, or rather unworthiness, displayed by agents in committing various crimes. A utilitarian might agree that penalties should be severe or light according to how serious the crimes are, but his standard of seriousness is typically the degree of harm done by the sort of act in question, rather than the moral blameworthiness of the agents. The second distinguishing mark of the extreme retributivist is a belief that the ultimate justification of having a system of punishment at all, as opposed (say) to a system of psychiatric treatment, is that the state should try, so far as is practical, to see that happiness and unhappiness are proportionate to moral desert. No utilitarian could hold that the *final* reason for punishment is to make the wicked suffer.

Did Kant hold the first opinion, namely, that penalties should be proportionate to the moral worth displayed by the criminal? The evidence is mixed, but the main trend of his thought seems to be opposed to the idea. It should be noted first that Kant regards certain acts outside the legitimate scope of law as displaying extreme unworthiness. "Wanton self-abuse," for example, is said to make one lower than the animals (MPV 86 [425]); but, as it violates only a duty to oneself, it is not a matter for legal concern. Refusal on principle to give to charity reveals negative moral worth (unlike mere neglect of charity) (MPV 48 [390]); but again the duty which is violated is merely "ethical," as opposed to "juridical," and so the state has no right to punish. The law then cannot try to proportion unhappiness to unworthiness in general. The question must be: within the class of acts that violate legitimate laws, should penalties be assigned according to the degree of moral unworthiness?

Prima facie evidence for a negative answer is the fact that Kant argues for *jus talionis* as the only non–fluctuating standard. By ordinary standards, the moral worth of agents who are guilty of any given crime, such as petty theft or even first degree murder, varies widely, depending on the circumstances and motives (love, political idealism, profit, vengeance, hate, etc.). Even Kant's limited remarks about degrees of demerit indicate that the fewer the "natural obstacles" to conforming to the law, the greater the demerit in violating it (MPV 28 [228]). A rich man's lesser temptations to petty theft, for example, make him worse for committing it than the poor man. If, therefore, penalties were to be assigned according to variable moral worth, we would not have the simple and fixed system of punishment Kant advocated but instead a complex system classifying murders, for example, not just in three or four degrees but in hundreds of different ways according to the possible motives and obstacles which affect moral worth. To be consistent, Kant should not count the difference between a profit motive and hatred as in itself relevant to moral worth, but at least the degree of temptation the criminal faced would be relevant. To suppose that a uniform application of "an eye for an eye" would take account of these differences is grossly unrealistic.

Further prima facie evidence against the view that Kant would have legislators and judges vary penalties according to their judgment of a criminal's moral worth is the fact that in works other than *The Metaphysics of Morals* Kant takes a dim view of secular punishment for evil. The wicked deserve punishment, but judgments of ultimate good and evil are reserved for God.[6] Some examples follow:

> Punishment in general is a physical evil accruing from moral evil. It is either deterrent or else retributive. Punishments are deterrent if their sole purpose is to prevent an evil from arising; they are retributive when they are imposed because an evil has been done. Punishments are, therefore, a means of preventing an evil or punishing it. Those imposed by governments are always deterrent. (LE 55)

> All punishments imposed by sovereigns and governments are pragmatic. They are designed either to correct or to make an example. (LE 56)[7]

Remarks from other works cannot establish that Kant's official view of punishment in *The Metaphysics of Morals* was similarly opposed to secular punishment for evil; however, if the pertinent passages in *The Metaphysics of Morals* are ambiguous, there is a presumption in favor of continuity.

The passages most quoted in favor of a moralistic interpretation are the following:

> Judicial punishment can never be used merely as a means to promote some other good for the criminal himself or for civil society, but instead it must in all cases be imposed on him *only on the ground that he has committed a crime*. . . . He must be found to be *deserving* of pun-

---

[6]My views on Kant's account of punishment owe much to Jeffrie Murphy's work, even though he may not agree. See his *Kant: The Philosophy of Right* (New York: Macmillan, 1970), chap. 4, pp. 109–49, and his "Does Kant Have a Theory of Punishment?" *Columbia Law Review* (1987): 509–32.

[7]See also R 16 [20] and Kant's letter to J. B. Erhart, Dec. 21, 1792, in *Philosophical Correspondence*, p. 199 [398–99].

ishment before any consideration is given to the utility of this punishment for himself or his fellow citizens. (MEJ 100 [331]; my italics)

Even if a civil society were to dissolve itself by common agreement of all its members (for example, if the people inhabiting an island decided to separate and disperse themselves around the world), the last murderer remaining in prison must first be executed, so that *everyone will duly receive what his actions are worth* and so that the *bloodguilt* thereof will not be fixed on the people because they failed to insist on carrying out the punishment; for if they fail to do so, they may be regarded as accomplices in this public violation of legal justice. (MEJ 102 [333]; my italics)

These remarks clearly show that Kant was opposed to the utilitarian theories that would make deterrence and other social benefits the sole standard of when, and how much, to punish. They do not, however, unequivocally state that punishment should be proportionate to moral deserts. In the first passage, for example, the ground of punishment is said to be, not the moral worth of the agent, but "that he has committed a crime." Both passages, as translated, imply that the criminal should get what, in some sense, he "deserves" or his actions are "worth"; but these terms do not always refer to the basic moral worth of actions. What a person "deserves," in one sense, depends on what is fairly allotted to him by a system of rules. We deserve the wage promised to us if we perform as expected; we deserve the prize if we win fairly over competitors in a race; and we deserve a parking ticket if, without excuse, we park illegally. Moreover, Kant's term, translated as "deserving of punishment" here and later, is *strafbar,* which might as well be rendered "punishable," which is less apt to suggest a judgment about the criminal's inner unworthiness. What is obviously intended is that the criminal intentionally violated laws which justly impose punishments; whether this is to be imposed *for* moral unworthiness, or meted out proportionately to such unworthiness, remains an open question. Similarly, our actions can be "worth" more or less by different systems of evaluation which are not concerned with basic moral deserts: for example, from an intellectual point of view, within a market system, or as contributions for or against a civil society. Kant thought at least that within a system of just laws the criminal should get what his actions were worth,[8] in some sense, but whether the system itself should try to measure such worth by the criteria of ultimate moral worth he refers to elsewhere is open to serious question.[9] Given his repeated doubts about the extent to which such worth can be known, we naturally suspect that he did not intend for the law to rely on judgments about it.

The reference to the "bloodguilt" of the murderers obviously suggests moral unworthiness, and we can hardly doubt that Kant believed murderers to be morally unworthy in some degree. However, his point concerns the shared guilt of those who refuse to carry out the penalties prescribed by law and does not imply that legislators or judges should try to fix penalties according to their judgment of degrees of moral worthiness.

The most impressive evidence for the moralistic interpretation is a passage in which Kant defends capital punishment for all who participate in murder. Even though he admits that they may have different motives and "inner viciousness," he argues that they should all receive the death penalty because "only in this way will the death sentence be pronounced on all criminals in proportion to their inner viciousness" (MEJ 102–3 [333–34]). The paradox is explained by saying that the death penalty is a more severe punishment for the more vicious because, lacking honorable motives, they would rather live than die, whereas the less vicious, having some sense of honor, would rather die than live in disgrace. Here Kant seems to imply that penalties should be proportionate to the degree of "inner viciousness," i.e., of basic moral worth. The passage, however, is not conclusive. Kant has already argued for *jus talionis* on the ground that it is the only non-fluctuating standard. Now he tries to rebut the obvious objection that this principle gives equally severe punishments to criminals of different moral worth. The conclusion argued for is uniform application of a rule that considers only intentional "external acts" without regard to motive; but, as a believer that from a divine point of view happiness should and will be distributed according to moral deserts, he

---

[8]The phrase is "was seine Thaten Werth seien" [333].

[9]These criteria are discussed, and pertinent passages quoted, in my paper "Kant on Imperfect Duty and Supererogation," reprinted in this volume.

naturally hesitated to admit that uniform application of *jus talionis* would cause the less vicious to suffer equally with the more vicious. The argument may be seen as an ad hoc, and not very convincing, defense of *jus talionis* against those who would see it as opposed to what God would do; but this does not mean that legislators and judges should try to imitate God by making penalties vary according to their judgments of moral worth.

Whatever the standard for assigning degrees of punishment, the final mark of a thoroughgoing retributivist should be his rationale for having a system of punishment at all. Here, I believe, Kant is consistently non-retributivist. That is, he holds that states are entitled to punish criminals not because they are morally unworthy but because the right to punish is an essential condition of maintaining a just civil society in which liberty is guaranteed equally to everyone under general laws. The first principle of justice, from which all rights are derived, is the so-called "universal principle of justice": "Act externally in such a way that the free use of your will is compatible with the freedom of everyone according to a universal law" (MEJ 35 [230]). Coercion is justified as a prevention of a hindrance to freedom (MEJ 35–36 [231]). This does not mean that authorities can be arbitrary in protecting freedom, for the right to punish as well as rights to ordinary acts by citizens must be considered as a part of a general system of laws. In a way admirably outlined by Jeffrie Murphy, the justification of punishment depends upon the idea of a social contract that would be accepted by rational persons for their mutual advantage. The agreements concern intentional "external actions," aside from motives; principles regarding inner motivation, and so ultimate moral worth, belong to "ethical legislation," outside the scope of law. In discussions of specific issues, such as the death penalty, Kant obviously let his moralistic sentiments show; but the structure of *The Metaphysics of Morals,* in the first part concerned with justice, clearly places the rationale for punishment in general under a principle of liberty, not a principle of moral desert.

III

What could explain Kant's anti-moralistic strain? That is, why would one who regarded positive moral worth as the most sublime achievement one could hope for be, relatively speaking, so cautious in allowing judgments of moral worth to influence our conduct? Certain answers must be ruled out at once; others are more promising but raise difficult moral questions.

One reason that many would cite for avoiding moral judgments on others is that God has preempted the field. "Vengeance is *mine,* saith the Lord," and "Judge not, that ye be not judged." This reason, however, will not do for Kant. He maintains that all we can reasonably believe of God is based on our prior knowledge of morality. He cannot then settle questions about what we should and should not do by reference to the word of God. And, of course, the argument would not move nonbelievers.

Another familiar reason for avoiding judgments of *blame*worthiness is that they are often destructive. We are plagued by guilt feelings enough as it is, some would say, and we would perhaps all be happier if we dropped blame in favor of behavior modification, psychotherapy, institutional reforms, and so on. Whatever the merits of these alternatives, however, the argument would hardly have appealed to Kant. It is an appeal to utility, which for Kant was a low priority when the issue concerns what moral judgments to make; and the ideologies behind finding substitutes for blame typically have the effect of denying what Kant thought very important, namely, that our acts can manifest more or less moral worth, and to act in the most worthy way should be our highest priority.

An argument which some philosophers give is that judgments of ultimate moral worth are incompatible with determinism. Everything which occurs has its causal explanation, and each cause can be explained in terms of further causes. A person may do what is right because he has a sense of duty but, it is argued, that sense of duty is itself a result of various causes, which in turn were caused by other factors, and so on. "Right" and "wrong," on this view, may usefully serve to classify actions according to whether their consequences are beneficial or harmful, and blaming and praising may be effective devices for changing behavior. But to judge that one person is more worthy, more deserving of happiness, not just within a set of conventional rules but in general, is to presuppose that our character and moral development are "due to us" in a way ruled out by causal determinism.

Whether or not this argument has merit, Kant could not have used it. Kant believed, in fact believed he had proved, a deterministic causal principle for all "phenomenal" events, but he held that one's *will* is not part of the phenomenal, or observable, world and that moral worth comes from what one wills. Despite causal determinism in the phenomenal world, our wills are regarded as "free" in several senses which are clearly meant to rule out the sort of causal determination of what we will which is presupposed in the argument above.[10] In fact it seems that the main reason moral worth was so important to Kant is that it is viewed as a reflection of the free commitments of rational agents. That is, a person gains merit by choosing, without coercion or hope of reward, to follow moral principles, which in turn are principles which rational persons would "legislate" for themselves if free from determination by various natural forces (including, alas, our own natural desires). The reason moral discredit, or negative moral worth, is so much to be avoided, it seems, is that it results from a "divided will": that is, a will which freely chooses to indulge certain natural desires contrary to exceptionless principles which it also freely adopts (or "legislates" to itself). The relevant senses of "free" are notoriously difficult to articulate clearly, but it is easy enough to see that Kant would not hesitate to rely on judgments of moral worth from fear that they might be incompatible with causal determinism.

One might try to build an argument on Kant's idea that a morally good attitude cannot be *taught* by reward and punishment. To have such an attitude is to have a "good will," which is a readiness to do one's duty without any inducements of the carrot and the stick. Kant cannot then consistently advocate making the wicked suffer to "teach them a (moral) lesson." Nor can he consistently urge us to reward the virtuous in order to foster a moral spirit in observers. In fact Kant repeatedly warns against trying to teach morality by examples. These points, however, though in line with Kant's beliefs, fall short of the explanation we want. They show that we lack a certain reason to reward and punish according to moral worth, but they do not establish that we should not. On the contrary, given Kant's view that the virtuous are *worthy* of happiness and the vicious are unworthy, it is natural to suppose that we

[10]See, for example, G 114ff. [116ff.].

should reward and punish according to desert unless there is a positive reason not to.

Readers of the *Groundwork* will have already thought of another reason for caution about judging others: we are so often ignorant of their true motives. Kant repeatedly stresses the difficulty of determining what a person's motives are and the impossibility of being *certain* that a morally good motive is at work (G 74–75 [407–8]). The problem is not simply that other people's motives are hidden from us; we cannot be certain even of our own motives. The problem arises with or without Kant's special metaphysical beliefs. Suppose, first, we set aside Kant's metaphysics and speak the language of common sense. Then the problem is a familiar one. How, for example, can we tell if the grocer gives correct change from a desire to be honest, from fear of reprisals, or from relishing the good opinion of others? How can we know whether the hero who throws himself on a live grenade, thereby saving others, does so from love, from a self-destructive impulse, from a longing to be a martyr, or from a sense of duty? When we move from common sense to Kant's metaphysics, the problem seems even more intractable. The ultimate source of action, and so of moral worth, is the agent's *will,* which is said to be noumenal, or unobservable. Even if we knew all the feelings and desires a person had prior to acting, we could not from this empirical information, apparently, determine why, in the appropriate sense, the agent did what he did. For that, it seems, depends on whether he *willed* to satisfy this or that desire, or none at all, and the will is not open to observation or even to introspection. Since we are unable to understand this crucial aspect of others' acts, then, it seems natural that we should not guide our conduct toward them by our opinions about their moral worth.

Our ignorance of others in fact even proves to be an obstacle in attempts to assess whether they have acted rightly (in accord with duty), quite aside from whether they have acted in a morally worthy way (from duty). For in order to use the Categorical Imperative, at least in its famous first formulation, we must know the agent's maxim. The maxim will reflect how the agent saw the situation, what his intention was, what general policy commitments he makes, as well as the nature of the "external act" (as he sees it). The same "external act," e.g., making a promise or killing a person, could be done from many different maxims, and whether the agent made the right decision depends upon which maxim he had. If, as Kant suggests, this is hard to be sure about in one's own case, it must be all the more so when one tries to judge another person. Partly for this reason, perhaps, Kant expresses the Categorical Imperative in the form of a command addressed to each agent ("Act as if . . . ") rather than in the more usual forms of rules of conduct (e.g., "Everyone should . . . "). Attention is focused on the agent's decision about what he will do, not on the grounds for judging in general whether people have acted rightly or wrongly. When assessing even the rightness of others' acts is so difficult, one should naturally be cautious about making the more complex judgment that an agent was, or was not, motivated in a morally worthy way.

But perhaps the problem has been exaggerated. It is true that, on Kant's view, we cannot be sure why a person did what he did in many, maybe even most, cases. For example, whenever a person fulfills an obligation but has some inclination (such as a desire for the good opinion of others) which leads him the same way, then presumably we could not tell whether he acted from duty or from inclination. That would depend upon whether he *willed* to act from duty or to satisfy the inclination, and such matters are not supposed to be empirically decidable. However, there are other cases in which, barring radical disconnection between the will and behavior, it should be evident that a person acted in a morally unworthy way. Suppose, for example, someone flagrantly violates one of the more obvious moral prohibitions, e.g., against murder, and then acknowledges that he did so intentionally and with full awareness that his was was wrong. We may be unable to determine for sure whether he was moved by greed, ambition, hate, love, political idealism, or whatever, but it should be obvious enough, even given Kant's metaphysics, that he did not will to conform to the principle which confers moral worth (i.e., "to do my duty"). Moreover, if (as Kant suggests) (MEJ 28 [227]) there is negative moral worth in willing maxims known to be contrary to duty, then one can reasonably assume that his act had such negative worth despite the fact that we may not be able to specify the maxim fully. The murderer cannot excuse himself on deterministic grounds, for on Kant's extreme view of free will any rational person can resist any temptation to do what he knows wrong. The only escape would be to push Kant's metaphysics of the noumenal to the extreme, claiming that, for all we know, he may have willed in the noumenal realm quite the opposite of how he behaved and how, by his own honest report, he intended to behave. But, whether consistently or not, Kant did not carry his noumenal metaphysics this far. In fact he even gave some guidelines to determine the degree of negative worth: the more stringent the duty and the fewer the natural obstacles to conformity, the greater the demerit (MEJ 28 [228]).

Ignorance, then, goes some way towards explaining why in ordinary circumstances we should not treat people according to our opinions of their moral worth; but it does not explain why we should not make it a primary purpose of punishment to deprive criminals of happiness because of the negative moral worth, or "demerit," which their more serious crimes display. Although we cannot make happiness proportionate to merit everywhere, why not try to do this so far as we can? Should we, in other words, view the proportionality of happiness to virtue as a practical goal, the way classic utilitarians view happiness: that is, as something to be promoted whenever possible, each contribution being better than none? Or should we, on the contrary, view it more like some utopian states: that is, an ideal to be wished for but such that a few steps towards it may be worse than none at all?

In favor of the latter view we might consider the following plea from a criminal resentful of society's moralizing about his depravity. "Admittedly I have done wrong and must pay a fair penalty," he says, "but stop rationalizing the punishment as a means of making happiness and suffering proportionate to moral worth; for there are millions of non-criminals who, for all you know, are no more worthy than I, who would have done the same as I in similar circumstances, and you cannot even begin to treat them according to their moral worth."[11]

Notice that the argument here is distinct from several familiar arguments which may have force in special circumstances but which are unlikely to have moved Kant. For example, the argu-

---

[11]Murphy suggests a line of argument like this but apparently believes it to be opposed to Kant's official theory of punishment.

ment is not that the criminal should be released because many others commit crimes without getting caught. Our criminal does not argue for release, or even a mild penalty; he only opposes using moral unworthiness as a rationale. Also he does not argue that the law is imperfectly enforced, or even selectively enforced; for the people he claims to be equally unworthy may have committed no crimes at all. Nor is his complaint that there ought to be laws which would make the moral offenses of other unworthy people punishable; for he can admit that there are practical difficulties in doing this and social costs in even making the attempt. The argument, moreover, is not that "people in glass houses should not throw stones"; for, let us imagine, he would put the same argument to the most upright legislators and judges. Again, though he claims that others similarly situated would have done the same as he, he is not trying to excuse himself on deterministic grounds ("My background made me do it") or because of unequal opportunity ("It is easy for the rich to be honest"). The argument, instead, is that many others who do not commit crimes, or even serious moral offenses, may have a will and character which is no better than the criminal's and so to punish him, and not them, *for* moral unworthiness is unjustified.

Several tempting replies seem inadequate from Kant's point of view. First, one might try to deny, on empirical grounds, the claim that many law-abiding citizens are prepared to do what the worst criminals do. Kant would no doubt admit that, happily, most people have inclinations which led them to conform to duty and so are unlikely, given a mere change in external circumstance, to commit the most serious crimes. But the crucial point in our criminal's argument is not that others would do just the same in externally similar circumstances, but that they are not morally more worthy. One's moral worth depends upon whether one's *will* is good, not upon the nature of one's natural inclinations. What matters is not what we desire but what we choose to do, given a set of desires. Fortunately endowed with sympathetic and conformist inclinations, the "good citizen" may remain law-abiding; but, without a will to do duty for duty's sake, he may be no more worthy than the criminal. That there are many such non-worthy conformists is, I think, a point Kant would concede. Second, one might reply that the unworthy but law-abiding citizen will be given his just deserts informally: that is, not through official punishment but through private censure and social pressure. But, again, this reply seems unavailable to Kant. For as long as people have inclinations that lead them to conform to duty, they may never identify themselves as unworthy. One can sometimes infer unworthiness from bad conduct, but one cannot infer its absence from good conduct. Third, a religious person might tell the criminal not to worry about the other unworthies because God will punish them in due time. Kant did argue that we can reasonably believe that God will reward virtue, but he also held that religion should be based on ethics rather than the reverse. To argue for certain human institutions (e.g., a system of punishment) from premises about what God will do is clearly against the spirit, if not the letter, of his position about the relation of moral and religious belief. Besides, the belief that God will punish according to deserts could equally well be used to argue against punishing the criminal for his unworthiness. Fourth, one might reply to the criminal that *crimes* reflect greater unworthiness than mere moral offenses and so it is justifiable to punish criminals for unworthiness even though other unworthy persons are not punished. This reply might be suggested by Kant's distinction between the strict "juridical duties," which are a matter of justice and include the obligation to obey the law, and "ethical duties," such as beneficence, which "leave a play-room for free action." But a glance at Kant's comments about violations of ethical "perfect duties to oneself" (e.g., self-stupefaction, "carnal self-defilement," etc.) (MPV 82ff. [421ff.]) makes clear that degree of unworthiness does not divide neatly between juridical and ethical duties, or crimes and non-criminal moral offenses.

The most forceful reply, however, would be that the proportionality of happiness and virtue is an absolute standard of justice, not a comparative one. That is, so long as the criminal is treated according to his own worth, he has no ground to complain; whether other unworthy people prosper or suffer is irrelevant to whether his treatment is just. This response, I think, has some persuasive force. At least it seems right that the criminal is in a poor position to complain about unfairness when he admits that he is worthy of no better treatment or less blame. On the other hand, he may have a point. When we shift attention from the individual criminal's complaint to the perspective of a designer of social institutions, punishing for moral unworthiness seems a peculiar idea (given our Kantian assumptions). If there is really no way to identify those who have a certain fault except in a few cases, and even no way to be sure that the fault is not shared by all, then to design an institution (of punishment) to make the few suffer for that fault seems unwarranted. To say that someone is unworthy of happiness does not imply that regardless of how others fare he should be deprived of happiness because of this. And designing a system to enforce an absolute standard in some cases when one knows that one cannot in principle enforce it in all does seem to raise legitimate questions of comparative justice. Given that one could instead design a system of punishment with fixed penalties for crimes we can hope to detect and that this would serve the aim of deterrence to preserve liberty, then that would seem the better alternative.

An analogy may be persuasive, though admittedly not a conclusive argument. Suppose that as a professor I want to assign grades according to academic merit, but it becomes a widespread practice for students to buy research papers (which are my only basis for grading). Since only good papers are sold, it is impossible for me to tell whether any student has positive academic merit. The authentic good papers are indistinguishable from those that are bought. The only time I can judge academic merit is when some dull-witted student submits a bad paper which he himself has written. But for all I know the rest of the students are just as academically deficient. Let us imagine that I have no moral concern about cheating: I am only concerned about academic merit. Now it may be that the dull-witted student who submitted his own paper is in a poor position to complain when he gets a low grade. But, assuming that I cannot stop the buying of papers or switch to examinations, would it not be more reasonable to give up the practice of assigning grades altogether (provided I have the authority)?

Whether this sort of consideration actually moved Kant is speculation, of course, but, given his radical views about our ignorance of moral worth in most cases, it would support the anti-moralistic aspect of his theory of punishment which I have tried to identify.

10

Making Exceptions without Abandoning the Principle: or How a Kantian Might Think about Terrorism

I. The Problem for Kantians and the Larger Issue

Terrorism poses a practical problem that is urgent and difficult. How, within the bounds of conscience, can we respond effectively to violent terrorist activities and threats, especially given the ideological fanaticism and non-negotiable demands that typically accompany them? The problem is partly instrumental and partly moral. The instrumental task is to find, among the morally permissible means, the best way to minimize terrorist violence, taking into account our other goals and values. The moral task is to determine what means of response are morally permissible. I shall focus here on this second problem, or rather on one way of thinking about it.

Terrorists, of course, often claim that their ends are morally worthy and that their means are morally justified in the context. Some of these claims deserve a serious hearing, and even the more outrageous claims can pose challenges that moral philosophers should not ignore. For present purposes, however, I shall simply

This paper was written for a conference on violence and terrorism sponsored by the Philosophy Department at Bowling Green University in November 1988 and subsequently discussed with faculty and students at the U.S. Air Force Academy, the College of Charleston, the College of William and Mary, U.C.L.A., the University of Colorado, and the North Carolina Triangle Ethics Group. I want to thank the participants at these meetings for their many helpful comments.

assume that terrorism is morally indefensible, at least in the cases to be considered; and I will not be discussing why this is so. My inquiry, instead, is about what *responses* are permissible when terrorists *immorally* threaten the lives of innocent hostages.

Even this somewhat more limited question is too large to undertake here. To give an adequate answer would require us not only to resolve deep issues in moral theory but also to investigate relevant matters of fact, make careful distinctions among cases, review our moral judgments regarding similar problems, and so on. Thus my remarks will address only one theoretical aspect of the larger moral issue, namely, how can a Kantian ethics, suitably interpreted and qualified, handle the life-or-death choices posed by terrorist threats? For example, can it ever permit the use of deadly force against terrorists even at the severe risk of killing innocent hostages? Can one refuse to negotiate for the lives of a few hostages in hope that a tough policy will in the long run save more people?

Although I shall explain the Kantian point of view I have in mind, my aim here is not to defend it either as a moral perspective or as an interpretation of Kant. Rather than presupposing the correctness of the Kantian perspective, I see my project here as preliminary to any final assessment of the relative merits of Kantian versus alternative perspectives: that is, it is simply an attempt to work out how a Kantian approach might direct us to think about some of the terrible choices forced upon us by terrorists. More specifically, can a person (rather like me) who is sympathetic to some main features of Kant's ethics make (intuitively) reasonable judgments about terrorism without, in effect, abandoning the fundamental Kantian principles? And if one admits that terrorism calls for "exceptions" to the straightforward applications of Kant's basic principles for normal circumstances, can one acknowledge these exceptions coherently, and not in an ad hoc manner, from a moral perspective that preserves much of the spirit of Kant's ethics?

My project, I should stress, is not to use Kantian principles to draw a precise line between permissible and impermissible responses to terrorism but rather to see whether a basically Kantian ethics has any reasonable and coherent way to approach the troublesome cases. Many of these cases leave me morally perplexed. I am not confident about what would be right to do. But even this uncertainty is enough to raise the problem, for it seems at first that basic Kantian principles leave no room for what generates the uncertainty. What pulls us even to consider, say, sacrificing a few to save many seems to be a kind of reasoning that makes sense only within a moral perspective radically opposed to Kant's. Even to acknowledge the reasoning in favor of the exceptions, it seems, is to abandon the Kantian perspective.

The issue here is an instance of a more general problem faced by many people who have never heard of Kant but who believe in taking a "principled stand" on moral questions. The problem is posed sharply by an old dialogue that could take many forms.[1] One person, *A*, asks another, *B*, whether for a million dollars *B* would do something against *B's* principles (e.g., go to bed with a stranger, tell a racist joke, or take hotel towels without paying for them). *B* responds, "Yes, I suppose I would." Then *A* asks, "How about five dollars?" *B* retorts indignantly, "What do you take me for!" "We have already established that," says *A*. "Now we are dickering over the price."

To those who take pride in standing on principle, the story poses a dilemma: either you hold rigidly to your principles for all circumstances or else you are prepared to suspend them, or open gaps in them, for special cases. In extreme abnormal circumstances the first course may begin to appear foolish, contrary to both common sense and reflective judgment; but taking the second option raises the suspicion that one's principle is just a rule of thumb and that one is open to persuasion by considerations that have nothing to do with the rationale for the alleged principle.

The sort of dialogue mentioned above was not meant to pose a serious moral dilemma, but more dramatic cases are not hard to imagine. Suppose, as in John Fowles's *Magus*, one were forced to choose between beating two Nazi resisters to death and having the vicious Nazi commandant shoot down a dozen or more resisters. Suppose one had to torture a terrorist in order to learn the location of a bomb set to blow up New York City? If we admit exceptions to familiar moral principles in these cases, then critics can start to push us down the slippery slope. How about if the bomb would

---

[1]Here I rephrase an often repeated dialogue, sometimes attributed to G.B. Shaw, because the original version exploits sexist stereotypes and the differences are irrelevant to my point.

only blow up the Bronx? Or half of that? Or a dozen people? Or two? If we take a hard stand on principle, refusing to make the exception, then the critics' move will be to "up the ante," asking, for example, whether we would kill the two resisters or torture the terrorist in order to save the whole world. The critics' objective here is to open a hole in the absolutist dike, leaving only consequentialist resources to hold back the flow of exceptions. They may even admit that it is almost always right to do as the principle prescribes, for the main issue is not how frequent the exceptions are. Rather, the critics want to raise a suspicion that there is no good reason to maintain the principle *as a principle,* as opposed to a flexible rule of thumb.[2]

One who insisted on standing by ordinary principles in all circumstances, despite the critics' challenge, could of course take a leaf from the consequentialist's book, denying the relevance of merely fictional cases and arguing that we do not actually face such stark alternatives. But, though options in the real world are rarely as clear-cut and certain as those in philosophers' examples, to insist repeatedly that each tough case is merely fictional seems a lame defense, one that appeals more to faith than to experience. Besides, since defenders of principle have so often used fictional counter-examples against utilitarianism, they should be more than a little embarrassed to resort to the wholesale rejection of hypothetical examples when trying to uphold their own position.

The history of ethics is full of subtle attempts to meet our imaginary critics' challenge to those who hold familiar moral principles as principles. I shall not review these attempts here, but one common strategy deserves special mention. This is the tendency to append a "catastrophe clause" to familiar principles whenever the consequences of adhering to the principles are so repugnant that it seems morally perverse to refuse the exception. For example, "Do not even threaten to kill innocent people, unless doing so helps to avert a nuclear war" or "Let justice be done, unless (thereby) the

[2]For simplicity I am imagining that my "critics" here are "act-consequentialists" and not "rule-consequentialists," for the latter might urge us in practice to treat certain rules as inflexible principles and yet defend this view at a "higher level" of deliberation by appeal to consequences. The Kantian alternative to be considered, however, is opposed to both forms of consequentialism because of the constraints it places on the role of consequences in justifying principles.

heavens should fall." This strategy of adding catastrophe clauses formally maintains the principle as nearly inflexible and yet allows us to side with common sense on extreme counter-examples. The problem with the strategy, however, is that it leaves our critics' main challenge unanswered: if the balance of consequences determines what to do in the extreme case, why not in the case slightly less extreme, and so on? If one may sacrifice a life to save a million and one lives, then why not save a million, or a million minus one, or a million minus two, or three, or four? Isn't it basically a matter of calculation, after all? This remains a serious challenge unless one can give a coherent common ground both for maintaining the familiar principle as nearly inflexible and for making exceptions for extreme cases.

Although my discussion is somewhat abstract and theoretical, the sort of problem raised here is not merely a philosopher's puzzle but a crisis of conscience for many people. Try to imagine, if you can, one of my typical undergraduate students whose talents and ambitions lead her into the inner circles of Washington where she faces decisions and a worldview more akin to those of Oliver North than to those of the local minister. Raised in a small peaceful community with shared values and limited global outlook, she has come to take for granted certain absolute prohibitions as the framework of any tolerable social life and of any decent person's conscience. Unreflective religious beliefs tend to reinforce her principles, but one suspects that it is not so much that her principles are derived from religion as that her theological beliefs are reinforced by the way they wrap an aura of authority around those principles. In the local world the hard cases did not force themselves upon her thinking. Removed to the tougher world of international conflict, power politics, terrorism, and constant compromise, however, she must live with the widespread opinion that her initial principles are foolishly rigid and face choices in which sticking to those principles seems unbearably costly. Making an exception here and there, perhaps with a bad conscience, may not at first force her to rethink her position; but after a while she may well wonder how she can continue to make what seem at each time justifiable exceptions without having, in effect, abandoned her principles. Ships with too many holes sink, and principles with too many gaps no longer function as principles.

II. Kantian Principles and the Presumption against Killing

For the would-be Kantian the challenge takes two forms: First, can the Categorical Imperative, in some form, be sensibly maintained as an inflexible principle in the face of extreme cases? Second, if one admits intuitively reasonable exceptions to the more specific principles about killing (lying, promise-keeping, etc.) commonly associated with Kantian morality, in what sense can these still be maintained as principles without abandoning the basic Kantian point of view? For example, can the exceptions themselves be justified by appeal to the Categorical Imperative, or are they, after all, partial concessions to a radically different moral point of view? My main focus is on the first question, but what I have to say is also relevant to the second.

Unlike many who are sympathetic to Kant's moral philosophy, I have little confidence that Kant's famous "universal law" formulations of the Categorical Imperative can function adequately as guides to moral decision making. More promising, I think, is Kant's principle that humanity in each person must always be treated as an end in itself, never simply as a means. This principle, Kant says, is unconditionally binding on all human beings, whatever their circumstances and regardless of what (contingent) ends must be sacrificed to satisfy it. It is, supposedly, not merely one "perfect" duty among others but an articulation of the comprehensive ground of all duties, "perfect" and "imperfect." As a foundation of a rational system of moral principles, it is not supposed to generate or allow any genuine conflict of duties or (what are often called) "moral dilemmas." If unresolvable conflicts of duty are derivable from it, then it cannot have the status Kant claimed for it.

Now despite the warm reception Kant's principle receives from non-consequentialists everywhere, its interpretation remains controversial. For our purposes, however, I simply take as given the following reconstruction.[3]

First, the "humanity in persons" that we are urged to respect is the "rational nature" of human beings, or human beings insofar as

[3]Some of these points are spelled out in more detail in my "Humanity as an End in Itself" and (in slightly modified form) in "Kantian Constructivism in Ethics," both reprinted in this volume. Many of Kant's works are relevant, but especially his *Groundwork of the Metaphysics of Morals*; see G 89 and 97.

they are considered rational agents with autonomy. The rationality and autonomy in question here are capacities and dispositions that virtually all sane adult human beings are presumed to have, not the full manifestation of these in actual conduct. Thus people who act foolishly and immorally are, in the relevant sense, rational agents with autonomy, and their "humanity" too must be treated as an "end in itself."

The status of infants and the mentally incompetent remains problematic under the principle, and the principle does not address the value of nonhuman animals. But we can set aside these special problems if we limit our examples to mentally competent, adult human beings and do not presume that the humanity principle alone is adequate to settle all moral issues.

Second, the injunction not to treat humanity merely as a means is incomplete and inapplicable without the contrasting phrase "always as an end in itself"; for without knowing what it is to treat humanity as an end in itself we cannot judge what would be, in the intended sense, treating it *merely* as a means. In contrast, if we succeed in treating humanity always as an end in itself, we automatically satisfy the prohibition against treating it merely as a means. Further, as Kant makes clear in his later writings, treating a person's humanity as an end in itself requires more than refraining from acts that would exploit the person as a mere means. Indifference to a person is also forbidden, and positive assistance may be required (MPV 54).

Third, the term "end" here, as Kant acknowledges, is a potentially misleading technical term, meaning roughly something giving a reason or "ground for determining the will." An "end in itself," or "objective end," is a ground of choice that would determine the will of a fully rational agent and should determine ours. In the ordinary sense, of course, neither persons nor the rational nature of persons are "ends."

Fourth, in saying that rational agents with autonomy are ends in themselves, I take it, Kant is saying that they have "dignity," which he defines as an "unconditional and incomparable worth" that, unlike "price," "admits of no equivalent." As an unconditional value, dignity does not depend on the contingent fact that something is useful, desired, or even liked. By contrast, things with mere "price," or conditional value, have a value that is dependent upon utility ("market value") or at least upon individual sentiments ("fancy value"). Anything with mere price has a value that "admits of equivalents" and so is subject to calculated trade-offs; however great its value, there can in principle be something else that could compensate for its loss and justify its sacrifice. Material goods, reputation, and pleasures as such have mere price, and so even great amounts of these things may at times be reasonably sacrificed for other things with the same sort of value. By contrast, dignity is "above all price" and so one can never act contrary to the dignity of someone for the sake of things with mere price, no matter how great the price.[4]

Fifth, Kant's fundamental principle is directly concerned, not with "external actions," but with the attitudes, or value priorities, that lie behind the ways we treat ourselves and others. Acts (e.g., of suicide and murder) and institutions (e.g., of slavery) are condemned not merely as kinds of intentional behavior with undesirable consequences but as manifestations of value priorities that are intolerable. The example of suicide is instructive here. In the *Groundwork*, for example, the suicide Kant condemns is terminating one's life because a hedonistic calculus predicts that one's future will contain more pain than pleasure (G 89, 97). Kant later says that to avoid suicide is a "perfect" or exceptionless duty, but he admits that it is an open question for casuistry whether we should *count as suicide* deliberate self-sacrifice for one's country or killing oneself to avoid an unjust death sentence or terminal madness from the bite of a rabid dog (MPV 84). The operative principle here is obviously not that intentional killing of a human being is always wrong but rather that (with a few conceivable exceptions) the reasons people have for killing themselves have only a conditional value ("price") which is not to be compared with human dignity.

This understanding of Kant's dignity principle fits well with Kant's other uses of the idea of humanity as an end in itself in the second part of *The Metaphysics of Morals*, which is concerned with ethics beyond questions of law, justice, and rights. For example,

---

[4]Because of the centrality of the idea of "dignity," I shall hereafter refer to my reconstruction of Kant's principle that we should always treat humanity as an end in itself simply as "the dignity principle."

the principle is used to condemn drunkenness and gluttony (which interfere with rational functioning), mockery (which treats people as worthless), and servility (which expresses the attitude that one's human worth is measured by one's utility to others) (MPV 88–90, 96–100, 132–33). The duty to respect others is grounded in the value of their humanity, not in their achievements or their moral conduct; and, significantly, the duty to promote the happiness of others is not grounded explicitly in the dignity principle (MPV 112–19). In summary, these principles say that one must seek to preserve, develop, exercise, and "honor" rational agency in oneself and to respect it in other human beings, no matter how immorally and irrationally they may behave. To preserve human life per se is not among the principles.

Now, though these applications illustrate the dignity principle, they are not concerned with the sort of life-or-death choices that terrorism can force us to confront. Regarding these cases, what Kant says about law and justice in the first part of *The Metaphysics of Morals* is more relevant. But before we turn to that, we need to face a further question about the interpretation of the dignity principle.

In brief, the problem is this: granted that dignity cannot be exchanged for price, can dignity be exchanged for more dignity? To put the question less cryptically: assuming, as already decided, that dignity is "above all price" and so cannot be sacrificed for things of merely conditional value, does the principle imply, further, that dignity itself is a non-quantitative value that does not admit comparisons like "The dignity of this (person) is greater than the dignity of that (person)" or "Two things of dignity are worth twice as much as one"? Does dignity merely "admit of no equivalent" among the things of conditional value or are there no equivalents even among things of dignity? Since dignity is the value attributed to human beings, these questions obviously have a bearing on the question of when, if ever, the dignity principle permits the sacrifice of one human being for the sake of one or more other human beings.

Now when we read that Kant approved of capital punishment, and sometimes killing in war, it is tempting to jump to the conclusion that Kant himself understood the dignity principle in the more permissive way, allowing us to justify some killing of human beings on the ground that the dignity of many persons outweighs the dignity of a few. However, for textual reasons I pass over here, I do not think that this interpretation is correct. More important for our purposes, the permissive interpretation would undermine what seemed to be the strikingly special character of Kantian ethics, namely, its refusal to reduce moral decisions to the weighing and balancing of commensurate values.[5] On the permissive interpretation, the theory would become just another version of an all-too-familiar type: namely, a theory that first assigns a quantity of intrinsic value to various possible outcomes and then treats the right decision as a function of these value assignments. Kant's theory, to be sure, would have the unique feature of having two scales of value (dignity and price), with any amount of value on one scale always "trumping" any amount on the other; and it would place the higher value on living as a rational agent as opposed to hedonistic values. But, nonetheless, like sophisticated forms of utilitarianism that place a higher priority on human life than on animal pleasures, such a theory would hold "the good prior to the right" and make moral choices fundamentally matters of calculation.

Thus, to further discussion, let us work with the alternative, non-permissive interpretation. On this account, dignity is still "above all price" in the previous sense: dignity must never be violated in exchange for things of mere price. But now dignity is not to be construed as a quantitative notion. Dignity is "without equivalent" even among other things with dignity in the sense that one cannot justify violations of dignity by claiming they are a necessary sacrifice to promote "more" dignity elsewhere. Thus the destruction of something with dignity, if ever justifiable, cannot be justified simply by weighing quantities of intrinsic value, even value of the highest order. The assignment of dignity to each rational agent, then, functions not to introduce a new kind of value calculation, but rather to block our tendency to treat rational agents as interchangeable commodities. Moreover, "the right" remains "prior to the good" in that the attribution of dignity to rational agents stems from a rational/moral command to adopt and

---

[5]Refusal to *reduce* moral decisions to weighing of costs and benefits does not, of course, imply that such weighing never has a legitimate role in moral thinking, even if some of Kant's more extreme remarks might suggest that he thought so.

act consistently with a certain attitude toward rational agents, not from a metaphysical claim about intrinsic values or from an empirical claim about preferences fixed by human nature.

Though the analogy is not perfect, we may say that the Kantian attitude toward preserving the lives of rational agents is rather like the attitude that some pious persons take toward an object they regard as "sacred" or "holy." They revere and treasure the object and seek diligently to preserve it. Even the thought that they might have to destroy the object is abhorrent, and so they make every effort to avoid situations where destruction would be necessary. They view the object as "irreplaceable," not merely in the sense that they would not trade it for an exact copy but in the sense that they would not view even its replacement by many other things revered in the same way as commensurate values compensating for the loss. If certain deplorable circumstances arose, however, they might nonetheless grant that they must destroy the object, for example, to keep it from being defiled by enemies. The attitude that such objects are "without equivalent" does not translate simply into an action-principle that they must never be destroyed but is more complex. It is also concerned with how one should view their loss, how one must work to prevent situations where losses will inevitably result from our choices, and how one should think about what to do when such tragic situations occur.

The attitude in question is perhaps more intuitively recognizable when one reflects how a loving parent would view the horrible situation of being able to save one of her children from drowning or to save two others, but not all. Surely she is justified in saving the two, but it is hard to conceive that she would accept that the rationale was that two are worth twice as much as one. The problem, of course, is to say what other rationale there can be.

It is the more radical, non-permissive reading of the dignity principle, I believe, that accounts for its wide appeal; but this reading is also what raises most acutely the consequentialist's challenge. The principle does not absolutely prohibit killing human beings, nor does it necessarily forbid us, when faced with no other option, to make the hard choice that results in the death of a few and the preservation of many. But, if such choices are morally defensible, they cannot be rationalized simply by the thought that "the lives of many people are worth more than the lives of few

people" or even "many innocent lives are worth more than fewer."
Even more obviously, the dignity principle does not permit the
choices to be justified by the thought that by preserving the lives
of more happy people we will bring about the most "intrinsically
valuable" experiences.

The problem, then, is how, despite this severe restriction on
consequentialist thinking, can the Kantian ever justify making the
hard life-or-death choices that seem intuitively compelling, particularly in cases where at some level of deliberation the numbers do seem to matter? The problem is far easier to state than
to answer, but some clues toward an answer, I think can be found
in Kant's views on state coercion and punishment, to which I
now turn.

III. Dignity, Punishment, and Deadly Force against Terrorism

Kant held that justice not only permits but even requires
capital punishment for murder. I disagree, but I think that what
Kant says in support of his view at least suggests how the dignity
principle can be reconciled with the use of deadly force against terrorists in some cases. It also opens up a way of thinking about
cases in which a response to terrorists would endanger the lives of
innocent persons. Once again I shall reconstruct Kant's views
liberally, without argument, but the purpose here is to focus
attention on the possible reconciliation, not on questions of textual interpretation.[6]

The background assumption is that we are dealing with agents
who are rational though not necessarily moral or ideally rational.
They know what they are doing, are capable of self-control,
and know well enough the difference between right and wrong.
Moreover, they are disposed, even when they act immorally, to

---

[6]Kant mentions punishment in several works but primarily in the first part of *The
Metaphysics of Morals*, translated as *The Metaphysical Elements of Justice*. My view of
Kant's position is presented briefly in "Kant's Anti-Moralistic Strain," reprinted in this
volume. For another view see Edmund L. Pincoffs, *The Rationale of Legal Punishment*
(New York: Humanities Press, 1966), chap. 1.

acknowledge moral requirements as rational and not merely imposed by others. When conscience and moral argument fail to dissuade them from their immoral projects, they are at least rational enough, as a rule, to be deterred by clear and credible threats to their own welfare. These assumptions, of course, are not always satisfied in the real world; and to the extent that they are not, the Kantian rationale may be vitiated.

Next, let us grant that, for various reasons, human beings need to join together into communities with common laws that assign to each rights and responsibilities. In a "state of nature" (or anarchy) individual reason and conscience would not in fact suffice to create and preserve the conditions necessary for people in close proximity to have lives appropriate to rational agents. So states are needed to define and secure to each person a reasonable opportunity for life and liberty as a rational autonomous agent. Thus there are moral as well as prudential reasons to form and support civil authorities with coercive powers.

This being so, the dignity principle must be applied not merely to relations between individuals isolated from others but, first and crucially, to the construction of a system of laws that can provide the framework for moral relations among individuals.[7] In working out the implications of the dignity principle for laws, one should take the point of view of legislators in the "kingdom of ends," that is, fully rational and autonomous persons, each with "private ends" but "abstracting from personal differences," and

---

[7] This is a crucial move in the Kantian line of argument I am suggesting. It is similar to Rawls's procedural commitment to first fixing the moral constraints on the basic structure of society and only then working out principles for interactions between individuals. The idea is to take the dignity principle, as initially presented, to be inflexible but abstract with its mode of application not yet specified. The examples in the *Groundwork* illustrate its application to interpersonal relations in a presupposed background of an ongoing society with a legitimate legal order. *The Metaphysical Elements of Justice* raises prior questions about the moral justification and limits of any system of public laws, with the assumption that day-to-day relations among individuals must conform to whatever justice demands regarding this necessary background. Thus the suggestion under consideration is that the dignity principle applies first to decisions about the basic system of public laws and only then to individual decisions remaining undetermined by those laws. Though the priority implicit here may be doubted, it is not the inconsistent view that the absolute dignity principle applies independently to laws and to individual conduct and that when these applications conflict we should make exceptions in the individual sphere.

making only universal laws.[8] From this point of view, Kant and Rawls agree, the first principle of justice adopted would be that the system of laws should try to ensure to each person, viewed in advance of particular contingencies, an equal and full opportunity to live out his or her life as a rational agent within the constraints of those laws. This is essentially what Kant calls "the universal principle of justice" and, of course, it is more or less Rawl's first principle of justice.[9]

Unfortunately, human nature being what it is, merely articulating laws that coordinate activities and define fair shares of liberty to each will not suffice to ensure compliance. Many would overstep the bounds and encroach on others' liberty. Thus coercion is needed as a "hindrance to hindrance of freedom" (MEJ 35–36). The coercive power of the state must provide incentives so that even without conscience everyone will have clear and sufficient reason not to violate the liberty of others (as defined by just laws). The aim of the coercive legal system is not to maximize welfare or to give the morally vicious their just deserts but rather to create the conditions in which each has, so far as possible, a fair chance to live out a life as a rational autonomous agent.

State officials cannot, of course, be present at each moment a person begins to invade someone else's freedom contrary to just laws, and so a system of punishment is needed. Though applicable only after a crime has been committed, the system can serve to "hinder hindrances to freedom" by credible threats that provide rational incentives, apart from conscience, for each to stay within the bounds of the freedom he or she has been fairly allotted. The threats must be genuine, enforceable, and public in order to be credible, and they must be carried out as legally prescribed for the sake of both fairness and efficacy.

The system of punishment, however, must not only be a rational deterrent; it must also honor the dignity of each rational agent.

---

[8]I draw here on a reconstruction of the Kantian legislative perspective that I sketch more fully in "The Kingdom of Ends," reprinted in this volume. This view is expanded (and modified slightly) in my "Kantian Constructivism in Ethics," also reprinted here. The basic idea is similar, of course, to the idea of the "original position" in John Rawls's theory of justice, but there are important differences.

[9]See MEJ 35, and John Rawls's *A Theory of Justice* (Cambridge: Harvard University Press, 1971), chap. 1.

This means that criminals must be treated with respect as human beings, not humiliated or manipulated like animals. It also means that the criminal, like every other citizen, must have had a fair chance to avoid the penalty. Thus ex post facto laws, strict liability, and unpredictable penalties must be avoided; the criminal law must be public, easily understood, uniformly enforced, and concerned with provable "external actions" rather than inner moral qualities. Ideally, the penalties would be just severe enough so that, given effective enforcement, reasonable self-interested persons could see that each crime is unlikely to be profitable and yet standards of proportionality of penalty to offense are maintained. The system must be defensible even to the criminal insofar as he or she is willing to look at the matter from the perspective of one rational agent, with dignity, among many.

Kant thought that the system that best satisfies these criteria relied on the *jus talionis,* or "an eye for an eye," as the rule that determines the degree and kind of punishment that should be attached to each offense (MEJ 101). Thus execution should be the punishment for murder. As I have argued elsewhere, this is not because the "inner viciousness" of the murderer deserves the death penalty, still less because the murderer has forfeited all consideration under justice and as a human being. Nor, I think, is Kant's main argument the implausible claim that in choosing the crime with a known penalty the criminal has actually willed his own punishment. The rationale implicit in the central features of Kant's theory of law is that capital punishment is a necessary part of a fair system needed to secure to each citizen, so far as possible, the opportunity to live out a life as a rational and autonomous agent.

We may doubt various assumptions, for example, that only the death penalty can provide adequate (nonmoral) disincentives to murder and that fairness requires inflexible application of the penalty. But let us grant these points for now. How does the reconstructed rationale for judicial killing of human beings square with the dignity principle? That principle, applied to legal systems, clearly implies that criminals should be treated with respect, that the death penalty should be imposed reluctantly, and that the systems should contain other features designed to prevent the crimes that call for capital punishment. The dignity principle also implies that capital punishment cannot be justified by the argument that it saves money, reduces fear, or promotes the happiness of most people. Nor can the rationale be simply "we will save more people than we kill" or "the people we save are worth more than those we kill."

But the justification sketched above was not of these kinds. It used the dignity principle to set standards for a general system of laws, concluding that a legal system expresses its respect for the incomparable worth of each rational agent by seeking to secure for each, in advance of particular contingencies, a full fair opportunity to live as a rational agent. A general system of laws acknowledges the worth of citizens, not as defined at a given time by character traits, social roles, achievements, and records of conduct, but as conceived more generally as rational agents extending over time, capable of choosing any number of roles and courses of action. In carrying out just punishment, one can argue that the system did, so far as possible, secure for even the criminal, in advance of his or her particular choices, a full life with as much liberty as possible in an impartial system of laws. Though the criminal does not wish for the courts to apply the punishment in his or her case, the system respects as far as possible what he or she wills, or would will, as a system of laws when looking at the matter just as a rational agent apart from a particular history and circumstance. If, as Kant thought, capital punishment for murder is a necessary part of that system, criminals should have no legitimate complaint that the law failed to respect their human dignity.[10]

This line of thinking, if cogent, can readily be extended to justify laws authorizing the police in some extreme cases to kill a terrorist who is immediately threatening the lives of law-abiding citizens. By my initial assumption, our terrorist, like the murderer, is a rationally competent agent who flagrantly and immorally crashes across the boundaries of freedom that a just system of

---

[10]It is worth reemphasizing here that the dignity principle does not say that *prolonging the life* of a rational agent is the supremely overriding value, though Kant's strong stand against suicide (with absence of cases of justified killing) in the *Groundwork* often suggests this to readers. The most obvious way to show that one treasures a physical object, say a "priceless" vase, is to do all one can to prevent its destruction, (almost) no matter what. But "rational agents" are not *things* like vases, and what it means to treasure them for what they are is accordingly more complex. Placing a supreme value on rational agents as such requires us not only to seek to preserve them but also to abide by the structures that they, as rational agents, endorse.

law tries to ensure for each, including him- or herself.[11] By authorizing police to use necessary force, even deadly force, against terrorists actively engaged in life-threatening activities, the system serves to "hinder hindrances to freedom" without violating anyone's dignity. In fact, the case here for deadly force against terrorists in action seems stronger than the case for capital punishment for murder because in the latter case prevention efforts have already failed and it remains controversial whether capital punishment is necessary as a deterrent.

IV. Dignity and Endangering Innocent Hostages

So far I have considered only how the dignity principle might be reconciled with policies that involve taking the lives of the terrorists themselves, given some strong assumptions about what the terrorists are like. This analysis suggests that a Kantian may admit legitimate exceptions to the rule "Do not kill human beings," even though there remains a strong presumption in favor of that rule in most circumstances. More controversial questions arise, however, when we consider responses to terrorism that endanger the lives of innocent people. In these cases we could not argue to the persons whose lives we endanger that they have knowingly overstepped the bounds of liberty allotted to them under a fair system of law. Moreover, in at least some of these cases common sense tells us that the numbers matter, that (for example) risking the life of one hostage to save hundreds is not unreasonable.

The issues here are complex. Many variables may be relevant. For example, do we have an option to negotiate without endangering anyone? If not, will the deaths result from our violent attack on the terrorists or from the terrorists themselves when we refuse to negotiate or attack? Are the persons we put in jeopardy already in danger from the terrorists? Is there a chance of rescuing

[11]These assumptions, of course, may not be satisfied in actual cases. Terrorists often claim high-minded motives and deny the justice of the legal systems they attack. Because of cultural differences we often cannot assume that the terrorists knowingly violate a shared moral framework, and in some cases they may not satisfy even the minimal rationality condition. To the extent that the assumptions fail, the line of justification we have been considering does not apply in any straightforward way.

the persons we put in danger? How do we estimate the odds of our killing the hostages, of the terrorists killing the hostages, of our rescuing the hostages, and of the terrorists killing other people? And how certain are we of these estimates? How many survivors and how many dead do we expect in each scenario? How pure are our intentions in imposing the risks? Is there publicly known and accepted policy concerning these situations?

We cannot review all variations, but let us begin with one of the easier cases. Suppose that negotiation to free the hostages is not an option, and so we must attack or stand by and accept the consequences. Suppose, further, that it is nearly certain that all the hostages will be killed if we do not make a rescue attempt. If we do make the attempt, there is a rather good chance that we can save all the hostages, but there is also a non-negligible chance that we may kill some hostages in the effort. For simplicity, suppose that the danger to the attackers and other innocent people is minimal.

Most people, I suppose, would say that we should make the rescue attempt and that if, despite our precautions, we kill innocent hostages in the effort we were still justified in doing what resulted in their deaths. After all, they might say, it is a question of some being killed or all being killed. So, it seems, the intuitive judgment is that the numbers matter here. Since the lives of non-threatening, law-abiding persons are at stake, the Kantian cannot accommodate the intuitive judgment by the same argument we considered for capital punishment and using deadly force against the terrorists themselves. The Kantian must refuse to permit the attack, contrary to common sense, or else find a new argument.

The case is made easier by the fact we stipulated that hostages who may be killed in the attack would be killed by the terrorists if we do not attack. We do not need to endanger one person in order to save others. We need only to justify risking our killing that person in an effort to prevent that person's nearly certain death at the hands of others.

Could the Kantian ever justify this? Again, the dignity principle implies a reluctance to kill or even risk killing human beings, and it implies we should make every effort not to be forced into situations where these actions might be required. But as the dignity principle does not absolutely prohibit killing human beings, it cannot absolutely forbid taking a serious risk that we may kill human beings. The question is, can we risk killing innocent persons in the sort of situation at hand?

Taking a clue from the argument for state coercion and capital punishment, the Kantian should consider the question not in the isolated instance but as it falls under general laws and policies applicable to everyone over time. Here the issue is: what public policies would it be morally legitimate for a community to adopt in authorizing official responses to terrorism? As before, the appropriate Kantian point of view for deliberating about this is presumably that of a rational legislator in the "kingdom of ends."

The legislators' commitment to the dignity principle means that they have a strong concern to preserve each person's opportunity to function as a rational autonomous agent. So they have an initial interest in saving lives. But the dignity principle also imposes constraints on how they can justifiably do this. For example, the legislators cannot simply assign a quantity of value to each life and then try to find the value-maximizing policy. Moreover, they must find policies that are justifiable even to those who will suffer under them (insofar as they, too, adopt the same legislative point of view). Further, since human dignity means more than merely preserving life, the legislators must consider other ways that policies can affirm that central value. They would, for instance, tend to favor policies that strongly express and encourage mutual respect, and oppose the opposite, independently of the policies' effects on survival rates.

Considerations of dignity alone are not always sufficient to resolve an issue. But nonetheless there may be a reasonable way of thinking about the problem from the Kantian legislative point of view. Each legislator not only values human dignity but also has a set of "private ends" which he or she can pursue only while living. (I set aside here beliefs about immortality.) Valuing each other person as an end, the legislator also has reason (Kant implies) to give some weight to the ends of others. From the legislative point of view lawmakers must "abstract from the content of private ends" and so cannot concern themselves with the details of who wants what. But that each has a general concern for his or her own survival seems to follow from the idea that members have private ends (and know so). To be sure, legislators are committed to seeking policies promoting their own survival only on the condition that the policy is equally acceptable to others. But others too have a similar concern for their own survival. Thus, one might argue, all would favor any policy that promised to prolong the survival of representative persons as rational autonomous persons, other things equal and provided the policy is otherwise consistent with the dignity principle. Each legislator would favor the policy when looking at it from his or her own perspective (abstractly conceived) and also when reviewing it from the perspective of each other person.

Now, if suitably hedged with restrictions, some policy that permitted authorized agents to endanger the life of a hostage in an attempt to save that hostage and others from almost certain death would be seen, in advance of particular contingencies, as enhancing each representative law-abiding citizen's chances for surviving terrorist situations. If so, the policy would be reasonable and, it seems, not inherently contrary to the dignity principle. If, in addition, the policy was decided upon in a legitimate political process, was known to all, and was carried out by authorized individuals, then (absent further objections) the dignity principle would seem to permit its execution, even at the serious risk of innocent lives.

This argument is too sketchy to draw any precise line between permissible and impermissible cases, but it suggests at least that the Kantian is not forced to choose between treating dignity as a measurable quantity and condemning all avoidable killing of innocent persons. The reasoning allows us to consider "chances of survival" and so (indirectly) the numbers of lives at stake, but this consideration enters the deliberation not as a basic principle ("many lives have greater value than few") but as pertinent information at a later stage. "Try to save the most lives" may become a highly qualified derivative principle for specified circumstances, but, if suitably restricted, this maxim is compatible with the dignity principle. And, of course, to deny that the chances of survival under different policies should ever in any way be a relevant moral consideration would be sheer madness.[12]

---

[12]Because of his rigoristic stand on certain issues (e.g., lying), contemporary discussions often simply label Kant an "absolutist" while treating any theory that allows that "the numbers count" as "consequentialist"; but this view is misleading. It matters how, for what reasons, and under what constraints a theory allows the numbers to count. An interpretation (or extension) of Kant's theory that admits that sometimes one should take into account, at some level of deliberation, whether one or a thousand will be killed does not thereby "reduce" to consequentialism.

A more difficult question arises when the persons endangered by our efforts to free the hostages are not the hostages already at risk but others. Even if the attack will save many lives, it cannot be defended as giving a better chance of survival to the very people endangered by the terrorists. To attack, it seems, would be to treat the fewer persons as exchangeable for a greater number of persons, contrary to the dignity principle.

Although I think there are strong reasons not to endorse a general permission to attack in such cases, the Kantian line of thinking we have been considering need not lead to an absolute prohibition. It might allow the attack in certain carefully circumscribed extreme cases but, of course, not on the ground that "more lives are worth more than fewer." The reasoning in favor of the attack, as before, would have to be that the policy of attack in exceptional cases of this kind could be defended from the general legislative point of view even to those who turn out to be the victims under the policy. The argument from that point of view would be that the policy, all considered, enhanced each representative (law-abiding) citizen's chances of survival, without violating any of the essential constraints of the Kantian legislative perspective. To show this we might need to establish that the chances of each citizen falling into the unfortunate hostage role, independently of his or her choice to take special risks, are more or less the same. We would also need to take into account the likelihood that the policy would undermine respect for life, would lead to foolish risk-taking, and would be abused by callous trigger-happy officials. A legal system or moral code that said, without careful qualification, "Authorities may risk killing one person whenever they think that they can thereby save more than one," would invite abuse and probably cost more lives in the long run. Moreover, prolonging human life is not the only value implicit in the dignity principle. Any policy must also be evaluated in terms of the way it expresses and encourages mutual respect, honors prior commitments, upholds just institutions, etc.[13]

[13]These other constraints are potentially important. My argument is not that any policy is acceptable if it would be approved by rational impartial legislators focused exclusively on survival. There is more involved in valuing human dignity than caring about prolonging the lives of rational agents. The point is that, unless circumstances

Nonetheless, a more circumscribed policy of this sort could conceivably give each representative citizen a better prospect for living out a full life as a rational agent than would an absolute prohibition on endangering innocent lives in such cases. Though the stakes may be higher, the argument for the policy would in principle be like the case for current laws that permit police to speed when actively pursuing armed robbers even though this imposes risk on law-abiding motorists. If all other constraints were satisfied, such policies might be approved by all from the appropriate point of view.

In this way of thinking, our calculation of each representative person's chances of survival under different general policies would be information relevant in the overall justification, but the fundamental principle regarding official responses to terrorism would remain "Public policies must conform to principles acceptable to all from the abstract legislative point of view that, among other things, regards each person as of incalculable worth." One way of respecting the dignity of all is to authorize police to impose grave risks only as permitted under public policies that they themselves, as rational agents would approve.

V. Intentional Sacrifice of Innocent Persons

My aim in reviewing this series of cases has been to suggest a (more or less) Kantian way of thinking that might reconcile the dignity principle with the common opinion that in some circumstances it is morally permissible to kill terrorists and to endanger innocent hostages. The scenarios we reviewed only posed questions about taking *risks* that we will kill innocent persons, *unintentionally*, as we try to save others. Reasonable people may differ about the degree of risk that is warranted, but almost everyone agrees that some such risks are worth taking. Unfortunately, we can imagine situations where terrorism confronts us with choices more horrible than those we have considered, and about these

---

reveal ways that a life-maximizing policy violates or undermines some other value implicit in human dignity, the dignity principle will allow and even encourage us to take into account whether the policy is likely to save the most lives.

cases philosophers will disagree more sharply. For example, suppose that the only way to prevent a terrorist from blowing up a building with many hostages is to shoot the terrorist *through* another innocent hostage who is held as a shield. Or, still worse, suppose that we could save the many hostages only by deliberately killing an innocent victim of his choice.

Here traditional morality draws the line, refusing to authorize the intentional sacrifice of an innocent person even to save others.[14] Kant too would be horrified at the thought, and no doubt many consequentialists would feel the same. But the question here is whether *the theories* in question could permit the killing, and how they could justify their conclusions.

These more extreme cases pose a challenge to the Kantian quite different from the one that has been my main concern. The worry now is not that Kantian theory cannot permit *enough* of what reasonable persons would allow; it is that the theory as construed here will permit *too much* to be morally tolerable, authentically Kantian, or significantly different from the consequentialist theory.[15]

These are important concerns, deserving a fuller treatment than I can attempt here.[16] A thorough response would require a more detailed characterization of the Kantian legislative perspective than I have given. But, even without that, it seems clear that our Kantian legislators have strong reasons for refusing to authorize the intentional killing of innocent persons in response to terrorism.

[14]To focus discussion, assume that the victim in question is either unable or unwilling to volunteer and that he or she is law-abiding and is not among those at serious risk of being killed by the terrorists. Further, from now on I shall concentrate on cases where the sacrificial killing in question would be intended, not merely a "foreseen unintended consequence." (Killing a chosen victim to placate the terrorist is a clear example; shooting the terrorist *through* the hostage is more controversial.). Also, as before, I am restricting my remarks to official (e.g., police) responses to terrorism and assuming the victims are "innocent" in an intuitive, but still undefined, sense. In a fuller discussion, of course, other variations would need to be considered.

[15]These worries have been often and well expressed at the meetings where I have presented this paper and by an anonymous reader. To these I owe not only thanks but, in time, a more fully developed response.

[16]It is worth keeping in mind here, as Larry Becker has reminded me, that *any* theory that attempts to resolve these dilemmas will leave conscientious persons unhappy because, despite the best of will, some things about which good people care deeply will be lost and our choices affect which these will be.

Most obviously, all the considerations making the Kantian legislators reluctant to *endanger* innocent hostages will be even stronger reasons not to authorize *intentional killing* of innocents. To
legitimize any such killing as public policy would be a dangerous
invitation to abuse by corrupt, self-deceiving, and bungling officials. The policy would likely lower everyone's sense of security
and trust. Those in authority could never honestly say even to a
loved one, "I would never kill you or turn you over to killers."
Worse yet, official readiness to kill innocent persons in response to
terrorists' threats would not only encourage such blackmail but
would also enhance the terrorists' power. By making convincing
threats to do a greater evil, terrorists could easily manipulate the
authorities into doing a lesser one. The lawless could thus enlist
the aid of law enforcement to get their dirty work done for them.

Few would deny that the general policy of killing innocents to
placate terrorists would have these bad consequences, and more;
but some may try to press an objection often posed to consequentialists. That is, they may argue that, in some extraordinary situation, a one-time, secret, unauthorized sacrifice of an innocent
person might save lives without incurring all the problems of
openly admitting a policy of negotiating with terrorists. Here, the
objection continues, the killing would still be wrong but not for
the reasons given above.

Now this counter-example may pose a problem for consequentialism of some kinds, but it does not apply to the limited use of a
Kantian legislative perspective that I have proposed here. This idea
was introduced not as a comprehensive moral decision procedure
but as a thought experiment to guide and constrain attempts to
justify public policies with regard to issues, such as murder and
terrorism, where not having enforceable public policy would be
disastrous. A crucial background assumption was that the procedure justifies policies only *as openly acknowledged and scrupulously administered.*[17] If any "exceptions" are to be justified by the

---

[17]The aim of the legislative thinking is to find public policies that officials *should*
scrupulously carry out. This does not mean, of course, that in their deliberations the
Kantian legislators should foolishly assume that in fact there will never be abuse and
corruption by public officials. The proposed use of the Kantian legislative perspective
here, I should note, differs in two important respects from the broader use considered
in my other discussions of Kant's "kingdom of ends" formula of the Categorical

legislative procedure, then, they must be justified as overt aspects of a general public policy, not as secret, one-time deviations.

A Kantian ethics must also take into account the following. The dignity principle requires that we *always* regard each person as having incomparable worth, and so not as a mere means even to worthy ends. This is an attitude to be maintained in daily living as well as a stipulated constraint on thinking from the abstract legislative standpoint. Thus, to be justified in a deliberate killing, a person would need to be able to face the victim and say, sincerely and truthfully, "I choose to kill you (when I have an option not to); but still I regard you as more than a *mere* means, in fact, as a person with a worth that is incalculable."[18] Now it is hard to imagine that a human being could maintain this attitude while deliberately killing another, even though apparently Kant thought that public executioners could and many think that doctors administering euthanasia can.[19] It seems even more unlikely that human beings in general could authorize, approve, and carry out public policies of deliberate sacrifice of innocent persons while continuing honestly to affirm an untarnished respect for human dignity.

Imperative (in Chapters 3 and 11). First, the proposal here is not to treat the legislative perspective as a comprehensive moral decision procedure but rather to consider it as a restricted perspective for reviewing general enforceable policies, assumed to be publicly acknowledged, for matters where there is good reason to have such policies. Second, my proposal here is not to assume "strict compliance" with the law but to review policies from the legislative perspective with full awareness that in fact even the best policies and laws are often ignored and abused. This last point helps to meet the "utopianism" objection raised in my fourth essay (and alluded to briefly in the eleventh), but there remain difficult questions about the relation between strict and partial compliance theory.

[18]Treating someone as more than a "mere means," in the ordinary sense, does not suffice to show that one regards them as an "end" in Kant's sense. One might, for example, regard a cherished old car as more than a "mere means" without attributing to it an "unconditional and incomparable worth."

[19]This was suggested to me by Andrews Reath. The point here is not that it is *logically impossible* to attribute an incomparable or incalculable worth to a person while one deliberately kills that person. Perhaps some community of superhuman beings, with complete self-control and purity of motive, could mutually agree on a policy of deliberate sacrifice when it will save more lives and then carry out the policy from pure devotion to duty, never once seeing this as an exchange of less value for more. But we are not like that. So, given human nature, it seems unlikely that we would, or even could, agree on and implement the policy "Deliberately kill innocent persons when it will save more" without coming to regard persons as things with a value subject to exchange.

As Kantian legislators they could not approve of any policy that they could not carry out consistently with the dignity principle. Thus it seems implausible that they could accept any policy involving deliberate sacrifice of innocent persons even if they predicted it would save more lives.

VI. Responsibility and "Clean Hands"

A final issue that calls for fuller discussion but can only be briefly mentioned here is how we should determine responsibility for the deaths in our terrorist situations. The worry is that our abstract deliberations about the numbers of lives saved and lost have not taken into account who will be responsible for the deaths. Mustn't we consider not only how many will die but also whether the deaths result directly from our acts (or omissions) or through another's immoral response to what we do (or refuse to do)?

Traditional morality does not impute to me, as the "consequence" of my action or inaction, every event to which my action or inaction was a causally contributing factor, even if that event would not have occurred but for my action or inaction. We are "responsible" for some of the effects of what we do but not for others. If, for example, prior to President Bush's inauguration someone had threatened to kill himself if Bush took up the presidency and Bush, knowing this, did so anyway and the threat was carried out, common sense does not impute the death to Bush but to the person who foolishly made and carried out the threat. Kant seems to agree, for he argues (in a far less convincing case) that even if one's refusal to lie to a murderer causally contributes to the murderer's finding one's friend and killing him, the death of the friend is imputed entirely to the killer, not to oneself for refusing to tell a lie. This suggests that, in a Kantian ethics, one must at least take into account whether deaths are a direct result of one's own actions (or inactions) or whether they result from someone else's immoral responses to what one does (or refuses to do). Judgments of responsibility after a death has been caused often take this factor into account, and so it seems also relevant as we deliberate before acting about what would be the right thing to do.

To expand our previous case, suppose that we have three options: submit to terrorist demands, attack the terrorists, or refuse their demands and do nothing further. If we submit, let us suppose, we will save the hostages but almost certainly encourage further terrorism that will cost even more lives. If we attack, we will kill some hostages but will save more other hostages. If we refuse to negotiate and do nothing else, the terrorists will probably kill all the hostages. In the first and third cases the deaths that occur will result through the agency of the terrorists themselves, even though our choice is a causal condition. In the second case (attack), the deaths will be a direct result of our actions (though we are responding to a problem posed by the terrorists). Prior to trying to figure out which course, all considered, is morally best, we need to ask whether, in addition to our intentions and the estimates of lives expected to be lost and saved, it is also relevant whether the deaths are directly caused by us or by the terrorists.

Extending our previous line of thought, we could also address this question from the abstract point of view of Kantian legislators. The dignity principle itself should make us extremely reluctant to risk killing human beings, but it should also make us very hesitant to do something when we are confident that others will respond by killing human beings. Perhaps the refusal to take action that may kill others, other things equal, is more directly expressive of the way we value human lives; but other things are rarely equal, and refusal to take extraordinary steps to save lives can also express inadequate concern. We cannot be certain, of course, that the terrorists would carry out their threats if we do nothing; but then we are also uncertain how other options would turn out, and our question now is whether anything but these estimates of probabilities and numbers should make a difference. If it is generally worse to risk killing someone than to do what has the same probability of someone else doing a killing, then there must be reasons for this policy that are cogent from the Kantian legislative point of view. But what could they be?

The policy in question is a fairly specific application of a more general principle that is often maintained, namely, that it is generally better to "keep one's own hands clean" than to do what would normally be wrong in an effort to prevent wrongs that one anticipates that others will commit. This says, vaguely, that one's primary responsibility is to worry about the direct consequences of what one does or fails to do, without excessive regard to whether others will take the occasion to respond immorally.

Now I can imagine four considerations that might be offered in support of this principle for a world in which most are conscientious and even those who are prone to crime are often amenable to reason. First, a public policy that gives you greater responsibility for what you cause independently of the immoral responses of others might work to minimize the damage so often caused by well-meaning people in their efforts to prevent the wrongdoing of others. If most people are conscientious and many are bunglers, we would perhaps all do better if we do not encourage people to anticipate and act violently to prevent the crimes of others. Second, the policy would curb the lawbreakers' power to get their way through blackmail. If authorities were prepared to harm innocent persons whenever someone made a convincing threat to inflict more harm, then by using manipulative threats criminals could in effect make the authorities their accomplices. Third, the policy might promote the opportunity for most people to live out their own lives as rational agents because it places a higher priority on "keeping one's own house in order" than on intervening in the lives of those who we expect will act badly. By contrast, a policy that required everyone to be a moral busybody, always ready to do a lesser evil to prevent others from doing a slightly greater evil, would leave less room for planning and living out one's own preferred life. Fourth, the policy that makes each person primarily responsible for his or her own actions expresses a hope or faith that others will, after all, listen to reason despite their threats and past records, and so affirming that policy is a way of expressing respect for them as rational agents.

Though relevant, these policy considerations do not decisively support an inflexible "clean hands" principle, even in good conditions; and they are even less persuasive when violent crimes become more frequent and criminals more oblivious to reason. Moreover, the reasons that favor a "clean hands" policy for ordinary citizens do not apply equally well to law enforcement authorities. There are fewer risks and interferences with rational life plans when responsibility to prevent crimes is restricted to selected officials who voluntarily take up the task.

Furthermore, I suspect that the "clean hands" principle gains much of its popular support from a confusion. Suppose it is assumed that a certain act, say, telling a lie, is always wrong. Then if someone is tempted to lie to prevent another person from doing something worse, it might be appropriate to admonish the would-be liar by saying, "No, forget what others may do, your responsibility is for what you do." Similarly, if we assume that any intentional killing of a human being is wrong in itself, then even when killing one person would prevent others from killing many, we may say, "Keep your own hands clean; what others do is not your responsibility." But the assumption in both cases is crucial. Unless we take as given that what we propose to do is wrong in itself, it remains an open question whether "what others do" affects one's responsibility. And, from the Kantian legislative point of view, what specific acts, if any, are always wrong and the degree to which we should take responsibility for preventing the consequences of others' crimes are matters about which we need to reason, not principles we can assume from the start.

VII. Conclusion

My conclusions are limited and tentative. First, the dignity principle, it seems, can be maintained without insisting that it is always wrong to kill human beings and to risk killing innocent human beings in response to terrorism. Second, there is a Kantian way of thinking about hard choices that admits, without abandoning the dignity principle, that at some level one must take into account the relative numbers of people whose lives can be prolonged by different policies. Third, though further discussion is needed, the objection that Kantian legislators would approve of deliberate sacrifices of innocent persons seems dubious. Finally, while this Kantian perspective may give some support to a limited "clean hands" policy for most people under good conditions, it does not endorse the absolute principle, "Regardless of what others threaten to do, your only responsibility is to ensure that *you* don't kill any innocent person."

Can the substantive principles "Don't kill human beings" and "Avoid endangering the lives of innocent persons" be maintained *as principles* in a Kantian morality even though they admittedly have exceptions? This depends on what "maintaining them as principles" means. Clearly not, if it means trying to keep the majority of people thinking of them as exceptionless rules while privately admitting that there are justified exceptions. But there may still be a sense in which the principles, with exceptions implicitly understood, might be held as quite fundamental principles, more so than others (like "Don't commit incest") that have far fewer justified exceptions. That is, though qualified, the principles are partial expressions, in action terms, of the very attitude that the dignity principle itself demands, and the exceptions they contain are not concessions to a radically different moral point of view but are rather refinements consistent with the basic Kantian viewpoint.

11

Kantian Constructivism in Ethics

Kant's ideas have influenced contemporary moral and political thought in many ways. This influence is exemplified most prominently in the work of John Rawls. In his now classic book, *A Theory of Justice*, and also in subsequent papers, Rawls develops an original political theory that is similar in important ways to Kant's ethical theory.[1] Rawls fully acknowledges, of course, that he draws from Kant's ideas, extending, specifying, and modifying them in ways appropriate to the aims and limits of his project. While some affinities between Rawls's political theory and Kant's ethics are familiar, the structural parallels between certain aspects of the two theories may be less evident. In this essay I highlight some similarities and contrasts between Rawls's "original position" and Kant's "kingdom of ends." This is not the usual point of comparison between Rawls and Kant, but nonetheless it can be illuminating. The kingdom of ends, I suggest, can be read as a constructivist model for deliberating about moral principles for individuals in a way that is analogous to the role of the original

I want to thank Richard Arneson, Bernard Boxill, and Geoffrey Sayre McCord for their helpful comments on an earlier version of this article.

[1]My discussion will assume that the reader is familiar with John Rawls's *A Theory of Justice* (Cambridge: Harvard University Press, 1971), hereafter referred to as TJ. The papers by Rawls most relevant here are: "Kantian Constructivism in Moral Theory: The Dewey Lectures 1980," *Journal of Philosophy* 77 (1980): 515-72, "Justice as Fairness: Political Not Metaphysical," *Philosophy and Public Affairs* 14 (1985): 223-51, and "The Idea of an Overlapping Consensus," *Oxford Journal of Legal Studies* 7 (1987): 1-25.

position as an ideal choice perspective for principles of justice regarding basic social institutions.

Rawls's constructivist theory of justice has had a wide appeal among those who reject utilitarianism and yet are dissatisfied with the common practice of relying on intuitions case by case. Rawls's constructivist methodology has also been attractive because it attempts to bypass linguistic and metaphysical disputes in which earlier "metaethics" had become entangled. The strong appeal of Rawls's political theory leads naturally to the desire to adopt his constructivism for thinking about issues in other areas. For example, writers sometimes assume uncritically that specific moral issues can be resolved by arguing directly from Rawls's original position. The danger in this assumption is that features of a theory that make it suitable for one purpose may render it unsuitable for other purposes. If so, modifications and alternatives need to be considered. My suggestion here will be, first, that Rawls's original position is not in general an appropriate standpoint for deliberating about ethical issues, and second, Kant's "kingdom of ends" offers the outlines of an alternative that is worth considering.

My aim, then, is to raise the question whether Rawls's work on justice offers a reasonable and workable model for ethical theory in areas apart from the special subject for which it was primarily designed. More specifically, does his particular version of Kantian Constructivism serve well the broader purposes of ethical theory when questions about the justice of basic political and economic institutions are not the central focus of attention? And, supposing the theory might be extended in this way, what modifications, if any, would be necessary or desirable?

These are large questions, and my comments on them will be admittedly quite incomplete and tentative. Since my discussion concerns the possible extension of Rawls's work, a road not taken by Rawls himself in recent papers, what I have to say is not to be construed as criticism of that work. Though my remarks will not presuppose that Rawls's theory is satisfactory even within its own domain, I do assume that the theory is richly suggestive of further extensions in ethical theory. At the same time, I sense the dangers of attempting to extend the theory uncritically. As will be evident, I take for granted some of Rawls's methodological assumptions: for example, that in moral philosophy we need for a time to deemphasize criticism and instead to work constructively to develop our alternative theories, painting at first with broad strokes, then filling in details, and only later assessing the comparative merits of the products as wholes. One-shot objections rarely demolish a moral theory, and premature demands for rigor of detail often impede progress. Any adequate ethical theory is likely to be complex and many-sided, and attempts to draw practical conclusions from a theory should be sensitive to its purpose and limitations.

My discussion will proceed as follows: First, I call attention to the explicit limits Rawls places on his project and the claims he makes for its results, but I also note widely appealing features of his theory that might encourage one to extend it beyond the purposes for which it was designed.

Second, I argue that, despite these attractive features, one cannot simply appropriate Rawls's theory, as it stands, for all purposes of moral decision making. Rawls's own reluctance to extend his theory suggests this conclusion, which becomes even more evident as we reflect on how the limited purpose of the original position has guided the selection of its defining features. Different moral questions call for different levels of reflection, and what features appropriately define a "moral point of view" for resolving a particular question depend importantly on the specific nature of that question. Rawls's original position is obviously not the appropriate stance for individuals facing immediate moral choices; and, I shall argue, it is also not a perspective from which we can justify and resolve disputes about our most basic moral values. If the original position is to be used to address ethical questions about matters beyond the justice of basic institutions, the only plausible alternative is to treat it as a perspective for reflecting about what intermediate-level moral principles would be suitable for certain ideal conditions. Even for this purpose, however, the original position, as currently defined, has serious drawbacks, which should at least lead constructivists to explore alternatives.

Third, for comparison, I sketch some features of an alternative "original position" drawn from Kant's idea of a kingdom of ends. Though incomplete and problematic in its own way, this Kantian perspective seems in some respects more appropriate than its Rawlsian counterpart when we go beyond Rawls's "primary subject" to raise questions about intermediate-level moral principles for individuals.

I conclude with a reminder that both Rawls and Kant use thought experiments with an idealizing feature which creates a gap between what we can conclude from those reflections and what we need in order to make reasonable moral decisions about immediate problems in the real world.

I. Extending the Theory: Warnings and Temptations

Despite his optimistic suggestions that the theory of justice might be expanded into a general theory of right conduct, Rawls never claims that one can resolve particular moral problems simply by putting the issues before deliberators in the original position. Nor does he claim that his two principles of justice, which he argues would be chosen in the original position, can be appropriately used to guide individual decisions about questions of justice in small groups. In *A Theory of Justice* he argues that certain principles of "natural duty" and "the principle of fairness," which apply to individual choices, would be adopted in the original position, and he suggests that this fact amounts to some kind of justification for them (TJ 108-17, 333-50). But these principles, as Rawls admits, are far from a comprehensive moral guide for individual choice; and, though Rawls speculates that his theory of justice might be extended into a general theory of right conduct, and even a theory of virtues, he does not develop these suggestions, (TJ 17, 436-37).

Several papers written after *A Theory of Justice* make even more explicit and unmistakable Rawls's intention to limit his theory, as presented so far, to questions about the justice of the basic institutions of large-scale cooperative societies.[2] Insofar as he comments on the moral decisions of individuals, this is to draw out the implications of his conclusions about this primary subject, not to propose a comprehensive moral theory. The Dewey Lectures might seem to be an exception, but they are not.[3] In those lectures

---

[2] See esp. John Rawls, "The Basic Structure as Subject," *American Philosophical Quarterly* 14 (1977): 159-65.

[3] Rawls, "Kantian Constructivism in Moral Theory," esp. the third lecture, "Construction and Objectivity," pp. 554-74.

Rawls sketches a type of moral theory ("Kantian Constructivism") that he says Sidgwick, and most subsequent moral philosophers, have overlooked, and he cites his own theory of justice as an illustration. But careful readers will readily notice that, though certain formal features of a constructivist type of ethical theory are described, Rawls makes no pretensions of having offered a comprehensive theory of this type. His theory remains, as before, a theory about how reasonably to assess and order certain conflicting views about the justice of the basic institutions of society. This is an ambitious, and urgently needed, project, but it is not itself a *comprehensive* ethical theory of the "Kantian Constructivist" sort which, Rawls says, Sidgwick and others have overlooked.

Two more recent papers also show that Rawls's current intention is to offer his theory of justice as something less than a comprehensive moral guide.[4] Not only is the subject restricted to "the basic structure of society," but the aim is also limited to finding a reasonable basis for "overlapping consensus" among those whose values are deeply formed by certain Western democratic traditions. The results are not claimed to be timeless moral truths but rather a core of political principles that reasonable adherents of different moral perspectives can publicly agree upon. These restrictions on the subject, aims, and hopes for the theory, as currently developed, need not detract from its value; nor do they preclude extensions of the theory for broader purposes. Yet when tempted to use Rawls's theoretical framework for more far-reaching moral purposes, we should at least take warning from Rawls's own acknowledgments that a theory carefully constructed with compromises and simplifying assumptions suitable for his limited purposes may not serve as well our grander ambitions for a comprehensive moral theory.

The fact that Rawls himself does not extend his theory is, of course, no absolute bar against our doing so. Appeals to authority are out of place here, and we may attribute Rawls's restrictions to excessive modesty or caution. Initial hopes for extending Rawls's work should not be lightly abandoned, for important features of that work still have a powerful appeal to those dissatisfied with other traditional types of ethical theory. Moreover, some of those

---

[4]Rawls, "Justice as Fairness" and "The Idea of an Overlapping Consensus."

appealing features are independent of other controversial aspects of Rawls's methodology that might deter some philosophers from trying to extend his theory.

Rawls's basic strategy is to attempt to determine the content and ranking of normative principles, and to justify them in some sense, by showing that these would be chosen in a specified hypothetical choice situation by persons conceived in a specified way. The choosers are not seen as seeking to *discover* a moral order, Platonic, natural, or divine, which exists independently of their reasoned choices; rather, we are to view principles as justifiable by virtue of their being what persons with the specified values would choose in the defined situation. Obviously the value of this general strategy depends upon the adequacy of the initial stipulations for the purpose at hand, and these purposes may vary.

"Kantian Constructivism," as Rawls presents it, uses this strategy in a way that gives a central role to a conception of persons as free, equal, and rational agents. Rawls's own theory is a particular version of Kantian Constructivism. Its "original position," in its final form, gives a specific interpretation of this Kantian conception of persons together with other features of the initial choice situation.[5] In addition, the Rawlsian theory is primarily focused on the justice of basic institutions, presupposes shared values in a public culture, uses a method of "reflective equilibrium" (TJ 20-21, 48-51), and claims only "reasonableness" in our times and not timeless "truth" for its results.

[5]The features of Rawls's theory mentioned so far, in contrast to those that follow, are the main ones that I shall be considering as I raise doubts about "extending his theory" in ethics. It is important to note, however, that other features associated with his methodology, especially his holistic approach and rejection of "foundationalism," will be set aside. Rawls does not suppose that ethics can proceed by deducing specific principles from self-evident starting points. He grants both that alternative descriptions of the initial choice situation could be employed and that the best description is to be selected in part by considering how its results match our "considered judgments" about more specific principles. Nonetheless he does present and argue independently for a preferred specific description (which is what I shall subsequently refer to as "the original position"), and he uses this to guide decisions about the principles of justice, "natural duties," "the principle of fairness," etc. When I later refer to drawing "more specific principles" from "basic moral values," I have in mind this guiding function of his original position as finally specified, realizing that the values built into the original position are not for Rawls "basic" in the foundationalist sense of "unrevisable," "self-evident," or "warranted altogether independently of the acceptability of their applications."

These additional features, I take it, are separable from Rawls's basic strategy and his Kantian conception of persons. The focus on the justice of basic institutions, for example, can be set aside in order to raise the question whether the original position can resolve moral questions *beyond justice*. One could use the basic strategy without the method of reflective equilibrium if one thought that a well-defined initial choice situation should not be modified to accommodate common sense "intuitions" about particular cases. And less modest versions of Kantian Constructivism could attempt to derive principles from the will of free and rational agents without conceding that one must rely on shared values in a culture and forgo claims to "moral truth." Controversies about these matters, then, need not prevent us from trying to use Rawls's basic strategy in its Kantian form for moral theory generally.

The reason for wanting to do so is the hope that certain appealing features of Rawls's theory could be preserved in inquiries of more far-reaching scope. Among the aspects of Rawls's theory which readers have found attractive, the following are perhaps most relevant for our purposes. First, the theory develops in a more thorough and contemporary fashion a line of thought deeply embedded in our intellectual history, most prominently in the works of Rousseau, Kant, and other social contract theorists. Second, by attempting to justify principles from the hypothetical choices of idealized agents, Rawls offers hope of a kind of moral objectivity missing in familiar emotivist and prescriptivist theories, such as those of Stevenson and Hare, while avoiding the strong metaphysical commitments of "moral realist" theories of the sort advocated by Plato, Moore, and others. Rawls may stretch one's imagination about *possible* agents, but he seeks to avoid ontological commitment to the existence of values and principles apart from hypothetical choices. Third, whereas prior to Rawls's work utilitarian moral thinking was opposed primarily by intuitionist critics who relied upon refutation by counter-example, Rawls has developed and defended a competing way of thinking that offers hopes of making anti-utilitarian sentiments more systematic and deeply grounded.

A fourth feature of Rawls's theory which I believe is intuitively attractive to many is that it seeks to contribute to the resolution of important disputes about substantive principles by first adopting a more neutral point of view appropriate for the purpose. It asks us to picture an ideal perspective, reflecting the more formal commitments shared by people of diverse moral opinions, and then to use this as a heuristic device for adjudicating more particular disputes. Like Kant, Baier, ideal observer theorists, and some rule-utilitarians, Rawls seems to offer a model of the basic features of a "moral point of view" which can be commended independently of one's position on specific moral controversies.[6] Such theories often attract or repel us, not so much by their results as by the way they envision the attitudes and procedures suitable for seeking specific moral conclusions. Though controversial in many respects, Rawls's model of the ideal choice situation seems to represent some of the most essential features of a widely shared moral point of view.

Our question, then, is whether the particular way Rawls works out the Kantian constructivist strategy can be extended for general moral theory without losing the appealing features just mentioned, even though Rawls himself has not taken this route. As a first step toward answering this question, I shall consider whether the original position *as currently defined* can serve this larger purpose. Later we can speculate about what alternative or modified perspective might be more suitable.

II. The Original Position as a Moral Guide?

Since we reflect on moral issues of different levels of generality, with appropriately different background assumptions, we need to sharpen our question by distinguishing different moral tasks which one might try to address from the original position.[7]

---

[6]See, e.g., *Groundwork*; Kurt Baier, *The Moral Point of View* (Ithaca: Cornell University Press, 1958); Roderick Firth, "Ethical Absolutism and the Ideal Observer," *Philosophy and Phenomenological Research* 12 (1952): 317-45; R.M. Hare, *Moral Thinking* (Oxford: Clarendon, 1981); Richard Brandt, *Ethical Theory* (Englewood Cliffs, N.J.: Prentice-Hall, 1959), chaps. 10 and 15, and *A Theory of the Good and the Right* (Oxford: Clarendon, 1979), chap. 15; and William K. Frankena, *Ethics* (Englewood Cliffs, N.J.: Prentice-Hall, 1973), pp. 107-14.

[7]In referring to "levels of generality" here, and elsewhere, I oversimplify somewhat. Moral issues can be divided along several dimensions: e.g., scope of the moral values in question (all moral values vs. justice vs. charity); order of justification (basic vs.

Most important, we should separate (1) the problems faced by particular individuals trying to decide what they should do in a specific context, (2) philosophical inquiry into the nature and grounds of our most basic values, and (3) the attempt to determine from our most basic moral values what "intermediate-level" principles of conduct are appropriate for ourselves and others who share a specified historical and cultural context. The question, then, will be: which, if any, of these tasks is appropriately addressed from the standpoint of Rawls's original position?

(1) Consider, first, moral choices faced by particular moral agents in concrete situations, for example, my decision whether to lie to a friend, Carla, about the past infidelities of her recently deceased husband, Floyd. Here I may find it helpful to be guided by principles which I believe rational agents in some idealized situation might adopt. In doing so I would be making *indirect* use of the idea of an "original position," but only by first trying to derive general principles from that position. (I return to this option below, under (3).) What is clear and obvious, after the least reflection, is that I cannot reasonably address my problem *directly* from the perspective of the original position. Indeed, to attempt to do so would be unhelpful and morally perverse. Why? Taking up the perspective of the original position would mean trying to make a choice while behind a thick "veil of ignorance," focusing exclusively on "primary goods," and thinking only of my own (abstractly conceived) interests (TJ 17-22, 118-50). This means not only that I would need to put aside my sympathy and the intuitive urgings of conscience but also that I must ignore my most reflectively considered moral policies as well my particular commitments to my friend. I must disregard my knowledge of the special things we value as *ends* and count as relevant only how the choice would affect the distribution of *means* which I can reasonably expect everyone to want, whatever their conception of the good life. The "veil" would, of course, free me from bias in favor of my own

derivative); degree of acceptance or controversy (commonly agreed vs. disputed); and domain of reference (institutions vs. individuals, all persons vs. our contemporaries vs. that person here-now). When I refer to "extending" Rawls's strategy for ethics, I have in mind mainly expanding the scope and reference from the justice of the basic structure of society to nonpolitical moral questions for individuals; but in this section I am also concerned with other distinctions, as I hope the context will make clear.

special interests, but it would also blind me to potentially relevant facts about the personal relationships in the case, my ability to sustain the lie effectively, and the sincerity of my friend's professed desire to know the truth. Indeed, if I take the "veil" seriously, I cannot even pose my problem from the perspective of the original position, for to understand that problem presupposes that I know more facts about particulars than the veil allows me to consider. The problem refers to real individuals in a concrete context on the other side of the veil; and it calls for sympathy, respect, and sensitivity to detail, not blind disinterest or judicial "ignorance."

In the original position the members have vast general knowledge but do not know particulars. Before the "veil" is lifted, they are ignorant not only of their own place in history but also of the particular course of history. One might suggest, however, that the members could contemplate *possible* historical scenarios, described in full detail, without identifying actual individuals. Then, it might be thought, the members could pass judgment on the problem of people just like Carla and Floyd in a situation exactly like theirs. The problem with this suggestion, however, is that the motivational structure attributed to the members is obviously insufficient to enable us to pick out a solution on which all members would agree for such particular problems. The difficulties in demonstrating agreement on even the abstract principles of justice are all too familiar, and the motives that typically move us in judging concrete moral cases have been explicitly excluded in order to promote that higher order agreement. Moreover, as I argue later, even if their exclusive concern for "primary goods" could generate agreement on (possible) concrete cases, there is little reason to suppose that decisions reached on *that* basis would reflect all the morally relevant criteria.

When critics reject Rawls's theory as "too abstract" and "impartialist," they may sometimes do so because of a failure to appreciate fully the fact that it was never intended to be applied directly to concrete moral problems. Rawls, however, is quite clear on the point. Even in his restricted domain of political questions, Rawls insists that the results of the original position be applied in successive stages (constitutional, legislative, judicial), each lifting the "veil" appropriately for the task at hand (TJ 195-201); and to do otherwise leads quickly to absurdity. If we want to extend Rawls's theory for broader ethical purposes, then, we need to consider whether the original position can be usefully extended in ethics at a higher level of abstraction, which might at least give us general guidelines relevant to concrete moral choices.

(2) Will the original position serve, at the highest level, to settle disputes about our most basic moral values? Here too the original position, as Rawls defines it, is inadequate, but for a reason quite different from what we have considered so far. The problem is that many of our most fundamental moral convictions are already built into the description of the original position. As Rawls says, it is a point of view designed to represent widely accepted assumptions about a *fair* way to determine and rank competing guidelines for constitutional and legislative choices.[8] Its defining features were selected partly for moral reasons: that everyone's interests count, that no one "deserves" his or her natural gifts, that conceptions of justice should be public, general, universal, and not tailored to special interests, that malicious envy should be discounted, that the welfare of future generations is important, and that procedural fairness, rather than particular visions of the good life, should provide the primary standard for our basic institutions. These are not, of course, arguments that are supposed to move us once we have adopted the point of view of the original position, for the "members" are to reflect prudentially, not morally. However, as Rawls often acknowledges, shared basic moral assumptions are *represented* by the overall characterization of the parties together with their choice situation.[9] Moreover, the justificatory force of arguments from the original position to the principles of justice is largely dependent upon audience acceptance of those basic moral assumptions.

Though more evident in the book, these points are not incompatible with Rawls's later insistence on the political and pragmatic nature of his project. For even then the aim is "overlapping consensus," rather than a mere "modus vivendi," among those with

[8]TJ 12-13; Rawls, "Kantian Constructivism in Moral Theory," p. 522; "Fairness to Goodness," *Philosophical Review* 84 (1975): 536-40.

[9]TJ 17-22, 120, 141; "Fairness to Goodness," p. 539; "The Basic Structure as Subject," p. 159; "Kantian Constructivism in Moral Theory," p. 529.

diverse *moral* viewpoints.[10] Although the theory of justice is not itself a "general and comprehensive moral philosophy," and perhaps not even a core of moral truth in the overlap of such philosophies, its status as a reasonable political compromise for our times rests upon its appeal to the basic moral assumptions of the diverse groups that would make up the consensus.

(3) The original position, then, is not and was never meant to be a morally neutral position from which our most basic moral assumptions can be justified. One consequence is that a familiar criticism, namely, that a rational amoralist could reject the original position, misses the point; arguments from the original position are meant to presuppose at least minimal moral commitments. The more relevant consequence for our purposes is that if the original position is to be of use in ethics it must be as a mediating device, enabling us to deliberate from our more basic, abstract, or uncontested moral values to more derivative, specific, or disputed principles. This is the only plausible use, and is suggested by Rawls's own procedures. The question remains, though, whether it is an appropriate use when we venture beyond Rawls's restricted subject. Does the original position adequately represent a "moral point of view" from which we can reasonably try to justify and order our moral guidelines for individual conduct, where the justice of basic institutions is not in question?

A thorough treatment of this question would require a critical examination of Rawls's arguments for "natural duties," and so on, in *A Theory of Justice*, a review of objections and replies in the subsequent literature, and a constructive effort to derive from the original position ethical principles beyond those that Rawls himself has discussed. This is more than I can attempt here, but I want nonetheless to mention several sources of doubt about the project of extending the original position, as currently defined, for ethical questions beyond its intended domain. These problems stem from a package of stipulations regarding the original position: that the members deliberate behind a thick "veil of ignorance," focus exclusively on social "primary goods," and are "mutually disinterested."

[10]Rawls, "The Idea of an Overlapping Consensus," pp. 1-25.

Consider, first, doubts concerning the *results* we may expect from extending the use of the original position (without modification). Will the original position give us *enough* guidance of the *right sort* when we raise ethical issues besides the justice of basic social institutions?

One consideration which raises doubts is that the thick veil excludes all knowledge, and even considered opinion, about what ultimate ends are most worth pursuing and what goods are in themselves most worth protecting. Members are supposed to focus exclusively on *social primary goods*, which are means or enabling conditions most directly influenced by basic political and economic institutions (TJ 90–95). Within Rawls's project there are good reasons for this stipulation, but it is doubtful that those considerations justify the same stipulation for the broader moral task now under discussion.[11] For example, Rawls sets aside "natural" primary goods, such as health, because, he says, these are not so directly influenced by basic social institutions as are wealth, liberty, and the bases of self-respect (TJ 62). One may question this judgment even for Rawls's purposes, but in any case it is clear that health, and other nonsocial goods, are often important concerns when we turn to moral questions about interpersonal relations within our social structure. Again, focus on primary goods instead of "happiness" or "intrinsic value" is a "simplifying device" warranted by the need for a publicly acknowledged "objective measure" in political processes on which we need agreement among people of widely divergent life-styles (TJ 95). But for purposes of guiding our individual efforts to reach tenable moral policies, within a basically just social order, public agreement is less crucial and there is less need for such simplifying devices. The liberal aim of establishing a constitution and economic order that mutually respecting citizens can publicly affirm without judging one another's individual ways of life may be an admirable one; it does not follow, however, that one should try to establish one's moral guidelines for friendship, family, charity, personal integrity, and so forth from the same restricted point of view. Here one's concern for the shared values of one's community and one's

[11] TJ 90–91, 142–43, 260, 433, 440, 447–48; "Fairness to Goodness," pp. 537–38; "Kantian Constructivism in Moral Theory," p. 526.

best judgment regarding the most valuable ends of life may reasonably play a central role.

Another consideration that may encourage our doubts is that members of the original position are devoid of any moral commitment to protect and respect other persons. They are *mutually disinterested* and barred by the veil from consulting even their most basic moral values. Moral values have, of course, guided the construction of the original position. For example, though an impartial regard for others is not an attitude which the members have, it has been built into the constraints on their choices: they must choose principles that are universal, general, and final behind the veil of ignorance. Only superficial readers will infer that Rawls tries to justify his principles from egoistic premises, for this impartiality constraint, though indirectly represented, is crucial and severe. One may question, however, whether this constraint is sufficient, and of the right sort, for our extended moral purposes. The impartiality needed in assessing the most basic social institutions may not be the sort appropriate in reflecting on principles of charity, family responsibilities, and personal loyalties. And one may well doubt whether impartiality in the distribution of social primary goods is the only other-regarding moral value relevant to these matters.

Furthermore, despite Rawls's arguments to the contrary, it remains controversial whether original position members would opt for utilitarian principles, which ensure impartial regard only for preferences (or satisfactions) detached from the individuals who have them. In principle, as often noted, this allows the sacrifice of a few for the greater good of many. Whether to adopt such utilitarian principles, or even (by default) permissive egoism,[12] at least remains on the agenda for members of the original position. While this is entirely appropriate when one's project is to assess the relative merits of utilitarian and alternative principles of justice, one

---

[12]TJ 135-36. My intention here is not to imply that utilitarianism or egoism would be adopted in the original position but rather to suggest that these basic questions should be taken as settled once we turn to the sort of mediating task we have been considering, i.e., working from basic moral values to more specific principles. My point is just that the original position itself leaves open too many questions for our purposes; but this does not mean that modified versions or later "stages" of that position would do so as well.

may reasonably doubt whether such questions should remain open when one is trying to characterize the appropriate moral point of view for applying basic moral values to more specific issues. For that purpose, more substantive moral commitments are in order, even if they are less widely shared than the assumptions of the original position.

Finally, any theory which throws a veil over historical and cultural information raises doubts about whether it can give adequate guidance that is sensitive to all morally relevant circumstances. Perhaps all conditions call for some sort of prohibitions against killing, bodily injury, infidelities, and so on as well as duties of aid, support of children, etc., but the practically important moral controversies about such matters arise because people disagree about how to make such principles specific. For example, what exceptions, if any, are allowed, how are the crucial terms to be interpreted, and to whom do the principles apply? Moral principles which specify answers to these questions are applications of more fundamental values to local circumstances, and the articulations of those principles may reasonably vary to some degree with historical and cultural conditions. Though moral principles are not simply whatever norms a community accepts, we cannot reasonably determine what should count as "infidelity" and "child neglect" while disregarding altogether the cultural context of the question. What one should regard as a justified killing may depend to some extent on the maturity and stability of the society, and even what is appropriately considered to be killing may vary with medical technology. The line between required and generous aid may depend upon the affluence of the community and alternative arrangements for meeting needs.

Now Rawls acknowledges the relevance of information about historical and cultural conditions even to questions of social justice, and he proposes a several-stage sequence of deliberations in which the thick veil of ignorance is gradually lifted (TJ 195-201). First we deliberate to the principles of justice in the original position behind the thick veil; next we reflect as members of a hypothetical constitutional convention to apply the principles of justice to our historical circumstances, broadly construed; then we assess laws from the point of view of an imaginary legislature with fuller knowledge of local conditions. The aim, Rawls says, is not to fix precisely one constitution and set of laws as just for a given society; it is rather to define a range of just institutions and legislative procedures so that further questions can be left to quasi-pure procedural justice and the ongoing processes of actual institutions (TJ 201). For Rawls it is important that there is wide agreement on the terms of the original position and the general principles derived from it; but it is not so important, or expected, that the theory dictate specific policies for particular historical circumstances. Accordingly, it is appropriate for the moral constraints in the original position to be minimal and many specific applications to be underdetermined.

One may doubt, however, whether this same strategy would work if we leave the political realm. There are no real constitutional conventions and legislatures for moral decision making, though perhaps we can imagine moral analogues of these institutions. But can we reach adequate specific moral principles, sensitive to historical conditions, by imagining ourselves going from the original position through a sequence of deliberations, each with more information about our place and times? The problem with this approach in ethics is that the stages seem to serve no function. Since, unlike Rawls, we are not working out standards for criticism of actual constitutions and legislatures, we would simply be applying the basic moral values in our original position in the light of more and more historical information. Whether the original position provides the guidelines we need depends entirely on how richly it is endowed with morally appropriate assumptions. Since Rawls intentionally makes only the minimal moral assumptions for his purposes, it seems doubtful that it could guide us, even with historical information, to many of the more specific moral answers we seek. Also, since the original position was constructed primarily to address questions of social justice, it seems doubtful that the answers it does give would reflect the full range of moral values that are relevant.

The considerations reviewed above raise doubts about whether the original position, as currently defined, will lead to sufficient and adequate results when applied outside its intended domain. But we need also to consider how well the original position *represents* the moral point of view appropriate for deliberating about ethical issues beyond social justice; for, as I have suggested, part of the appeal of ideal models of deliberation in ethics lies in the heuristic value of the *way* they picture the moral deliberator, quite aside from any specific advice we derive from them. In this respect, too, the original position seems inadequate when extended beyond its primary subject.

The fact that members of the original position are concerned exclusively with social primary goods, and make no judgments about the relative importance of ends, tends to undermine its value as a general model for moral deliberators to emulate. Respectful acceptance of individual differences is an admirable trait, particularly when one is designing coercive institutions; but suspending all judgments about what is valuable, besides social primary goods, would not be admirable if one were working out moral policies, within the limits of just laws, for governing oneself and one's voluntary dealings with others. But the main problem stems, not from focus on primary goods, but from the fact that members of the original position are *mutually disinterested.*

This stipulation, that the parties take no interest in each other's interests, means that the deliberators in the original position have no other-regarding motives, moral or otherwise. It simplifies the decision process, and it does not prevent Rawls from representing the impartiality of justice, indirectly, in the constraints on members' choices (especially the veil). This way of representing impartiality admittedly has some advantages. For example, it enables Rawls to use decision theoretic principles for individual rational choice which allow theoretically neater arguments; and when such arguments run out, he is able to substitute "prudential intuition" for "moral intuition" (TJ 44, 94, 152-58). Some ideal observer theories represent the moral point of view as a position of full information with impartiality ensured by the observer's vicarious identification with the interests of each agent (and lack of other motives), but this simply encapsulates the utilitarian perspective and makes agreement on specific principles unlikely.[13] Rawls also avoids the vagueness of the common sense notion that a proper moral perspective is *somewhat* other-regarding and impartial on *some* matters but not all.

Despite these advantages, representing the agents of the original position as mutually disinterested reduces its heuristic value as

[13]See TJ 184ff.; and Hare, esp. chap. 3. For a different sort of ideal observer theory, see Firth.

model for the attitude one should try to approximate in deliberating about how to specify (intermediate-level) moral principles. Exclusive concern with one's own welfare, even if severely constrained by limited knowledge, is so deeply associated with common paradigms of amoral egoists that, I suspect, the best intentions and most careful explanations cannot mold it into an intuitive model of a general "moral point of view." The image of "blind justice," weighing self-interested claims without knowledge of *whose* claims they are, is a powerful and time-honored symbol, when the only issue is *fairness*; but this is hardly an adequate general representation of the proper position and attitude for those who would deliberate from their more essential moral values to specific policies for a wide range of interpersonal issues. Rawls does not claim that the original position is a general representation of this sort; but for the broader purposes of constructivism in ethics it would be advantageous to have an alternative model which represented the deliberative point of view in a more intuitively appealing way.

Such an alternative, I imagine, would picture the ideal moral deliberator as more informed than Rawls's veil permits but still prepared to disregard morally irrelevant considerations of gender, race, and social status, as respectful of individual differences but not ready to ignore firm convictions about the relative value of various human ends, and as committed to advancing the happiness of others but unwilling to merge all interests into a pool for distribution by a utilitarian archangel. Kant suggests a model of this sort, which I shall sketch for comparison.

III. An Alternative Model

One version of Kant's Categorical Imperative says that one must act as if one were a legislating member in an ideal "kingdom of ends."[14] Kant offers this principle as a combination of the main ideas expressed in previous formulations of the Categorical Imper-

---

[14]G 100-102. Some of the points summarized in the next few pages are discussed in my papers "The Kingdom of Ends" and "Humanity as an End in Itself," both reprinted in this volume. My discussion, it should be noted, follows Paton's rendering of

ative. Thus the kingdom of ends is meant to summarize certain basic moral values, for which he argues independently; it is not a morally neutral rational standpoint from which those values might be justified. Kant also suggests that the kingdom of ends is not the best stance for making everyday moral decisions, for he implies that the "universal law" formula is the stricter method for that purpose. It seems, then, that the "laws" one is to legislate in the kingdom are neither one's specific maxims nor the supreme moral principle itself. Thus it is natural to regard these "laws" as the sort of intermediate-level moral principles which we have been considering. On this reading, the kingdom would be a heuristic model of the appropriate moral attitude to take when deliberating from basic moral values to moderately specific principles. Kant does not himself follow through this suggestion when he works out his own system of moral principles in *The Metaphysics of Morals,* and in the *Groundwork* he implies that the main function of the kingdom is to make his abstract moral principles more intuitive. Nonetheless, it may be useful to compare this model with the original position.

The kingdom of ends, like the original position, is an "ideal," not a description of an actual state of affairs. Kant sometimes speaks of it as the ideal world that would result if everyone made *and followed* moral laws and if God arranged nature so that everyone's permissible ends would be satisfied. But Kant also speaks of the kingdom as an ideal moral legislature, a point of view for adopting principles one should follow regardless of what others may actually do.[15] This ideal, which is the one relevant here, is not offered for the purposes of assessing the basic structure of society but rather as an intuitive model of the morally appropriate attitude to take when reflecting on all but the most general "moral laws." As in Rawls's theory, normative conclusions follow from

---

"Reich" (in the *Groundwork*) as "Kingdom" even though this has some unfortunate connotations. "Realm" or "state" is perhaps a better translation, but Paton's has become the familiar one.

[15]Kant implies, I think, that members of the kingdom, as such, conscientiously obey its laws (G 100–101, 105–7). Thus, in legislating from the perspective of the kingdom, we are to imagine that we are making laws for perfect law-abiders, i.e., we assume "strict compliance." However, Kant also implies that once the "laws" are settled from this ideal perspective, we (as individuals in the real world) must follow those laws even if others do not. This gives rise to the problem I mention in my concluding paragraph.

hypothetical choices: one *should* act according to the "laws" one *would* adopt if one were legislating in the kingdom.

The main features of this legislative point of view, reconstructed liberally, are these. The members are rational and autonomous; they "abstract from personal differences"; they make only "universal laws"; they are "ends in themselves," and presumably recognize each other as such; they are all both "authors" and "subjects" of the law (except God, the sovereign, who is not "subject"). Like Rousseau's citizens of an ideal state, they are bound only by laws they give themselves. Each of these conditions requires interpretation, but for present purposes it is best to focus on the most significant ways in which the model compares and contrasts with the original position.

Kant's idea of "rationality" is broader than Rawls's but also less clearly defined. It includes taking the necessary means to one's (rationally adopted) ends, and it also encompasses dispositions to preserve, develop, and respect oneself as a thinking agent. Rational beings, Kant says, necessarily view their "rational nature" as an "end in itself," which implies placing a stringent priority on realizing these dispositions over satisfying various contingent ends when these two values ("dignity" and "price") conflict. Kant also held that rational consistency demands the same priorities in dealing with others, but the other-regarding attitudes of kingdom members are also stipulated more directly, as I explain below, by the characterization of all the members as "ends in themselves."

Autonomy is a controversial notion but implies, I think, at least the following: the members view each other, for practical purposes, as able to make and follow rational principles which are not simply a product of their strongest desires and impulses. They are not causally or rationally constrained to adopt as their ultimate guide "Do whatever most efficiently satisfies your desires." They are not under obligation to independent authorities; obedience to God is required only because God's commands are supposed to coincide with the voice of their own reason. They are principled, but they cannot "discover" moral principles in nature, custom, or social institutions. Apart from the values inherent in being a rational agent, they acknowledge no fixed "intrinsic value" in the nature of things. Particular ends, such as fame, power, and wealth, are "relative" to individual tastes; they are morally important only when and because autonomous agents choose to make them their ends. Even pleasure and avoidance of pain, which are natural concerns of all human beings, have value only to the degree that autonomous agents incorporate them into their (permissible) projects; and they are subordinate to the values implicit in acknowledging rational agency as an end in itself.

In thinking of the kingdom, Kant says, we "abstract from the differences" between rational agents as well as from the "content" of their particular ends. This is Kant's analogue of the "veil of ignorance," but how far does it extend? Clearly one is to disregard gender, race, social rank, special talents, degree of wealth, and the like, and we are not to think as music lovers, birdwatchers, or sports fans. Unlike Rawls, however, Kant does not specify fully what other sorts of considerations we must set aside. Since all rational agents are potential "members," it seems that "abstracting from the differences" may require us to ignore not only the special values of particular communities but also any other distinguishing historical conditions. If so, some of the doubts I raised about extending the original position would apply equally well to Kant's model, unless the latter contains some compensating feature. (I return to this problem shortly.)

The stipulation that the members make "universal laws" may be construed as similar to Rawls's idea that members adopt only principles that are general in spirit as well as in form. That is, they do not direct orders to particular individuals, and they do not arbitrarily design their principles to ensure the outcomes they especially favor for their own immediate situation. Since members make "universal laws," which for Kant must be (practically) "necessary" as well as general in scope, we can infer that the members will not make laws without sufficient reason. They choose only what, given their situation, they see as rationally compelling.

The conditions so far tell us little about what would motivate members of the kingdom to select one principle over another. We need an analogue to the original position members' concern for social primary goods. This must be drawn from the idea that members of the kingdom acknowledge each other as "ends," with "dignity" above all "price." The idea is not simply that "everyone should be considered," still less that the moral legislators' task is to satisfy the maximal set of individual preferences when these are "impartially" pooled together. Nor is Kant's idea merely the empty formal notion that people should be granted all the rights and consideration that are morally due to them. In calling rational agents "ends in themselves," Kant implies at least three points, all imprecise but nonetheless important.[16]

First, the "humanity," or rational nature, of each person is a rational value that has strict priority over contingent ends. That is, preserving and respecting the rational agency of the members is a central aim of the kingdom's legislators, and this has a higher priority, in case of conflict, than promoting the various particular ends that the members may adopt. In Kant's terms, "dignity" is an unconditional value that always takes precedence over "price."

Second, the "dignity" of rational agents is a value that has *no* equivalent. That is, we not only must avoid subordinating this value to less essential ends (with mere "price"); we also cannot justify sacrificing one rational agent for others on the grounds, say, that two persons are worth twice as much as one. (This does not necessarily mean that hard choices cannot reasonably be made, but only that they cannot be based on comparisons of quantities of value.) Persons are not to be treated as "mere means," even to the preservation and rational development of other persons.

Third, regarding rational agents as ends in themselves, Kant says, implies some degree of commitment to furthering their contingent ends (within the other constraints of moral law). This is not because those ends, or their satisfaction, have intrinsic value as such but because one cannot ignore the concerns and projects of agents whom one respects and values. Kant never specifies the extent to which one must care for the ends of others, and his principles in *The Metaphysics of Morals* place the priority on promoting the liberty and mutual respect needed for rational agents to pursue their own ends.

This sketch of Kant's legislative model is admittedly both incomplete and controversial, and the model itself raises serious problems. But, as my main purpose is not to explain or defend Kant, perhaps enough has been said to make way for some useful comparisons.

---

[16]For further references and applications, see my "Humanity as an End in Itself," reprinted in this volume.

To review, the main sources of doubt about extending the original position behind its domain were these stipulations: (1) that its members focus exclusively on primary social goods, (2) that they are mutually disinterested and so lack moral regard for others, and (3) that they are ignorant of historical circumstances and too thinly described to give us adequate guidelines for when the veil is lifted. On each of these points Kant's model provides an interesting contrast.

First, the Kantian legislators have values beyond social primary goods. Since they value rational nature as an end in itself, they are committed to the value priorities that Kant thought essential to being rational: that is, preserving, developing, exercising, and respecting rational agency takes precedence over other (contingent) ends. These priorities hold for self-regarding as well as other-regarding policies.

Second, and most striking, the Kantian legislators are not mutually disinterested. To the contrary, they are viewed as committed to furthering the ends of others and as valuing, above all, the dignity of each rational agent. Significant moral values are thus built into the attitudes of the deliberators, not merely represented in the stipulated constraints on their choices. Because their motives are complex and not morally neutral, they do not reason prudentially, using (say) a maximin strategy. This no doubt makes it harder to argue that all members will agree on exactly the same principles. For Rawls's project it is important that original position members publicly agree on the same general standards for the basic institutions of a heterogeneous society. But that every deliberator reach the same moral policies is less important if one's aim is to model an ideal point of view for applying basic moral values to more specific circumstances. And for this purpose, as I have suggested, it is helpful to represent the ideal deliberators as morally committed and (to some degree) other-regarding.

Third, and finally, since the Kantian model abstracts from all differences between rational agents, its deliberators must initially disregard historical and cultural conditions; but this initial abstraction may not be as severe a problem with the Kantian model as with the original position (taken outside the political sphere). This is because the Kantian model (as represented here) itself reflects a fuller, less modestly described moral viewpoint. The moral commitments implicit in the Kantian conception lead rather directly to general moral guidelines that may be used in deliberations about more specific policies when historical circumstances are taken into account. For example, the stipulated attitudes of the kingdom members ensure that, even before they consider historical information, they would accept a strict principle of respect for persons, an indefinite principle of beneficence (enjoining us to make the ends of others to some extent our own), and principles forbidding the sacrifice of the lives and liberty of any rational agent merely for an increase in general welfare. These and perhaps other principles in Kant's *The Metaphysics of Morals* are, as Kant suggests, implicit in his idea of humanity as an end in itself (G 95-104). Though they may be disputed, they are not without practical import.

The price for building more value assumptions into a constructivist model is, of course, the risk of generating more controversy about the model itself. Many may reject the strong initial commitments in the Kantian model, for example, and even those who find that it expresses their moral viewpoint may well ask for independent justification. Kant himself was not unmindful of this demand and in fact devoted more attention to deeper issues of justification than to developing or applying his heuristic model of the kingdom of ends. These other aspects of Kant's moral philosophy, which I have ignored here, may also be construed as constructivist; but that is a topic for another time.

To conclude, my aim has been to explore some possible extensions of Rawls's basic strategy in ethics, not to defend Kant or to criticize Rawls. The doubts I have raised have concerned the extended use of Rawls's current version of the original position and not possible modifications of this. Other extensions may be more promising, and my remarks on both Kant and Rawls are regrettably abstract and inconclusive. One further point, however, should not go unmentioned. This is the fact that the thought experiments which Rawls and Kant suggest, for different purposes, presuppose that we are deliberating about principles for an ideal world of conscientious agents. In Rawls's terminology, we assume "strict compliance." But there is an important gap between the policies that we would make for such a world and the policies that may be morally best for the real world. This world, unfortunately, includes people who refuse to comply with just institutions and moral principles, no matter how well these are explained and defended; and this creates a situation in which rigorous adherence to the principles for an ideal world may prove disastrous. To his credit, Rawls seems well aware of this; but one cannot confidently say the same of Kant.

Index

Library of Congress Cataloging-in-Publication Data

Hill, Thomas E.
  Dignity and practical reason in Kant's moral theory / Thomas E. Hill, Jr.
      p.   cm.
  Includes bibliographical references and index.
  ISBN 0-8014-2514-X (cloth : alk. paper).—ISBN 0-8014-9748-5 (pbk. : alk. paper)
    1. Kant, Immanuel, 1724–1804—Ethics.   I. Title.
B2799.E8H55   1992
170—dc20
                                                        91-23543